Twayne's United States Authors Series

Sylvia E. Bowman, *Editor*

INDIANA UNIVERSITY

Henry Wadsworth Longfellow

HENRY WADSWORTH LONGFELLOW

by CECIL B. WILLIAMS

Texas Christian University

 68

Twayne Publishers, Inc.   ::   New York

TO MY WIFE
MARY BETH

Preface

I GAVE AN EAGER WELCOME to the invitation to write a book on Longfellow, for I had long wanted to learn more about a poet I had enjoyed in childhood and found attractive ever since. The fact that his reputation had been buffeted rudely during my own middle years had left me wondering who was naïve: Longfellow, I, or his detractors. As a long-time teacher of literature, I had of course learned that literary reputations ebb and flow, with or without discoverable reasons. But Longfellow had been loved and respected in his own time beyond the meed of most, and later he had become perhaps more than any other major figure a butt of ridicule or a yardstick for measuring sophomoric literary taste. I decided that it would be a challenge to study him and all of his writings to see what he was and was not. What I found is set forth in this book.

Since the man and his life have become shadowy with time, I thought it advisable to begin with an examination of the popular Longfellow image and to compare it to the actuality as I had observed it as teacher and casual student. And, as the man and his milieu have now become too distant for a modern reader's easy perception, I decided to divide my book roughly into two halves, with the first devoted to the author's life and the second to his writings. Although his journals and letters have still not been published in their entirety, I found that I could base my study largely on primary materials. Such rather recently published works as James T. Hatfield's *New Light on Longfellow;* Lawrance Thompson's *Young Longfellow;* the collection of Fanny Appleton Longfellow's letters, edited by Edward Wagenknecht and published as *Mrs. Longfellow;* Andrew R. Hilen's edition of the *Diary of Clara Crowninshield;* and Hilen's *Longfellow and Scandinavia* are invaluable supplements to the still indispensable three-volume official *Life* by the poet's brother Samuel Longfellow. All these works are rich in quotations from or about Longfellow. I have read most of the scholarship and profited from some of it, but have preferred to let my imagination dwell on the writings of Longfellow himself— both those published by him and those written in his journal or in letters to friends and relatives—and on letters to and comments about him by those who knew him well in his own time. I have some reason to think that I have presented a truer picture of the real man and writer than any available hitherto.

My comments on the writings are relatively full. For major prose works and the long narrative poems, I have devoted considerable space to genesis, composition, and reception, as well as to the qualities I perceived in them.

Although I began this preface with an admission of affection for Longfellow, I do not believe I have manipulated evidence for the sake of a favorable portrait. I have tried throughout to let the chips fall where they should. I have made no extravagant claims for him, but have meant to assign him to the place in America literary history and American literature which his writings and other literary services warrant. Because his academic career affected his career as a writer, I have devoted considerable space to it and hope I have evaluated rightly the interrelationships of his two principal occupations. Also, since they too are important, I have given attention to his associations with his relatives and friends. Longfellow was even more a product of all that he met than is true of most authors.

A few acknowledgments are in order. I have admitted above the special usefulness of certain books. The librarians of Texas Christian University have been cheerfully helpful to me in many ways. My wife, to whom the volume in dedicated, provided encouragement and indispensable editorial aid. My sons Philip and James have been constructively interested in the project throughout. A group of seminar students who wrote papers on Longfellow while my work was in progress were more helpful than they realized. They supplemented my own researches considerably and strengthened my belief in Longfellow's present-day readability. Other students and several colleagues have been interested and have thereby encouraged me. As is true of all scholarly books, this one is indebted to more persons than can be named. I wish I could express gratification to all who have helped me in one way or another. Particularly, I wish Longfellow could know how agreeable a constant companion I have found him.

C. B. W.

Texas Christian University
June 18, 1964

Contents

4

Chronology

1807   Henry Wadsworth Longfellow born in Portland, Maine, February 27, second son of Stephen and Zilpah Wadsworth Longfellow.

1821   Passed Bowdoin College entrance examinations with older brother Stephen. Studied at Portland Academy, 1821-22; entered Bowdoin, 1822.

1825   Graduated from Bowdoin, ranking fourth in a class of thirty-eight.

1826- Studied in France, Spain, Italy, and Germany to prepare
1829   himself for professorship of modern languages at Bowdoin.

1829- Professor of Modern Languages at Bowdoin. Translated and
1835   prepared texts for his students; wrote scholarly articles for journals.

1831   Married Mary Storer Potter, daughter of Judge Barrett Potter of Portland.

1835   Accepted Smith Professorship of Modern Languages and Belles-Lettres at Harvard.

1835- Studied abroad, especially in Scandinavia and Germany, to
1836   prepare for Harvard position.

1835   *Outre-Mer* published. Mary Longfellow died in Rotterdam.

1836   Began Harvard professorship.

1836- Harvard duties and social activity.
1839

1837   Reviewed Hawthorne's *Twice-Told Tales.*

1839   *Hyperion* and *Voices of the Night* published.

1841   *Ballads and Other Poems* published. Translation of Tegnér's *The Children of the Lord's Supper.*

1842   Several months in Germany for his health. Formed friendship with Ferdinand Freiligrath, German poet. *Poems on Slavery.*

1843   Married Fanny Appleton. Received Craigie House as a present from Fanny's father. *The Spanish Student.*

1845   *The Waif. The Poets and Poetry of Europe,* an anthology of translations, including many of his own. *The Belfry of Bruges.*

1847 *Evangeline, A Tale of Acadie.*

1848 "Hymn for My Brother's Ordination."

1849 *Kavanagh: A Tale.* Father died.

1850 *The Seaside and the Fireside,* containing "The Building of the Ship," read publicly by Fanny Kemble.

1851 *The Golden Legend,* afterward Part II of *Christus.* Mother died.

1854 Resigned Harvard professorship. Worked on *Hiawatha.*

1855 *The Song of Hiawatha.*

1856 Planned European visit with family; abandoned because of an injury to his knee.

1857 Became a member of the Saturday Club.

1858 *The Courtship of Miles Standish and Other Poems.*

1859 LL.D. from Harvard.

1861 Tragic death of Fanny Appleton Longfellow. Resumed translation of Dante's *Divine Comedy.*

1863 First part of *Tales of a Wayside Inn.* Went to Washington to care for wounded son.

1865 Founding of the Dante Club.

1866 *Flower-de-Luce.*

1868 *The New England Tragedies,* later Part III of *Christus.*

1868-
1869 Made last visit to Europe, with members of his family; a triumphal tour including honorary doctoral degree at Cambridge and Oxford.

1867-
1870 Translation of Dante's *Divine Comedy* (3 vols.).

1871 *The Divine Tragedy,* Part I of *Christus.* Second edition of *Poets and Poetry of Europe.*

1872 *Christus: A Mystery,* the collected edition of what he had hoped would be his magnum opus. *Three Books of Song,* containing second part of *Tales of a Wayside Inn, Judas Maccabaeus,* and translations.

1873 *Aftermath,* containing third part of *Tales of a Wayside Inn* and other poems.

1875 *The Masque of Pandora and Other Poems,* containing "The Hanging of the Crane," "Morituri Salutamus," and other poems. Delivered "Morituri Salutamus" at fiftieth anniversary of his Bowdoin graduation.

1876- *Poems of Places.* He edited this anthology of thirty-one
1879   volumes.

1878   *Kéramos and Other Poems.*

1880   *Ultima Thule.*

1880- Birthday widely celebrated in the public schools.
1882

1882   *In the Harbor.* Died in Cambridge, March 24.

1883   *Michael Angelo* published posthumously.

1884   Bust unveiled in Poets' Corner of Westminster Abbey.

CHAPTER *1*

Image and Actuality

I *The Popular Image*

ANYONE UNDERTAKING TODAY a new evaluation of Longfellow almost perforce begins with an attempt to relate the modern image to the man. It has been said that Cotton and Increase Mather barricaded themselves from re-evaluation by the huge rampart of thorny reading erected by their tireless pens.[1] Longfellow is also formidably guarded—not so much by the bulk of his writings or the difficulty in reading them as by the extraordinary fluctuations in his reputation, both as author and as man. In his own time, he gradually won for himself, both at home and abroad, the undisputed top place in American letters. His American contemporaries paid him homage; European authors and artists who came to America did not consider their visits complete until they had enjoyed the famed hospitality of the Craigie House. In the last two decades of his life, he was so besieged by autograph seekers and aspiring writers that he managed to carry forward his own work only with the utmost difficulty. Throughout the world of Western culture, he was known as a gifted author, a wise philosopher, and a great man.

But it has been many years since it was fashionable to look upon Longfellow as great. He has had defenders in every age, to be sure, and there are signs that a mild Longfellow revival may be under way. Yet the newest full-length biography asks no more than that we "agree once for all, that he is a minor writer."[2] The popular image, which fortunately schoolchildren and their teachers have never fully accepted, has been that of a bewhiskered fuddy-duddy who provided popular entertainment for our grandparents (especially our grandmothers) in a naïve age of American culture which had not yet shed its milk teeth, figuratively speaking. No redblooded American who had experienced World War I and World War II, and the Great Depression, the birth of the Atomic Age; and who had found his literary entertainment in free verse and the fiction of the Lost Generation could visualize an age when reading Longfellow was respectable, even mandatory.

Who was he, anyhow? If curiosity impelled them to look him up in a biographical dictionary, they were probably most impressed to learn that he had married the daughter of Boston's wealthiest citizen and lived a soft life from then on. It was easy to believe that he had never known hardship, had never suffered in war or peace. What, then, could he know about the real heights and depths of human thought and emotion? A pleasant singer for children, perhaps—children either in terms of their age or the age of their nation—that was all, if even that. Twentieth-century America was too sophisticated to waste its time in reading the facile verses of a nineteenth-century Victorian American. The nineteenth century could have Longfellow; he had nothing to say to the twentieth.

II *The Actuality*

This book will examine how Longfellow became the kind of writer he was and evaluate not only his role in literary history but also his literary accomplishment. It is pertinent, therefore, to consider how Longfellow as a person differed from the persona, the modern image. First of all, he was not naïve. He had much of the shrewdness that had made his father a successful lawyer, a leading citizen of Portland, Maine, and an influential Bowdoin College overseer. How many young men of nineteen in his day would have had the boldness to undertake solitary life in four European countries while he studied their languages? Not many. Still fewer would have had the resourcefulness and fortitude to live abroad for three and a half years without friends save those he made, in countries with alien languages. From his youth, Longfellow was urbane, if not sophisticated; he could live with all sorts of people and, while in Europe, achieve both his primary object of learning languages and his secondary (perhaps largely unconscious) object of acquiring inspiration and subject matter for later writings.

Longfellow was not only a descendant of New England Puritans but also a Yankee. He may not have carried a Greek head on Yankee shoulders, as Lowell said of Emerson in his "Fable for Critics"; but in the head of the scholar and poet that sat on Longfellow's sturdy Puritan shoulders there were always little corners where Yankee traits continued to abide, emerging to assert themselves from time to time. Perhaps the most dominant Yankee trait was frugality, which took the form of making limited resources of time and talent achieve maximum results. Modern critics have condemned Longfellow because he did not make on-the-spot investigations of the settings of *Evangeline* and *Hiawatha*. He did not because he realized that his full schedule would not permit both traveling and writing. So he used Banvard's pictures of the Mississippi and School-craft's on-the-scene descriptions of Indian life—and wrote while he kept school and lived with his beloved family. Actually, who has ever proved that *Evangeline* and *Hiawatha* would have been better if Longfellow had visited the scenes he portrayed rather than let his imagination evoke them from the authentic sources he studied?

Possibly Longfellow was too frugal, too intent on making too little talent go too far. One is tempted to quote his fellow household poet, Whittier, who described the early Puritans as

> Saving, as shrewd economists, their souls
> And winter pork with the least possible outlay
> Of salt and sanctity.[3]

The soul Longfellow sought to save through intellectual frugality was his own poetic soul. He had learned that he would have to carry, at least through much of his life, a full vocational burden. Perhaps he could be a poet despite this, but he could not be a poet in the pattern of François Villon or Edgar Allan Poe.

Another modern misconception is that he was an effeminate weakling, a Caspar Milquetoast. This view certainly runs counter to the evidence. His best friends in America were a United States Senator, Charles G. Sumner; a sturdy Professor of Greek, C. C. Felton; a cosmopolitan botanist, Louis Agassiz; and a notable historian, George W. Greene. In Europe he made friends with the great Anglo-Saxon scholar Joseph Bosworth, the outstanding German poet Ferdinand Freiligrath, and the English novelist Charles Dickens. In Cambridge he was on familiar terms with Hawthorne, Emerson, and others of the Boston circle, in addition to the close friends named above. But he could also hold his own with men of affairs, such as his father-in-law Nathan Appleton, his brother-in-law Tom Appleton, famous Harvard President Josiah Quincy, and the wealthy banker Samuel Ward.

The misleading popular image derives partly from the famous white whiskers. It may be a shock to some to learn that Longfellow went smoothshaven through most of his life. An 1839 portrait presents a debonair young man more suggestive of Shelley than of Father Abraham, and portraits taken much later show no more facial foliage than the sideburns fashionable at the time. When as a young Harvard professor he roomed at the Craigie House, "he ... was considered rather a dandy, and I believe Mrs. Craigie, when he first came to board with her, thought his gloves of much too light a shade to be worn by a strictly virtuous man."[4] He had no white whiskers then. William Dean Howells, whose admiration of the older author was little short of idolatry, perhaps did his reputation a bad turn by applying to him the Norwegian dramatist Björnsterne Björnson's phrase, "The White Mr. Longfellow."[5] It is ironic that this misleading hirsute symbol should have resulted partly from the tragic accident of his life. Burned on the face in 1861 when trying to save his wife's life, he found shaving thereafter "impossible or inadvisable."⁶ So the flowing white beard, however appropriate or inappropriate, was not a pose but a necessity.

Possibly the person who did most to create a misleading modern image of Longfellow was one who not only greatly admired him but sought diligently to perpetuate his good name. This was his own brother Samuel, who perused journals, letters, and unpublished literary manuscripts and then presented to the world the image he himself admired and wanted the reading public to have of his famous deceased brother. But Samuel Longfellow was a clergyman, and although considered liberal he never had his Longfellow-Wadsworth ancestral Puritanism liberalized, as his brother had, by European residence and lifelong interest in a rich variety of cultures. More recent and less biased examination of these papers shows that Samuel Longfellow overemphasized the gentle, the placid, and the resigned in the poet at the expense of his more robust qualities; his resistance to injustice, his almost fierce loyalty to friends and cherished beliefs, frank admiration for pretty women, business acumen, and, with some allowance for the mores of the time, very human reactions in emotional crises springing from triumphs and disappointments, joy and grief.

The actual Longfellow was a man far different from the modern image. From young manhood, he was regarded as a strong, masculine individual. He walked purposefully, with the spring in his gait of a man who knew where he was bound and enjoyed going there. He was bright-eyed and handsome in an unassuming way, and he loved to be well dressed. In maturity, he had the respect of the great men and women of his time. He entertained an amazing proportion of them in his home, and many felt honored in turn to have him as their guest. His Harvard friend C. E. Norton has given us a memorable portrait of him: "The rare social gifts with which Nature had endowed him, cultivated by his experience in Europe, made Longfellow a delightful host, or guest, or companion. He possessed the first requisite of all fine social art,—a real desire to give pleasure; he was quite free from vanity, and while he was master of large resources in conversation, he did not use them for display, but with the light touch and kindly humor which gives ease and grace to talk."⁷

Fellow poet Oliver Wendell Holmes also found him admirable, as his comment in a letter to Motley, the historian, shows: "I find a singular charm in the society of Longfellow,—a soft voice, a sweet and cheerful temper, a receptive rather than aggressive intelligence, the agreeable flavor of scholarship without any pedantic ways, and a perceptible soupçon of the humor, not enough to startle or surprise or keep you under the strain of over-stimulation, which I am apt to feel with very witty people."[8]

III *Fallen Prince of Popularity*

In this twentieth-century era of prose fiction and prose articles on the new science and the old politics, it is hard to imagine how popular poetry in general and Longfellow's poetry in particular were in the late years of his life. One has only to compare a few late nineteenth-century issues of the *Atlantic Monthly* or *Harper's Magazine* with issues of today to see what has happened. In Longfellow's old age, poetry—the best poetry which Europe or America was producing—was *popular;* it was widely read and well paid for. Longfellow himself had done much to bring about this halcyon state of affairs. He had been paid pittances (as were Poe and others) in his early days: $15 for "The Village Blacksmith," $25 for "The Wreck of the Hesperus."[9] His total literary income mounted from $219 in 1840 to $1,900 in 1850, the date his records stop (*Life,* III, 435). There are later entries recording exciting payments for single poems, culminating in the $3,000 he received for "The Hanging of the Crane" in 1873. What poet has been paid a comparable sum for a poem in our time?

But it was not only in coin of the realm that Longfellow achieved recognition. For his sixtieth birthday, James Russell Lowell, his friend and successor as Smith Professor at Harvard, wrote a verse tribute containing this stanza:

> Surely if skill in song the shears may stay
>   And of its purpose cheat the charmed abyss,
> If our poor life be lengthened by a lay,
> He shall not go, although his presence may,
>   And the next age in praise shall double this.[10]

In this tribute Lowell was proving himself more a loyal friend than a good prophet. But the next year, 1868, Longfellow, with an entourage of relatives, made his fourth and final visit to Europe. Perhaps no other American visitor to Europe except Mark Twain ever received so warm a welcome. He was feted in the home of Charles Dickens; Queen Victoria received him at Windsor; he dined with the Prince of Wales. Queen Victoria was greatly impressed. She said: "The American Poet Longfellow has been here. I noticed an unusual interest among the attendants and servants. I could scarcely credit that they so generally understood who he was. When he took leave, they concealed themselves in places from which they could get a good look at him as he passed. I have since inquired among them, and am surprised and pleased to find that many of his poems are familiar to them. No other distinguished person has come here that has excited so peculiar an interest. Such poets wear a crown that is imperishable."[11]

Oxford and Cambridge both conferred doctorates upon him while he was abroad; he had already received the LL.D. from Harvard in 1859 and in 1874 was awarded another by Bowdoin. In 1874 he was nominated for Lord Rector of the University of Edinburg and received a large complimentary vote. Such honors are evidence of the esteem in which he was held during his lifetime.

A flood of additional tributes came shortly after his death in 1882. Whittier wrote a poem ending:

> He heard the Summoning Angel
> Who calls God's children home!
>
> And to him in a holier welcome
> Was the mystical meaning given
> Of the words of the blessed Master:
> "Of such is the kingdom of heaven!"[12]

Another fellow American poet wrote for publication in *Puck* magazine:

> If this be dying, fair it is to die:
> Even as a garment weariness lays by,
> Thou layest down life to pass, as time hath passed
> From wintry rigors to a springtime sky.
>
> Are there tears left to give thee at the last
> Poet of spirits crushed and hearts downcast,
> Loved of worn women who when work is done
> Weep o'er thy page in twilights fading fast?[13]

Poet H. C. Bunner, in an age when women (and some men) tearfully read the English *Jane Eyre* and the compassionate novels of Dickens and the American *The Lamplighter* and *The Wide, Wide World*, did not hesitate to praise Longfellow for the comfort he brought to the sad and the weary. Whether or not there was more sadness in those times than now is debatable, but certainly there was far more physical weariness before modern technology turned over most of the hard work to machines.

Even in 1882 news crossed the ocean by cable, so it was possible for a Mrs. E. B. Prideaux to write in Modbury, England, only three

days after Longfellow's death, a pathetic tribute including the
following stanza:

> For in spirit he dwelt amongst us;
> . His name is a "household word:"
> Where liveth the Anglo-Saxon
> Whose feeling he hath not stirred?[14]

These are only a few of the numerous tributes paid at his death.[15]
The crowning accolade, however, came two years afterward in 1884
when a handsome bust of Longfellow, presented by "his English
admirers," was mounted in the Poets' Corner of historic Westminster
Abbey. Longfellow is still the only non-British author to be represented in that famous gallery.

While searching in bookstores for a standard set of Longfellow's
works, I accidentally came upon one impressive testimonial to his
popularity at the end of his career. A bookseller placed before me
a Longfellow item which he thought might prove irresistible to an
admirer. This was a two-volume set of the *Poetical Works,* published
in 1879-80. Surely few finer editions of a poet's work have ever
been published. The page size of the two volumes is 9 x 12 inches.
They are elaborately bound in embossed leather, with richly
marbled endpapers. On the highly-calendared, gold-edged paper
one finds not only the household poet's poems but also literally
hundreds of illustrations, many of them full page, by F. O. C.
Darley, Mary Hallock Foote, and numerous other artists of the time.
These volumes were to be treasured and leafed through, with
children or friends peering over one's shoulder, rather than read
in bed or in paperback irreverence. But they could not be held
comfortably in the hands of anyone smaller than a titan, for the
two volumes weigh almost twenty pounds! The publisher must
have risked a mint of money in bringing them out, but he probably
found them a good investment.

No piling up of evidence or testimony can create a faithful picture
of how famous he once was, but the following quotation is
indicative:

> Longfellow's following was incomparable. The statistics are stag-
> gering: more than seventy British publishers, largely piratical,
> nearly three hundred editions in England alone in the second half
> of the century, at least a hundred separate book translations into
> eighteen different languages by 1900, and in Latin America at
> least eighty-seven of his poems in one hundred seventy-four
> separate versions by fifty-three translators. He surpassed Tennyson
> as the household laureate; and *Evangeline* (1847), *The Golden*

Legend (1851), *Hiawatha* (1855), and *Miles Standish* (1858) became the common property of Englishmen everywhere. . . . On the Continent his popularity was unmatched.[16]

The rising tide of Longfellow's reputation as a poet must have crested at his death or shortly afterward, but his fame continued high for at least another generation. Craigie House became one of America's most visited literary shrines, and his long and short poems continued popular in homes and schools. In 1902 his biographer Thomas Wentworth Higginson, summing up an impressive array of facts and testimony about Longfellow's worldwide fame, could conclude: "It is safe to say that up to the present moment no visible reaction has occurred in the case of Longfellow."[17] William Tirebuck, in an introduction to a new edition of his works, wrote in 1909: "He occupies more space in the popular imagination than any other author. In connection with literature his personality springs first to the minds of the people; moreover, he is the American author most quoted without the label of his name" (*Works*, I, 15).

IV *Nadir of Reputation*

What caused the decline in his popularity? It must have been a combination of the birth of the free-verse movement in the second decade of the nineteenth century and the simultaneous growth of wide interest in the poetry of Walt Whitman, along with the turbulence inspired by World War I. Certainly the "retreat from Longfellow" began to be apparent at this time, and by the 1920's it had become almost a rout. By 1931 Russell Blankenship, one of the new historians of American literature, could dismiss Longfellow in three deprecatory pages while according fourteen pages of praise to Emerson and eighteen to Whitman. In 1932 another historian, Ludwig Lewisohn, was even more contemptuous. He said in part: "Who, except wretched schoolchildren, now reads Longfellow? . . . The thing to establish in America is not that Longfellow was a very small poet, but that he did not partake of the poetic character at all."[18] To be sure, there were other historians who presented him more favorably at about the same time, but there is no denying that Longfellow had not only lost his halo, but was beginning to be characterized as just about everything an American poet should not be.

The severest critics of Longfellow in the 1930's were either nonacademic persons or very young academics. Mature critics were staunch in his defense throughout. Soon after H. S. Gorman held him up to ridicule in *A Victorian American* (1926) and Lewisohn said he was no poet, such university professors as Howard Mumford Jones, University of Michigan (now at Harvard), and Odell Shepard, Trinity College, rose to defend him. Jones said: "He grew out of the beautiful life which a Puritan civilization had made possible";[19] and, in analyzing numerous poems, he found, in addition to occasional bathos, many fine literary qualities. Because he summarizes the situation in 1934, when the battle over Longfellow was at its height, Shepard invites quotation at some length:

> The retreat from Longfellow, which has recently become almost a stampede, has been caused by nothing connected with the art of poetry. He is obnoxious to some as a representative of the prosperous middle class, to others as a New Englander, and to a third group as a "Puritan"—however little that deeply colored word may be understood. His enormous popularity has worked in some ways as a misfortune to American letters because it has recently suggested to many writers that whatever he had they must avoid. Now he had good sense, moderation, simplicity, reticence, faith in his country, tradition, sense of form, and some learning. It is not well for us to avoid quite all these traits.[20]

Shepard continues by asserting that reading Longfellow is still good for Americans, especially the young, and he concludes: "To every educated American it should be a pride and a pleasure to know Longfellow well, to defend him wisely, and to hold him dear."

V *Longfellow in Our Time*

Although Longfellow was never without defenders and is now experiencing a mild revival (two full-length biographies in the last decade, a paperback edition of selected poetry, and a paperback collection of "Tales"), there is no doubt that he has lost, probably permanently, most of his once widespread and admiring audience. Why? Professor Shepard's analysis is illuminating, but additional points may be noted.

Some decline was, of course, inevitable. Authors of a given age compete as time goes on not only with their predecessors and contemporaries but also with their successors. Longfellow was bound to be pushed aside to make room for such conventional poets as Edwin Arlington Robinson and Robert Frost and also (which he would not have liked) for free-verse writers like the resurgent Whitman and new talents like Edgar Lee Masters and Carl Sandburg. Moreover, if a pendulum swings far in one direction, its return swing tends to take it equally far in the opposite direction. Longfellow's excessive popularity in his own time was almost bound to generate a corresponding swing of unpopularity at a later date. Undoubtedly many children, especially those who are disinclined toward poetry, conceived an antipathy for him because they had to memorize his poetry; they retained this dislike as adults, and were only too glad to express it when they discovered it was not considered irreverent to do so. Also, as already mentioned, poetry has lost out heavily in modern times to fiction and other prose.

However, the matter is not quite as simple as this. Longfellow was voicing the America of his own time, and he knew it. America was characterized by a buoyant belief in the progressive quality of Western civilization, especially as it was developing in the New World, and this helped popularize his lyric expressions of faith. But the America that turned against him was a nation rudely jolted from its dream of faith in man's progress. Mother Europe had been racked by a world war heavily destructive of life, limb, and property, but even more shattering to faith in society. America was not to remain untouched by this war; its President's slogan of "Too Proud to Fight" had to give way to other slogans: "War to End War," "We Must Make the World Safe for Democracy."

America, especially young America, strove mightily, if often blindly or uncertainly, for reorientation in the years following the initial defeat of Western society in World War I and the continuing reverses of the Great Depression. The voice of America, which had been buoyant with faith in man and nation, was lost in the disillusioned, cynical chorus of the Lost Generation. Longfellow was caught in the search for new values and certainties. The American Adam had not, to be sure, been driven out of his new Eden; but, worse, he had found that it was no longer Eden—if indeed it ever had been. Who or what was the serpent? Casting about angrily, young critics, with H. L. Mencken the bellwether of many, identified as enemies the idols of a former time—both abstractions and persons. Puritanism and Victorianism especially became anathema. And was Longfellow not both Puritan and Victorian? He was a descendant of several generations of New England Puritans, and he continued loyal to their ideal of strict morality. In late life he had received the Victorian accolade from no less a person than Queen Victoria herself.

In 1826, soon after he went abroad for the first time, Longfellow wrote to his mother: "I . . . am delighted with Paris, where a person if he pleases can keep out of vice as well as elsewhere; though, to be sure, temptations are multiplied a thousand-fold if he is willing to enter into them" (*Life*, I, 80). For the benefit of his continuing reputation in the twentieth century, perhaps he should have entered into them at least once. One can only conjecture how different

Longfellow's position in American literature might have been in the 1930's if some scholar had been able to discover for the young Longfellow an "affair," the counterpart of Wordsworth's with Annette Vallon. But no such discovery has been made, and a search for one seems singularly unpromising.

Also unfruitful has been the search for Freudian oddities in Longfellow. He had no complexes and only the inhibitions of a Victorian gentleman. A biographer could write a book centering on a supposed Freudian repression in Whittier,[21] but Longfellow obviously cannot be made into a Freudian subject. Moreover, his recurrent affirmations of faith and belief in eternity were painfully antithetical to an age which cherished the death wish and thoughts of total annihilation.

In the final analysis, he became unpopular chiefly because Americans no longer liked people such as they believed him to have been. That he had never been just that kind of person but in many ways its opposite was irrelevant. The writer who attempts to assess Longfellow today must perforce relate the image to the man. The aim of the following chapters is to make clearer the kind of person Longfellow really was and to re-evaluate his contribution to American literary history and to American literature.

CHAPTER 2

Boyhood and Background, 1807-25

I *The Longfellow Family*

DESCENDED FROM well-established New England families, Henry Wadsworth Longfellow was proud of his heritage. His earliest American paternal ancestor was William Longfellow, who came to Newbury, Massachusetts, from Yorkshire, England, about 1651. The line of descent traces through William, a merchant; Stephen, a blacksmith; Stephen, a judge; Stephen, a lawyer and legislator; to Henry Wadsworth, professor and poet.[1] Judge Stephen Longfellow was the first Longfellow to live in Portland, Maine. In his day and well into the poet's boyhood, Maine was not a state but a territory of Massachusetts, with close cultural ties to Boston.

Henry's ancestry went back to even earlier colonial days on his mother's side. Her maiden name was Wadsworth. Christopher Wadsworth came from England to Duxbury, Massachusetts, about 1632. The poet's maternal grandfather was General Peleg Wadsworth of Revolutionary War fame. Some of his ancestors on his mother's side went all the way back to the *Mayflower* Pilgrims, and included Elder William Brewster and, more important for his poetry, John Alden and Priscilla Mullins.[2] Henry was named for his uncle, his mother's brother, Lieutenant Henry Wadsworth, who had died a naval hero in Tripoli Harbor in 1804 in the war with the Barbary pirates; he and his companions blew up an American vessel rather than be captured (*Life*, I, 3-4). Henry's later pacifism did not stem from lack of military ancestors, at least on the maternal side.

On both sides the stock was of sturdy, industrious, large-city, coast-dwelling New England Puritans. However, unlike the ancestry of Emerson, Holmes, and Lowell, it did not exhibit a preponderance of clergymen. The Longfellows and the Wadsworths were predominantly enterprising laymen rather than clerical intellectuals. No writer of consequence was included among them.

Henry was born in Portland, Maine, February 27, 1807. He had an older brother (named Stephen like his grandfather and great-grandfather), two younger brothers, and four younger sisters. Samuel Longfellow, twelve years his junior, was to become a Unitarian clergyman and ultimately the poet's biographer. That Henry felt close to all members of his family is indicated by his correspondence with all of them during his first stay in Europe; separately to his father, mother, and brother Stephen, and collectively to his sisters. Of his sisters, he seems to have been closest to Anne (whom he called Annie), who was three years his junior.

Longfellow's relationship with his father was very important. He kept in close touch with his father by letter while in college, on all of his first three European tours, and during most of his Harvard professorship. Whether or not either father or son was aware of this fact, it is apparent that much of the pressure that made Longfellow an academic person and kept him one until after his father's death was applied by his father. His relationship to his mother was important too, but in a very different way. According to her youngest son's account, "From her must have come to her son the imaginative and romantic side of his nature. She was fond of poetry and music, and in her youth, of dancing and social gayety. She was a lover of nature in all its aspects. She would sit by a window during a thunder-storm, enjoying the excitement of its splendors. Her disposition, through all trials and sorrows, was always cheerful,—with a gentle and tranquil fortitude" (*Life*, I, 4). If his father gave him industry, seriousness of purpose, and tenacity, his mother helped point him toward imaginative contemplation and ultimately the writing of poetry.

II *The City by the Sea*

It is significant that Longfellow was born in Portland, a major Maine seaport. It was to become the first capital of the new state in 1820. In 1960, Portland had 77,634 inhabitants, about 5,000 fewer than a decade earlier. A figure for 1807 is not available, but, then as now, it was Maine's largest city. A description written not long after Longfellow's death by his biographer W. S. Kennedy invites somewhat extended quotation, especially for its inclusion of testimony by Portland residents:

At present it is a flourishing seaport city, beautifully situated on the broad Casco Bay, with its quiet waters and numerous beautiful islands. Landward the landscape stretches away for eighty miles to the White Mountains, with Mount Washington indistinctly visible on the far horizon. The town, as it was in Longfellow's boyhood, is thus described by Mr. Edward Henry Elwell: "It lay on the narrow peninsula, or Neck, in the depression between the two hills which mark its extremities,—Munjoy and Bramhall. In a square house, standing on the one hand within a stone's throw of the spot where the first settler landed and built his cabin in 1632, and on the other

not much farther from the site of old Fort Loyal, our poet was born. . . . It was a pleasant site, not then, as now, hemmed in by new-made land encroaching on the sea. It looked out on the waters of our beautiful bay, commanding a view of those
—'islands that were the Hesperides
Of all my boyish dreams.'
Nearby was the beach, the scene of many a baptism on 'the Lord's day.' "

No doubt a boy living there would sense the bustle and accomplishment, along with his enjoyment of the natural beauty. Elwell continues: " 'With the revival of commerce, after the war, trade with the West India Islands sprang up, and low-decked brigs carried out cargoes of lumber and dried fish, bringing back sugar, rum, and molasses. This trade made lively scenes on Long Wharf and Portland Pier.' " Kennedy quotes another resident: "Rev. Elijah Kellogg, jun., gives a lively picture of Portland at the time: 'Portland was a lumber-port, driving a brisk little trade with more tumult and hurrah than now accompanies the transaction of ten times the amount of business then done. In addition to its lumber-trade it had its distilleries, its tanneries, its rope-walks, and its pottery,—the latter two of which so impressed themselves upon the memory of the boy Longfellow that in after-years they suggested his poems, "The Ropewalk" and "Keramos," the song of the potter.' "

Kennedy gives his own description of the intellectual life of Portland: "There was a good deal of intellectual life in the town. In 1790 the Rev. Dr. Samuel Deane published his New-England Farmer, or Georgical Dictionary, which was for a long time a standard work on matters of agriculture. In 1816 Enoch Lincoln of Portland published his poem, 'The Village,' containing over two thousand lines, and 'remarkable for its advanced moral sentiment, anticipating many of the reforms of our day, as well as for its erudition and its evenly sustained poetical merit.' "[3]

Portland was a good place for an author's boyhood—metropolitan enough to inspire a longing to see more of the world, quiet enough for meditation. It is easy to note parallels between Portland, Maine, and Hannibal, Missouri, where Mark Twain grew up. Both were on waterfronts; both were places of considerable intermittent bustle, created mainly by the coming and going of ships; both were cities of considerable importance in their own right, but were more or less in the shadow of a greater metropolis nearby: for Hannibal, Saint Louis; for Portland, Boston.

At first called Falmouth, Portland was almost as old as Boston. Unforgettable events which took place there during Longfellow's boyhood included the seafight in 1813 between the American

Enterprise and the British *Boxer,* in which the American ship captured the British and both captains were killed.[4] Doubtless this greatly impressed the six-year-old boy; Longfellow records it with other reminiscences in the short lyric which many readers consider his finest, "My Lost Youth." Later, in 1824, when Longfellow was a college student, the aging Revolutionary hero, the Marquis de Lafayette, visited Portland. Henry must have been at home on vacation at the time, for he also made literary use of this event later in one of his few short stories, "The Bald Eagle."

Longfellow's boyhood home was built by his maternal grandfather, Peleg Wadsworth, in 1784-86, and was the first brick house in Portland (*Life,* I, 3). It still stands, a memorial to the poet. The house was then almost by the seaside, where Longfellow could hear the rhythmic roar of the surf. Probably much of his facility for verse rhythms came to him through his responsive listening to the lapping of the waves and to the sighing of the wind in lofty pines nearby. Longfellow always loved Portland and often visited there, especially up to the time of his father's death in 1849.

III *Youth of a Poet*

It is a little hard to imagine that the "White Mr. Longfellow" was ever a child. Actually, his early boyhood was not remarkably different from that of thousands of other American boys. He was a "good" boy, but does not seem to have been offensively so. A friend of the family wrote reminiscently in 1877: "Most distinctly do I recall the bright, pleasant boy as I often saw him at his father's house while I was living in Portland, in the years 1816-17" (*Life,* I, 9). His brother wrote: "Henry is remembered by others as a lively boy, with brown or chestnut hair, blue eyes, a delicate complexion, and rosy cheeks; sensitive, impressionable; active, eager, impetuous, often impatient; quick-tempered, but as quickly appeased; kind-hearted and affectionate, —the sun-light of the house. He had great neatness and love of order. He was always extremely conscientious. . . . He was industrious, prompt, and persevering; full of ardor, he went into everything he undertook with great zest."

In brief, he was a rather typical boy in a Puritan household of somewhat extraordinary liveliness and charm. The industry and conscientiousness are noteworthy; both were to be dominant traits throughout his life. However, he was not without playfulness: "He was fond of all boys' games,—ball, kite-flying, and swimming, in summer; in winter, snowballing, coasting, and skating" (*Life,* I, 10). He also enjoyed the circuses and menageries that frequently came to Portland. When he was eight years old, he suffered from an infected leg, which got so bad that there was talk of amputation (Thompson, 16-17). Like Hawthorne at about the same age, he had this added incentive to turn from games to reading. He probably reach much more, and more intently, than the average boy. Like his admirer Howells, he had "literary passions," and was fortunate enough to be able to indulge them: "In the home, there were books and music. His father's library, not large, but well selected for the time, gave him, as he grew up, access to Shakespeare, Milton, Pope, Dryden, Thomson, Goldsmith; the Spectator, the Rambler, the Lives of the Poets, Rasselas, Plutarch's Lives; Hume's, Gibbon's, Gillies's and Robertson's Histories, and the like" (*Life*, I, 11).

Sunday reading was different from that of weekdays. On Sunday the home library offered Hannah Moore's *Works* and Cowper's poetry, but apparently not Bunyan's *Pilgrim's Progress,* perhaps because it was theologically objectionable. Longfellow did have access to most of the perennial family favorites: "Robinson Crusoe, of course, and the Arabian Nights were read by the children together; and Henry took delight in Don Quixote, and Ossian, and would go about the house declaiming the windy and misty utterances of the latter."

One can see responsiveness to poetry gradually awakening in the sensitive boy, encouraged no doubt by his mother, though probably not by his ultra-practical father. The general atmosphere was favorable to literary awakening: "He had access, also, to the shelves of the old Portland Library. And sometimes, of evenings, he got permission to go down to Mr. Johnson's bookstore to look over the few new books that from time to time arrived from Boston. There the boy might listen, also, to his elders, John Neal and Nathaniel Deering, talking about literature" (*Life*, I, 11). John Neal (1793-1871) was one of the earliest historians of American literature and a novelist of some distinction. There were also Neal's contemporaries, the once popular Nathaniel P. Willis (1806-67), born in Portland but reared in Boston, and the prolific novelist J. H. Ingraham (1809-60), whose curious literary output and its wide reception seem to have puzzled Longfellow, to whom Ingraham dedicated one of his novels without Longfellow's permission and to his annoyance.[5]

Just when Longfellow began to write verse is not known. His brother denies that he wrote the jingle, often attributed to him, about Mr. Finney and his turnip which grew behind the barn (*Life*, I, 22). Probably he made some preliminary attempts before he sought publication at the early age of thirteen. Using only his first name, he submitted a poem published November 17, 1820, in the poet's corner of the *Portland Gazette*. It is revealing:

THE BATTLE OF LOVELL'S POND

Cold, cold is the north wind and rude is the blast
That sweeps like a hurricane loudly and fast,
As it moans through the tall waving pines lone and drear,
Sighs a requiem sad o'er the warrior's bier.

The war-whoop is still, and the savage's yell
Has sunk into silence along the wild dell;
The din of the battle, the tumult, is o'er
And the war-clarion's voice is now heard no more.

The warriors that fought for their country—and bled,
Have sunk to their rest; the damp earth is their bed;
No stone tells the place where their ashes repose,
Nor points out the spot from the graves of their foes.

They died in their glory, surrounded by fame,
And Victory's loud trump their death did proclaim;
They are dead; but they live in each Patriot's breast,
And their names are engraven on honor's bright crest.

(*Life*, I, 21-22)

A lover of the melancholy and oratorical strains of Ossian would naturally write such a poem. There are clear echoes in it, too, of Lord Byron, whose popularity reached its height while Longfellow was growing up. More important, the poem already shows Longfellow's lifelong facility in achieving meter and rhyme, but, probably fortunately for his poetic growth, publication brought little praise and one stinging criticism. One of his father's best friends, a Judge Mellen, presumably unaware of the poem's authorship, commented on it in the boy's presence: "Did you see the piece in to-day's paper? Very stiff, remarkably stiff; moreover, it is all borrowed, every word of it" (*Life*, I, 23). According to his brother, who could have known only from family hearsay, "there were tears on his pillow that night."[6] However, he was not discouraged for long; he had other pieces, none of which he reprinted later, published from time to time in the *Gazette*. This was the beginning, not an especially promising one, of his career as a poet. His was a normal, happy boyhood, with only modest suggestions that world-famous authorship might lie along the unseen road in the distance.

IV *Early Education*

The scanty records of his early education show that Longfellow was a precocious student, though perhaps not more so than many children in New England Puritan families of intellectual bent. He is said to have started school when he was three years old, with his brother Stephen, two years older. By the age of six he had entered the Portland Academy; apparently he also attended other private schools. An early Academy report by his teacher, a Mr. Carter, was very favorable: "Master Henry Longfellow is one of the best boys we have in school. He spells and reads very well. He also can add and multiply numbers. His conduct last quarter was very correct and amiable."[7] His brother paints his days at the Academy as having been very enjoyable. Boys sat on one side and girls on the other, all of the romantically inclined (which could not have failed to include Henry Longfellow) covertly very much aware of the proximity of the other sex.

And "Deering's Woods also afforded lovely opportunities in its leafy glades, which our school-boy frequented, not only with his boy companions in search of autumnal acorns and walnuts, but with the pretty maidens, his sister's friends, when April winds stirred the blossoming of the rosy-white May-flowers under their blanket of rough leaves" (*Life*, I, 25). In mid-life Longfellow, in "My Lost Youth," was to recall these "early loves" and the "long, long thoughts" of the schoolboy. No doubt he was at least as sentimental as the average boy, differing chiefly in being even more thoughtful, with many a partly bold, partly timorous imaginative effort to envision what the future might hold in store for him.

In 1821, only a year after he had published "The Battle of Lovell's Pond," he passed the Bowdoin College entrance examinations, as did his older brother (*Life*, I, 26).

V *Bowdoin College*

Although he himself was a Harvard graduate, Longfellow's father was determined to send his sons to Bowdoin. Not only was he a Bowdoin trustee; there was much pride in Portland in the new college at Brunswick, only a little more than twenty miles up the coast to the northeast: "The college itself was but twenty years old, and Maine had only just become an independent State of the Union, so that there was a strong feeling of local pride in this young institution."[8] Moreover, his own father, old Judge Longfellow, had been one of the founders of Bowdoin.

Probably because of the youth of the boys, fourteen and sixteen when they passed their entrance examination, the decision was that they should pursue their freshman studies at home at Portland Academy rather than at Bowdoin. That Henry at least was eager to see Bowdoin is proved by the fact that he snatched an opportunity to visit there with another boy (not his brother) in May, 1821.

The stagecoach ride over a winding woodland road of thirty miles must have been an adventure in itself. In the little village of white houses, the three buildings of the new college formed three sides of a quadrangle. There seems to be no record of what Longfellow thought when he saw his prospective Alma Mater for the first time. He must have visited the chapel building, which housed the four thousand volumes—mostly concerned with theology, history, and classical literature—of the library. He probably felt a growing eagerness to begin residence studies immediately, but the sons of Stephen Longfellow did not question their father's judgment. Instead, Henry returned to Portland and with his brother studied freshman subjects at the Academy. But he kept in touch with certain more fortunate classmates already residing in Brunswick, notably George Pierce, who was later to become his brother-in-law.

Finally, in the fall of 1822, the Longfellow brothers took up resident study in Brunswick. As newcomers, they were not entitled to dormitory housing, which could accommodate only fifty of the one hundred and twenty boys enrolled. Their father arranged to have them and their friend Ned Preble live in the home of Benjamin Titcomb, a former Portland resident and now a Baptist minister. The boys were not greatly pleased with the austere quarters furnished by Parson Titcomb, and they probably found it a bit arduous to arise in the cold to hustle to the college for six o'clock prayers before breakfast at their lodgings. The library was open only during the noon hour; Longfellow must often have had to choose between a book and a meal.

A college rule required all students to remain in their rooms during the evening, but it could not be enforced. A neighboring tavern was a favorite resort, which Stephen frequented more than Henry, who did not, however, report his brother's night prowling to their parents (Thompson, 31). A classmate named Bradbury has given his impressions of the new sophomore:

> I met him for the first time in the autumn of 1822. . . . As we both had our rooms out of college and in the same vicinity, we were often together in passing to and from the recitation-room, and became well acquainted. He was genial, sociable, and agreeable, and always a gentleman in his deportment. . . . He had a happy temperament, free from envy and every corroding passion and vice. In personal appearance, according to my present recollection of him, . . . his figure was slight and erect, his complexion light and delicate as a maiden's, with a slight bloom upon the cheek; his nose rather prominent, his eyes clear and blue, and his well-formed head covered with a profusion of brown hair waving loosely. While he was understood in college to be a general reader, and more especially

devoted to the Muses, he never allowed himself to come to the recitation-room without thorough preparation. . . . His class was one in which there was a large amount of ambition and an intense struggle for rank in scholarship. . . . In this class Longfellow stood justly among the first (*Life*, I, 27-28).

In September, soon after his arrival in Brunswick, Henry wrote his "Dear Parents" some first impressions and put in some requests for items from home which he wanted or needed:

I feel very well contented, and am much pleased with a College Life. Many of the students are very agreeable companions and, thus far, I have passed my time very pleasantly. The students have considerably more leisure than I expected. . . . I expected, when I got here, that I should have to study very hard to keep a good footing with the rest of the class; but I find I have sufficient time for the preparation of my lessons and for amusement. . . . I wish some one would get a brass ferrule put on to my cane and send it to me as soon as possible—If you have any good apples or pears I wish you would send me some—and tell the girls to send a whole parcel of Gingerbread with them (Thompson, 31-32).

In a postscript, he added a request for a good watch, since it was hard to hear the chapel bell off campus. The letter shows rather typical student reactions to the college experience. Longfellow was apparently as much interested in his cane, an accessory of the well-dressed young man, and in creature comforts as in his studies and other responsibilities.

His letters to his mother indicate satisfaction in his work, especially in the study of poetry. He expressed admiration for Gray's Odes and the Elegy (*Life,* I, 29-31). In 1823 he was finding very interesting Heckewelder's book on the Delaware Indians, which Cooper was using at about that time as a source for *The Pioneers.* Shortly afterward he wrote his father that he was tackling Locke's *On the Human Understanding* and finding it "neither remarkably hard nor uninteresting." It is probably significant that he wrote his mother about poetry and his father about philosophy.

For a time he was a member of a self-constituted military group called the "Bowdoin Cadets," which drilled regularly with patriotic fervor. This was probably the only time Longfellow entered voluntarily into any military activity, and he soon lost interest in it; but his brother Stephen, finding the group transforming itself into a convivial club, retained membership. If Henry engaged in walking, he preferred to do it at his own pace and inclination: "More appealing to Henry than soldiering was the quiet diversion of walking through the shaded forest paths with such congenial companions as Preble, Greenleaf, and his classmate Eugene Weld. Occasionally they walked through the town to the falls of the Androscoggin, where great logs, carried down by the spring freshets, pitched and rolled out over the steep ledges of the falls to the quiet waters beyond" (Thompson, 39). Longfellow was so impressed by these falls that a dozen years later, when visiting the famous falls of Trollhättan in Sweden, he found them inferior to his memories of the falls of the Androscoggin.[9]

Meanwhile he was making a favorable impression on his classmates, apparently without arousing their envy. Later one of them, the Honorable J. W. Bradbury, described him as "a slight, erect figure, [with a] delicate complexion and intelligent expression of countenance." He added, "He was always a gentleman in his deportment, and a model in his character and habits." Another, the Reverend David Shepley, wrote: "He gave urgent heed to all departments of study in the prescribed course, and excelled in them all; while his enthusiasm moved in the direction it has taken in subsequent life. His themes, felicitous translations of Horace, and occasional contributions to the press, drew marked attention to him, and led to the expectation that his would be an honorable literary career."[10] Shepley had observed, perhaps after the corroborating evidence was already available, two significant points: his early facility in translation, which was to be lifelong; and his continuing desire to achieve publication.

Returning to Bowdoin for their junior year, the Longfellow brothers were given a corner room in a new dormitory, with a view of a nearby dark grove of whispering pines. An important event late in their sophomore year had been their election to the two Bowdoin literary societies. By chance or otherwise, each brother got into the society most congenial to him. Henry was chosen for the Peucinian Society, which then enrolled the best students; Stephen for the Athenian Society, which had more convivial inclinations but also a great deal of talent —Franklin Pierce, Horatio Bridge, and Nathaniel Hawthorne were members. It was probably their memberships in these rival literary societies, rather than any lack of congeniality, which prevented Henry Longfellow and Hawthorne from becoming good friends until long afterward when both were struggling authors.

Living in the dormitory, Henry could make the most of his membership in the Peucinian Society. Now that campus "literary societies" exist only in history, it is hard to imagine what they meant in Longfellow's day. However, it is obvious that they combined the appeals of social fraternities, debating clubs, library browsing rooms, and honor societies. No doubt Longfellow reveled in reading the new books made available by the Peucinian Society. The Society "subscribed to *Blackwood's*, the *North American Review*, and the *American Monthly*, so that they might decide which books to buy for the society library" (Thompson, 41). A collection of new books containing the still-new romances of Sir Walter Scott; the first novels of James Fenimore Cooper, the American Scott; and the works of two still earlier American romancers, Charles Brockden Brown of Philadelphia and Longfellow's fellow citizen John Neal, were bound to excite the bright-eyed college junior.

About this time, he wrote his mother a letter about his reactions to reading Brown's *Arthur Mervyn*, and took the opportunity to make his earliest of several pleas for the recognition and encouragement of American authorship. That he was reading *Blackwood's* at the time is indicated by a reference to a *Blackwood's* writer's comments on Brown's writings. A letter to his sister Anne a week later shows that he was excitedly immersed in his reading: "You must know I have no time to spare—for what little time I can steal from my college exercises, I wish to devote to reading" (Thompson, 41). Probably few, if any American college students have found the campus intellectual adventure more enthralling than Longfellow did, once he discovered that he could indulge a voracious reading appetite comfortably and with no limitation other than time.

For Longfellow the writer, the most important single adventure stemming from his Peucinian activity was no doubt his participation in the Junior Exhibition in December. The exhibition was a public debate between two persons, in this instance Longfellow and his classmate J. W. Bradbury. The title announced by the college president was "English Dialogue between a North American Savage and an English Emigrant." Each contestant had four minutes in which to make his case. Longfellow drew the part of the savage, though he would have preferred the other. He appeared as King Philip and Bradbury as Miles Standish. Longfellow did his best to make a case for the Indian. He was probably already acquainted with Irving's sketch, "Philip of Pokanoket," and it was about this time that he discovered John Heckewelder's big volume on the Pennsylvania Indians. That Longfellow entered into the spirit of the performance and even dimly foreshadowed his *Hiawatha* of a generation later is shown by his peroration: "Alas! the sky is overcast with dark and blustering clouds. The rivers run with blood, but never, never will we suffer the grass to grow upon our war-path. And now I do remember that the Initiate prophet, in my earlier years, told from his dreams that all our race should fall like withered leaves when Autumn strips the forest! Lo! I hear singing and sobbing: 'tis the death-song of a mighty nation, the last requiem over the grave of the fallen" (Thompson, p. 47).

Apparently Longfellow gave a quite creditable performance, to his own relief. Now he could go back to the more leisurely, less purposeful reading he preferred. A number of his classmates taught school in rural communities during the winter vacation; Longfellow considered this, but decided against it on the ground that it would be more profitable for him to continue his reading. Presently, however, it became apparent that there was another reason. He had learned of a Shakespeare Jubilee to be held in Boston in February, 1824, with a prize competition for an ode to be read as a feature of the Jubilee. He had secretly submitted an ode, and hoped to be in Boston to hear it read. He wrote his father for permission to spend a week in Boston, since "I am of an opinion, that it is better to know the world partly from observation than wholly from books" (Thompson, 51). His father replied with a homily on the danger of travel for an inexperienced youth: "To travel with advantage requires a maturity of understanding & an extensive knowledge of books. Youth is therefore the proper period for study, manhood for traveling, & intercourse with mankind." But he was permitted to go to Boston. He did not win the contest, the honors going to one Charles Sprague, an experienced occasional poet; but he did make interesting acquaintances, and he returned to his home in high spirits.

Often one teacher proves influential enough to play a decisive role in a boy's life. For the young Whittier, it was Joshua Coffin, who taught him Burns and fed his interest in New England balladry. For the young Longfellow, it was Samuel P. Newman, Bowdoin professor of languages, who was in effect also professor of rhetoric. Newman showed the young student how to discover the human personality in the poetry of Horace and taught him that the study of Latin and Greek could be much more than a mere analysis of words and sentences (Thompson, 48-49).

In his senior year Longfellow continued the serious application to duty that had always been characteristic, with results generally satisfactory to himself, his parents, and the college authorities. One matter at the very end of his college career deserves emphasis: he was selected to deliver one of the Commencement Day orations (Thompson, 67ff.). After wavering between the assigned subject, "Our Native Writers," and an essay on his current literary passion, the newly discovered poet Thomas Chatterton, he finally decided to speak on "Our Native Writers."

This speech was a remarkable performance, especially when one considers that it was uttered in 1821 by an eighteen-year-old college boy, only six years after Washington Irving's remarks on American culture in the *Sketch-Book* and twelve years before Emerson's celebrated declaration of intellectual independence in "The American Scholar." The seven-minute oration warrants extensive quotation:

To an American there is something endearing in the very sound,—Our Native Writers. Like the music of our native tongue, when heard in a foreign land, they have power to kindle up within him the tender memory of his home and fireside; and more than this, they foretell that whatever is noble and attractive in our national character will one day be associated with the sweet magic of Poetry. Is, then, our land to be indeed the land of song? Will it one day be rich in romantic associations? . . . as yet we can boast of nothing farther than a first beginning of a national literature: a literature associated and linked in with the grand and beautiful scenery of our country,—with our institutions, our manners, our customs,—in a word, with all that has helped to form whatever there is peculiar to us, and to the land in which we live. We cannot yet throw off our literary allegiance to Old England, we cannot yet remove from our shelves every book which is not strictly and truly American. English literature is a great and glorious monument, built up by the master-spirits of old time. . . .

Poetry with us has never yet been anything but a pastime. . . . We are a plain people, that have had nothing to do with the mere pleasures and luxuries of life: and hence there has sprung up within us a quick-sightedness to the failings of literary men, and an aversion to everything that is not practical, operative, and thoroughgoing. But if we would ever have a national literature, our native writers must be patronized. . . .

We are thus thrown upon ourselves: and thus shall our native hills become renowned in song, like those of Greece and Italy. . . . Our poetry is not in books alone. It is in the hearts of those men, whose love for the world's gain,—for its business and its holiday,—has grown cold within them, and who have gone into the retirements of Nature, and have found there that sweet sentiment and pure devotion of feeling can spring up and live in the shadow of a low and quiet life, and amid those that have no splendor in their joys, and no parade in their griefs. . . .

We may rejoice, then, in the hope of beauty and sublimity in our national literature, for no people are richer than we are in the treasures of nature. And well may each of us feel a glorious and high-minded pride in saying, as he looks on the hills and vales,—on the woods and waters of New England,—

"This is my own, my native land."[11]

Much about the young Longfellow is revealed in this quotation. A few points need emphasis. The language reveals more than the conventional desire of the orator to sound impressive. It shows that Longfellow was thinking seriously, and rather shrewdly, about the state of literature in America. It shows too—despite later accusations that his house had only Eastern windows—that, from the outset, he believed that American literature needed to be more than a mere outgrowth of the literature of Europe. Also, with Poe, Hawthorne, and others, Longfellow recognized that lack of patronage was a serious limiting factor for authors. It is apparent in the next-to-last paragraph that Longfellow was already thinking of poetry as the poet's expression of the feelings of inarticulate, humble folk. Finally, it is interesting, though in no way surprising, that the young orator should conclude with a line from Scott's *Marmion.*

VI *I Will Be Eminent in Something*

Mention has already been made of the ode Longfellow entered in the Shakespeare Jubilee contest during his senior year at Bowdoin. This poem was by no means his only poetic effort while in college, and he was more successful with others. He actually sold poems to editors in Boston and Philadelphia, and he continued to have poems published in the *Portland Advertiser.* He published also in the *American Monthly Magazine* and in the important *United States Literary Gazette,* a vehicle for Bryant and Percival, among others. He must have been especially gratified to receive a letter from the *Gazette* editor, Theophilus Parsons, containing this tribute: "almost all the poetry we print is sent to us gratis, & we have no general rule or measure of repayment. But the beauty of your poetry makes me wish to obtain your regular aid. Will you be good enough to let me know how large & how frequent contributions it will be agreeable to you to furnish us, & what mode or amount of compensation you would desire" (Thompson, 62). Thus encouraged, Longfellow contributed during his senior year to the *Gazette* alone sixteen poems, five prose essays, and two book reviews. There can be no doubt that he was beginning to envision for himself the kind of career as a "native writer" for which he had expressed hope in his commencement oration.

However, free-spirited young man that he was in most respects, he seems not for a moment to have considered striking out on a literary career without his father's consent and approval. More a wide reader than a devoted Bible student, Longfellow nevertheless knew and revered the commandment, "Honour thy father and thy mother." There may have been less religion in his attitude than genuine respect for his father's views, but whatever the reason, the correspondence between father and son during Henry's last year and a half in college includes much discussion of the important subject of Henry's vocational choice. He wanted to be a literary person; his father distrusted literature as a vocation. His father would have settled for divinity or medicine, but expressed a natural preference for his own profession, the law.

Just when the serious discussion of Henry's vocation began is not certain, but it was no later than the middle of his junior year. On March 13, 1824, Henry wrote to his father: "I feel very glad that I am not to be a physician,—that there are quite enough in the world without me. And now, as somehow or other this subject has been introduced, I am curious to know what you do intend to make of me,—whether I am to study a profession or not; and if so, what profession. I hope your ideas upon this subject will agree with mine, for I have a particular and strong prejudice for one course of life" (*Life,* I, 50).

He did not state his preference at this time, either out of tact or in deference to his father's still unvoiced choice; but preceding events and later expressions proved it to be professional authorship. By April 30, however, his father must have named the law, for Henry wrote in protest: "in thinking to make a lawyer of me, I fear you thought more partially than justly. I do not, for my own part, imagine that such a coat would suit me. I hardly think Nature designed me for the bar, or the pulpit, or the dissecting-room" (*Life,* I, 52). Perhaps playfully, he then suggested the farmer's life. Several months later, December 5, 1824, he expressed his own preference forthrightly and vigorously. First he would spend a year at Cambridge studying history and language. Then:

> After leaving Cambridge, I would attach myself to some literary periodical publication, by which I could maintain myself and still enjoy the advantages of reading. . . . The fact is . . . I most eagerly aspire after future eminence in literature; my whole soul burns most ardently for it, and every earthly thought centres in it. . . . Surely, there never was a better opportunity offered for the exertion of literary talent in our own country than is now offered. . . . Whether Nature has given me any capacity for knowledge or not, she has at any rate given me a very strong predilection for literary pursuits, and I am almost confident in believing, that, if I can ever rise in the world, it must be by the exercise of my talent in the wide field of literature (*Life,* I, 53-54).

Here is no Milton burning to write works which the world would not willingly let die—but a young man aspiring to achieve success and fame through writing. It should be recognized, however, that the young man was trying to impress a reluctant parent; his passion for literary art was almost certainly, therefore, deeper than his phrasing might imply. At the same time, he was clearly in sympathy with his father's insistence on a vocation in which he could achieve success. There was enough Yankee in both of them for that.

About two weeks later, he wrote again to his father, yielding ground with obvious reluctance: "Even if it should be found necessary for me to study a profession, I should think a twelve-months' residence at Harvard before commencing the study would be exceedingly useful. Of divinity, medicine, and law, I should choose the last. Whatever I do study ought to be engaged in with all my soul—for I *will be eminent* in something" (*Life,* I, 55-56). The italics indicate that Longfellow did not lack ambition. His college performance had whetted a desire for distinction. His growing preference was for eminence in literature, but he seems to have been determined—and certainly he wanted his father to believe he was—to be eminent in some field. This resolution evidently made a strong impression on his father, but it did not persuade him to acquiesce in his son's choice. The opening sentence of Stephen Longfellow's letter is important in showing the father's genuine affection for his keen, promising son: "The subject of your first letter is one of deep interest and demands great consideration. A literary life, to one who has the means of support, must be very pleasant. But there is not wealth enough in this country to afford encouragement and patronage to merely literary men. And as you have not had the fortune (I will not say whether good or ill) to be born rich, you must adopt a profession which will afford you subsistence as well as reputation" (*Life,* I, 56).

Henry seems to have found his father's reply as satisfactory as could be expected. He accepted gratefully the offer of a year at Harvard and resigned himself to the study of law—though not at the cost of giving up "the pleasures of literature." In a letter of January 24, 1825, sent from Portland to Washington, where his father was serving as a congressman from the new state of Maine, he thanked his father and then said he planned to spend much of his Harvard year studying the languages of France and Italy, both of which he intended to visit "before I die." This statement was to prove significant, but not so significant as the following one: "The fact is, I have a most voracious appetite for knowledge. To its acquisition I will sacrifice everything. . . . Nothing delights me more than reading and writing. And nothing could induce me to relinquish the pleasures of literature, little as I have yet tasted them. Of the three professions I should prefer the law. I am far from being a fluent speaker, but practice must serve as a talisman where talent is wanting. I can be a lawyer. This will support my real existence, literature an *ideal* one" (*Life*, I, 58). What had happened meantime to his announced resolution to become eminent is conjectural. Perhaps he consoled himself with the thought that this way he would have two possible avenues to distinction.

A little earlier, he had written to a friend, George W. Wells, "Somehow, and yet I hardly know why, I am unwilling to study any profession. I cannot make a lawyer of any eminence, because I have not a talent for argument; I am not good enough for a minister,—and as to physic, I utterly and absolutely detest it" (*Life*, I, 52). Longfellow was skeptical of achieving "eminence" in the law, but he could resign himself to studying and practicing it to please his father.

But even while resigning himself to becoming a lawyer, Longfellow was possibly sensing an avenue of escape. He concluded his letter of January 24, 1825, with this observation: "I purchased last evening a beautiful pocket edition of Sir William Jones's Letters, and have just finished reading them. Eight languages he was critically versed in; eight more he read with a dictionary; and there were twelve more not wholly unknown to him. I have somewhere seen or heard the observation that as many languages as a person acquires, so many times is he a man" (*Life*, I, 58). Longfellow was already expressing the germ of an idea which was to motivate all his language study and teaching: the real objective in language study is to enter into the culture of the people who developed the language and used it to express themselves.

On February 7, 1825, he wrote again from Portland to his father in Washington. He estimated the total expenses of his year at Harvard at $184. He went on to lament the state legislature's failure to make any donation to Bowdoin College in the current session, mentioning particularly that the petition for a grant had stipulated that part was for the establishment of a professorship of modern languages (*Life*, I, 59). A few months later this professorship was to open a way for resolving the partial impasse which he and his father had reached. Although the legislature was not interested in it, Madam Bowdoin, for whose husband the college had been named, was. She contributed $1,000 toward it, and at the commencement in 1825—Longfellow's commencement— the Board of Trustees voted to establish it. A professorship would need a professor, and qualified professors of modern language were then almost nonexistent in America.

CHAPTER 3

Poet Submerged in Professor:
Bowdoin College, 1826-34

I *Bowdoin Wants a Department of Modern Languages*

IN VOTING TO ESTABLISH a professorship of modern languages, Bowdoin's trustees were surprisingly progressive. Latin, Greek, and Hebrew had been respectable college studies in America from the first, but modern languages were something else. The Bowdoin department would be only the fourth in the United States. Through the influence of Thomas Jefferson, the first had been opened at William and Mary in 1779-80 (Thompson, 82). Harvard's was the second, but much later, in 1819, at the instigation of George Ticknor. The third had been established at the University of Virginia, also through the influence of Thomas Jefferson, in 1825, the very year in which the Bowdoin trustees acted.

It was one thing to vote a professorship and another to establish a department. All three earlier modern language departments had been pioneer enterprises. George Ticknor, an able language scholar, especially in Spanish, had built a department at Harvard only slowly and with much difficulty, partly because of what he considered the provincial attitude of the president.

Where could the Bowdoin trustees find a professor of modern languages? Sometimes an individual's destiny hangs on a slender thread. Benjamin Orr, a trustee, had been greatly struck by young Henry Longfellow's translation of an ode of Horace at his senior examination. If a young scholar could show brilliance in the classical languages, Orr seems to have reasoned, he must have the ability to learn and teach the modern languages. In any case, he presented Longfellow's name for the new chair (*Life*, I, 67).

Longfellow must have been dumfounded at this turn of events. He had been going forward with his plans for a year of study at Harvard; in August, 1825, he had written to Theophilus Parsons, the Boston editor who had been so receptive to his contributions for the columns of the *United States Gazette,* applying for a position as assistant editor during his year in the community (Thompson, 74-75).

Although sympathizing with his talented correspondent, Parsons did not encourage Longfellow's literary aspirations. He himself had turned from the law to magazine publication, and had found the going difficult and precarious. Quite independently, Stephen Longfellow and Parsons gave the young writer substantially the same advice: write if you feel you must, but don't expect to make the principal part of your living through writing. Parsons wrote:

> I should think it would be exceedingly difficult for any one to earn a living by literature, just now. . . . You can easily earn a little anywhere, but I think you will find it difficult to earn much as a mere scholar. . . . There is a stage in the progress of a bright mind, when the boy has thrown away his toys and marbles, but the young man is still so far a child as to value things more by their elegance and power of amusing, than by their usefulness. He plays with his books, and thinks he is working when he is only playing hard. . . . Get through this present delusion as soon as you can, & then you will see how wise it will be for you to devote yourself to the law. . . . There is no fear of your losing your hold upon letters; at least, the danger of any young man's neglecting literature too much if he really loves it, is so remote, it hardly needs to be guarded against (Thompson, 76-77).

Longfellow must have been sadly taken aback by this letter. He had been trying to convince a general audience in his commencement oration and then his father in a series of letters that the time was at hand when literature would have full status as a profession in America. If his favorite editor had voluntarily come to the support of his father in urging the law upon him, what chance had he to escape? But the avenue of escape was nevertheless to open up promptly and to prove not only an acceptable alternative, but, at least in its preliminary stages, a highly exciting adventure.

Although there seems to be no written evidence, one suspects that Longfellow's father may have been almost as relieved as Henry at this resolution of the impasse between him and a son of whom he was extremely fond. Indeed, he may even have taken some initiative in the matter. Certainly it was he who, returning from a meeting of the trustees, bore to Henry the news that "an informal proposal had been made that he should visit Europe for the purpose of fitting himself for the position, with the understanding that on his return he should be appointed to the Professorship" (Life, I, 68). Apparently there is no written record of how the young graduate received the news, but he must have been almost beside himself with joy. Lawrance Thompson summarizes his probable reaction and its background as follows:

Europe! The land of his dreams! Since boyhood Longfellow had revelled in thoughts of mouldering castles, the ruins of ancient temples, the snow-capped wonders of Alpine peaks, the soft breathing of musical night-winds over moonlit waters in Italy. Europe and poetry were one to him—all the mystery of antique tradition and legend was wrapped up in the very sound of the name. At Portland Academy one of the poems he had copied into his commonplace book had been Samuel Rogers's "Venice, an Italian Song." His discovery of Scott had rapidly developed his fondness for tales of chivalry and legends of medieval times. Just what Europe was like, he had no definite idea, because his visions were blurred by mists of romance. But *The Sketch Book* had transformed his vague imaginings into a persistent longing to travel in those regions of quaint peculiarities (Thompson, 79).

Eager as he was to go, however, he had to exercise considerable patience before setting out. Ocean travel in those days depended on sailing ships, and the season was not favorable. The year of post-graduate study at Harvard having been automatically ruled out, Longfellow filled in the autumn and winter reading law in his father's office—perhaps partly to make his father feel better about the turn of events, partly to hedge against a new turnabout, for the romantic Longfellow was always in some measure a realist. Evidently he did not take his Blackstone very seriously, for during the same time "he undertook to write for the *Portland Advertiser* a series of papers after the fashion of Irving's Salmagundi" (*Life*, I, 68). These sketches were printed anonymously. He was also writing verse, mostly musings on nature subjects; one of these was "The Burial of the Minnisink." Some of this verse was published in the *Atlantic Souvenir* (Philadelphia), one of the numerous gift-book annuals of the time.

With the coming of spring, Longfellow began his plans for the great adventure; he sailed in May. On the eve of his departure, while en route to New York to board his packet-ship, he exchanged letters with both his parents. He wrote his mother from Boston that he had heard Dr. Channing preach and had dined with Mr. Ticknor: "He is exceedingly kind and affable. He has supplied me with letters to Washington Irving, Professor Eichhorn in Germany, and Robert Southey. He strongly recommends a year's residence in Germany, and is very decidedly in favor of commencing literary studies there" (*Life*, I, 71). He also met President Kirkland of Harvard, "a jolly little man." His mother's reply was full of maternal solicitude, but evidently she fully approved of his going: "I will not say how much we miss your elastic step, your cheerful voice, your melodious flute. I will say, farewell, my dear son, may God be with and prosper you. May you be successful in your pursuit of knowledge; may you hold fast your integrity, and retain that purity of heart which is so endearing to your friends. I feel as if you were going into a thousand perils" (*Life*, I, 71-72).

His father's parting counsel was similar, but more specific: "It is impossible, with all my solicitude, to give you all the instructions which your youth and inexperience require; but permit me to conjure you to remember the great objects for your journey and keep them constantly in view. . . . Be careful not to take any part in opposition to the religion or politics of the countries in which you reside. . . . In all your ways remember the God by whose power you were created, by whose goodness you are sustained and protected."

Tennyson's dictum, "I am a part of all that I have met," was especially applicable to Longfellow. He arrived in New York long enough before the sailing of his ship to make a short visit in Philadelphia, and, while strolling the streets, came upon the Pennsylvania Hospital, which over twenty years later he was to utilize for the final scene in *Evangeline* (*Life*, I, 73). The day before he sailed, he wrote his sister Anne from New York: "I was not so much pleased with Philadelphia as I expected to be," apparently not realizing the significance of at least one of his impressions. He also gave her a bit of business news, which may well be the explanation of the Philadelphia visit: Carey and Lea had informed him that the second volume of the *Atlantic Souvenir* would appear in October with four of his poems.

II *First Visit to Europe*

The voyage from New York to Le Havre took a month, allowing the young man of nineteen plenty of opportunity for long, long thoughts. His first letters to his relatives do not show as much excitement as might be expected, but there were to be significant echoes when, almost a decade later, in 1835, he published his first literary book, *Outre-Mer*, an Irving-like sketchbook about his travels. He explained that he had named the book for "The Pays d'Outre-Mer . . . a name by which the pilgrims and crusaders of old usually designated the Holy Land" (*Works*, I, 28). The Old World was in a sense a holy land for him, and he was making a pilgrimage to it. Fortune's wheel had indeed turned in his favor; no longer compelled to enter a profession in which he had no interest, he was now granted the privilege of not just briefly visiting but actually living in those countries he had once told his father he hoped to see before he died.

In his first letter to his mother, he admitted that he could not describe his sensations on taking his farewell look at his native land or on first glimpsing a foreign one. This reaction is not surprising if we remember that Longfellow was not primarily a landscape viewer; it was immersion in the cultural atmosphere of the foreign countries that he desired, and this was not to be achieved through the eyes of a tourist. A few days later he wrote to his father from Paris that he had "arrived in this great Babylon of modern times" and had settled in a boardinghouse in which all English was forbidden on penalty of fine. Three weeks later he wrote to his parents that he was attending public lectures, "though not understanding one sentence out of fifty." Even so, he thought he could note an improvement in his comprehension, and he assured them, "I have not forgotten what I came to Paris for" (*Life*, I, 79-83).

Shortly after he wrote to his more Bohemian brother Stephen, "After five weeks in Paris, I have settled down into something half way between a Frenchman and a New Englander,—within all Jonathan, but outwardly a little of a *Parlez-vous*" (*Life*, I, 83). He went on to describe the boulevard life, with the "quality crowd in their coaches" and "musicians singing and playing the harp; jugglers; fiddlers; blind beggars, and lame beggars, and beggars without any qualifying term except importunity.... On the Boulevards are several minor theatres, where parodies and farces are performed. A little while ago I attended the Variétés, and saw Apollo in red hat and striped pantaloons, and Vulcan dressed in a flame-colored coat" (*Life*, I, 84).

In the heat of summer, he left Paris for the village of Auteil, where he took up lodgings in what turned out to be a private hospital, thus adding an experience he had not anticipated (*Life*, I, 84-86). He concluded that the situation was a pleasant one, for he could hear an abundance of French conversation: "the French are always talking." The inmates of the "house of health" included some notable personalities: "an old Gentleman who was of the household of Louis the Sixteenth, and a Madame de Sailly, daughter of a celebrated advocate named Berryer, who was the defender of Marshal Ney in his impeachment for treason." He had the good fortune to become friendly there with a young French law student (the law seemed to follow him even here) "who corrects all my mistakes in speaking or writing the French." He seems to have decided that the best way to learn a language was to seize every opportunity to mingle with the people, with a minimum of formal instruction. In October he wrote to his father that he had met Lafayette (whom his father had had the recent honor of introducing in a Portland celebration and who now sent greetings) on the streets of Paris and had been surprised to observe that the Marquis was not such a celebrity in his own country as in America (*Life*, I, 89).

Much of October, "my favorite month of the twelve," he spent in a walking journey from Tours to Orleans. On one occasion, he fell in with a group of villagers and sought to obtain lodging, Goldsmith fashion, by playing his flute for it: "So I addressed the girl who was walking beside me, told her I had a flute in my sack, and asked her if she would like to dance.... She said she liked to dance, but she did not know what a flute was!" Whether Longfellow was more intent on a mild flirtation or on finding lodging for the night is not clear, but he was squelched: "I said no more about a flute, the whole journey through" (*Life*, I, 91).

By November he was back in Paris, and could report to his brother Stephen that "French comes on famously. I have now got to enjoy the society around me; but it was dull enough at first, as it must necessarily be to one who cannot speak French and does not wish to speak English. I have been here five months!" (*Life*, I, 94). In December his father wrote to emphasize the importance of mastering French and Spanish and of ranking German language and literature higher than the Italian—and he added, "I hope and pray that you will have virtue and prudence. I commend you to the care of your Heavenly father." At the same time, his mother wrote at length to console him for the disadvantages under which he had studied and to express regret that he could not have had "the company of some one older and more experienced than yourself in the ways of the world." His Puritan parents were obviously concerned about his moral welfare, but his mother expressed confidence "in your uprightness, and in that purity of mind which will instantly take alarm on coming in contact with anything vicious or unworthy." She nevertheless warned him to be "careful and watchful." Writing to her at about this time, he admitted homesickness; when he thought of reunion with his family, "my heart swells into my throat and tears into my eyes." However, by now he was attending the theater and the opera, taking Italian lessons from an Italian, and going more into society. He might sometimes be lonely, but he was making the most of a great opportunity.

Rumors of danger to travelers in Spain caused him to consider proceeding directly to Germany, but reassured by Americans recently arrived from Spain, he decided to go there first as planned. In late February, eight months after his arrival in Paris, he wrote his father that he was satisfied with his knowledge of French: "I shall leave Paris for Spain on Wednesday, day after tomorrow" (*Life*, I, 99). He called Bordeaux the most beautiful city he had seen in

France. Even so, he left France with little regret, despite his impression that "the French are a hospitable, kind-hearted people." Although doubtless he followed his father's injunction not to meddle in local religion or politics, he could not quit France without commenting on the unfortunate state of the government: it was under "the dark and dangerous policy of the priesthood." It seemed reasonable to him to "look forward to a happier life in Spain than I have led in France."

On March 20 he wrote to his father that, despite "the tales of bloody murder and highway robbery" he had heard in Paris, he had arrived without misadventure in Madrid, where all was "as quiet and peaceful as France itself" (*Life*, I, 102). There were rumors of war, however, and "the country is infested, nook and corner, with hordes of banditti." Despite the unrest, he was delighted with Madrid, where he soon took up residence with a Spanish family. He enclosed an extract from his journal, in which he paid special tribute to the Basque girls who served as guides to travelers. "I said that the Basque girls were handsome. They have most beautiful dark eyes, fine teeth, a sun-burnt complexion, and glossy, black hair parted over the forehead, gathered behind the ears, and falling down to the knees in a large, beautiful braid ... one, in particular; whose image haunts me still,—a most cheerful-looking girl, in the dress of the peasantry, her hair braided, and a large gypsy straw-hat thrown over her shoulders" (*Life*, I, 105). It seems mildly surprising that Longfellow would send to his solicitous parents a journal describing so feelingly one particular girl "whose image haunts me still," but they probably judged rightly that he was only an admirer—and probably from a safe distance.

Longfellow wrote to his family at length about his life in Spain, for it was clearly an adventure to him. He remarked on the poverty of the peasants in north Spain, and the huge covered wagon drawn by six mules, in which he traveled. This equipage reminded him (perhaps to the surprise of most of his readers, who believe him uninterested in American pioneering) "of the backwoodsman of our own country, when, sick of the quiet of the fruitful valleys of New England, he bundles his wife and children, together with pots and kettles and household goods, into a lumbering wain, and shouldering his axe, trudges off to Ohio" (*Life*, I, 110). He was pleased to find lamps like those of the plates in *Don Quixote*. He was much impressed by the Escorial, that combination of "a palace, a church, a convent, and a sepulchre." He called the church "magnificently grand," and heard mass said in the twilight in its aisles. He was particularly pleased with his residence in the Spanish family, where the "whole house is goodness." But he admitted that part of his pleasure came from the presence of the daughter, "'sweet sixteen,' with the romantic name of Florence," who "supplies the place of a sister much better than I had thought could be possible" (*Life*, I, 116). Obviously he liked the Spanish people better than he did the French. The content of his early letters shows more interest in the people than in their language, but he does note linguistic curiosities, especially in expressions of courtesy.

No doubt one reason he was happier in Madrid than in Paris was that he was better introduced. He bore letters to Mr. Alexander Everett from an American friend, which paved the way for a welcome in the Everett family; and he was especially gratified by his association with the American writer he had admired most and imitated in his own prose writings, Washington Irving, who at the age of forty was "engaged upon his *Life of Columbus*" (*Life*, I, 117). He was much impressed to learn of Irving's industriousness; he seemed to be writing constantly and informed Longfellow that he was always at work in his study "as early as six." Longfellow was not disillusioned when they met: "he is one of those men who put you at ease with them in a moment ... a very fine man in society, all mirth and good humor ... and says very pleasant agreeable things, in a husky, weak, peculiar voice" (*Life*, I, 108).

As a New England Unitarian, Longfellow was much impressed by the religious observances of the Catholic Spanish, and wrote to his father at length about them: "The religious ceremonies of the Roman Catholic Church are still celebrated in Spain with all the pomp and circumstance of darker ages. The Spaniards, in their faith, are the most obedient people in the world. They will believe anything a priest tells them to, without asking why or wherefore. But at the same time ... they have as little pure religion as can be found upon the face of the earth" (*Life*, I, 119). The doctrine of transubstantiation had evidently been unknown to him, and he was much impressed by the "passage of the Host," which the Spaniards believed to be "the body of God himself."

In a letter to his father about a month after his arrival in Spain, he wrote candidly about his language studies: "Do not believe what people tell you of learning the French language in six months and the Spanish in three. Were I guided by such counsellors I should return a sheer charlatan; and, though I might deceive others as to the amount of my knowledge, I cannot so easily deceive myself. Whatever vanity I may possess with regard to my natural abilities, I have very little with regard to my acquisitions" (*Life* I, 120-21). This sounds more like the honest self-appraisal of a sincere student than a young man's plea to his father for more money for a lark abroad.[1] Longfellow certainly had more than average ability in languages, but he had learned that, even for him, time and effort were required to master a new tongue. However, in a letter of the same date to his mother, he confessed "that I feel very little desire to leave Madrid," and he intimated that he would stay longer except that he had had to throw his purse out of the window because it was full of holes and empty.

Longfellow spent only the summer of 1827 in Madrid, not long enough by his estimate to master the language. By September he was working his way through the south of Spain en route to Italy. Both Professor Ticknor and his father had urged upon him the importance of Germany and the German language, but Italian had been one of the first languages to intrigue him; he had no intention of foregoing Italy to please anyone. Perhaps he was all the more determined to go because he knew that much of the road lay through parts of Spain which he also wanted to visit. His route included La Mancha, where for him the spirit of Don Quixote still lived. He also enjoyed the blooming country of Andalusia and the vineyards and olive trees of Cordova, but he was disappointed in Seville, despite visits to its impressive cathedral and to the beautiful Moorish tower. But of Granada, in which he spent five days, he wrote: "There are moments in our lives to which we feel that romance could add nothing, and which poetry itself could not beautify. Such were those I passed in lingering about the Alhambra and dreaming over the warlike deeds of other days" (*Life*, I, 132). In all, he spent eight unforgettable months in Spain. Though he traveled to Europe three more times, he was never to visit it again, perhaps, as his brother surmised, because "He was unwilling to break the spell of that early time" (*Life*, I, 134).

In late November, Longfellow sailed for Genoa, by way of Marseilles and Toulon. It was his good fortune to have as traveling companions several other young men, including three officers of the U. S. Schooner *Porpoise,* and, more important, another young man named George Greene, the grandson of the Revolutionary General Nathanael Greene. He and Longfellow were destined to become lifelong friends, and many years later Greene dedicated his biography of his grandfather to Longfellow. They spent much of their time in Italy together.

Longfellow spent Christmas Eve in Genoa. He thought it a "superb city," with its beautiful Strada Nuova lined with palaces— "But what misery at their gates!" Five days later he left Genoa for Pisa, and on New Year's Day, 1828, "Left Pisa for Florence; beautiful country, and beautiful peasant girls" (*Life*, I, 136). In Florence he was pleased to find lodgings in a house near a scene he remembered from Boccaccio's *Decameron.* He wrote his father that he planned to stay a month or six weeks there and had little idea "how long it will be necessary to remain in Italy in order to acquire its language and see its wonders" (*Life*, I, 137). At first he found the language easy to read but difficult to understand when spoken, and it was hard to keep from confusing it with his newly-acquired Spanish. The carnival was commencing, and theatricals were available at half price. Here he had his first experience of vaudeville, which he described as "a genteel kind of farce interspersed with songs." But he assured his father that he was carrying on his French, Italian, and Spanish studies regardless of the distractions.

Despite the historic associations and other attractions, Longfellow experienced some of his worst homesickness during the early part of his stay in Italy. On January 18, he wrote his mother from Florence that he did not find Florence and the Arno River as full of romance and poetry as he had expected: "Can you believe that the Arno . . . is a stream of muddy water, almost entirely dry in summer, and Italian boatmen, and convent bells, and white-robed nuns, and midnight song and soft serenade—are not altogether so delightful in reality as we sometimes fancy them to be?" (*Life*, I, 140). He confessed that he was traveling through Italy without excitement or enthusiasm: "The fact is, I am homesick for Spain. . . . The recollection of it completely ruins Italy for me. Next to going home, let me go to Spain!" Perhaps his homesickness was actually more for home and family than for Spain.

However, he must have been pleased to be able to move in high society in Florence. He had a letter of introduction to the Princess Charlotte, daughter of Joseph Bonaparte, and he received and accepted an invitation to pass an evening in her home. There he met the Duchess of Istria, "a beautiful Frenchwoman"; the Countess de Survilliers, wife of Joseph Bonaparte, who invited him to dinner; and "an Italian lady of the family of Michael Angelo, with her daughter, who sang in the evening most divinely." Later in the evening the Princess Charlotte dropped in with other guests—and played "Yankee Doodle" to make the American guest feel at home! (*Life*, I, 141).

Arriving in Rome, he had the good fortune to be lodged in the Italian home where his new friend Greene was already staying. He described the Persiani's as "a delightful family," with "three young ladies, who have all been excellently educated and speak, besides their native tongue, both English and French. They are great musicians also" (*Life*, I, 144). In the same letter to his mother in which he describes this happy situation, he tells her that his sisters ought to be "studying French, or one of the languages" and that

Spanish would be easiest to start with. He continues: "The fact is, with this study of the languages I am completely enchanted. Indeed I am passionately fond of it." In a later letter to his sisters, he returned to the subject: "Are you studying French, or Spanish, now-a-days? If not, you should lose no time in commencing, for I assure you that, by every language you learn, a new world is opened before you. It is like being born again; and new ideas break upon the mind with all the freshness and delight with which we may suppose the first dawn of intellect to be accompanied" (*Life*, I, 151).

However, one suspects that Longfellow did more sightseeing than language studying in Italy. In Naples he visited the Elysian fields and Lake Acheron, which evoked reminiscences of his college studies in Virgil. The visit to Naples with Greene marked a high point of travel experience for both young men. Later, Greene recalled a long talk they had had as they walked on their flat roof with its view of the crowded street and the bay, including Capri and Sorrento and a distant glimpse of Vesuvius—all in the splendor of an Italian sunset: "We talked and mused by turns, till the twilight deepened and the stars came forth to mingle their mysterious influence with the overmastering magic of the scene. It was then that you unfolded to me your plans of life, and showed me from what 'deep cisterns' you had already learned to draw. From that day the office of literature took a new place in my thoughts" (*Life*, I, 147). The last statement is tantalizing; one wonders what sort of "office of literature" Longfellow portrayed to Greene at this time. In college he had apparently pictured literature as a compound of patriotism and emotional release, and as an avenue for personal advancement. It was in Naples that he met Nicander, the young Swedish poet whom he found to be such a kindred spirit; he was keenly disappointed not to be able to arrange a reunion with him when he later went to Sweden.

Returned to Rome, he continued his observation on life in the Imperial City. To his brother Stephen he wrote of something he was probably too shy to communicate to either of his parents: his shock at the dissoluteness of manners: "There seems to be no kind of shame attached to it. Whenever I go to the principal street of the city at the hour for promenade, I see a lady of the highest ton [*sic*] (who has a rich young banker for her 'cecisbeo') driving in her carriage with her daughter, her husband, and her lover!" He is pleased to note, however, that, "there are many families, of manners and morals as uncorrupted as ours." He continued with remarks on the superstition evident in religious observances: "But I have been so long in Roman Catholic countries that the abuses in this religion have little effect upon me. Its *principles* are as pure and holy as could be wished" (*Life,* I, 148). He blames the evils on the folly of mingling religion and politics.

Longfellow lingered in Rome considerably longer than he had intended. His brother attributes most of the delay to a severe illness that began as a cold and developed into a dangerous fever from which he might not have recovered except for the ministrations of the Persiani family, especially the oldest daughter, "who, having the freedom of a married woman, was his especial nurse" (*Life,* I, 149). Lawrance Thompson, who had full access to the Longfellow papers, drew a somewhat different inference. He thinks Longfellow exaggerated the illness and lingered chiefly because he had fallen in love with Julia, who was probably either unmarried or a young widow (Thompson, 124-27). The evidence seems inconclusive, but it may be significant that after Longfellow was well enough to leave Rome for Ariccia, where he stayed a month, he returned to Rome to remain through September, October, and November in the Persiani home.

Thompson's view is that Longfellow was shocked out of a developing romance by a letter from his father bringing the news that the Bowdoin Board of Overseers had voted that his position at the college on his return should not be the proffered professorship but an instructorship. Thompson's case for the romance seems to be weakened, however, by the fact that Longfellow was already in Venice en route to Germany when he received the disturbing letter. On December 19, he wrote indignantly from Venice. It was especially unfair, he thought, that the board should say he was too young—they had known his age from the beginning. He concludes: "If they think I would accept the place which they offer me, they are much mistaken in my character" (*Life,* I, 155). The gentle Longfellow could stand up for himself when necessary.

Stephen Longfellow's role in the Bowdoin appointment is not entirely clear. As a trustee, he was caught in the middle. The evidence indicates that he wanted his son to have the appointment, even though this meant abandonment of the law. At the same time he must have realized that his own prestige required that the youthful Henry should be fully qualified. He kept a good deal of pressure on his son to master the languages. As early as December, 1826, he had written Henry: "Your ulterior objects cannot be accomplished unless you obtain an *accurate* knowledge of the *French & Spanish* Languages. *The situation you have in view cannot be obtained unless you qualify yourself to teach both these languages correctly*" (Thompson, 102). Apparently Stephen Longfellow was keenly aware of how young his son was and the distractions he was probably encountering; he used his great paternal influence to make as certain as possible that Henry would return fully qualified for a position they both regarded as important. After sending his son the bad news of the overseers' vote, he wrote again to say that in his judgment the professorship would be offered within a year, if not immediately on Henry's return. He ended with a shrewd hint that Henry was intelligent enough to use successfully later: "Indeed I think they will likely do it next commencement, if you should return qualified for the station and they find you will not accept a subordinate position" (Thompson, 374).

Longfellow sought to reassure his father about his progress in languages: "With the French and Spanish languages I am familiarly conversant, so as to speak them correctly, and write them with as much ease and fluency as I do the English. The Portuguese I read without difficulty. And with regard to my proficiency in the Italian, I have only to say that all at the hotel where I lodge took me for an Italian until I told them I was an American" (*Life*, I, 156). Despite his affection for Venice, he indicated that he would cut short his stay there and proceed to Dresden because "I do not wish to return without a competent knowledge of German." However, he stayed in Venice long enough to visit the Palace of the Doges, to have Lord Byron's residence pointed out to him by a gondolier who was himself a poet and had written a sonnet to Byron, and to observe that "The Venetian ladies are not handsome, but they have a great deal of vivacity." After an unpromising beginning, Italy had proved fascinating to him, though it was apparently not the fulfillment of a dream as it was thirty years later for his classmate Hawthorne.

Longfellow's attitude toward Germany was mixed. Before he left home, Ticknor had tried to impress on him the importance of German studies. His father had been ambivalent in the matter, at one time thinking German important but most of the time emphasizing French and Spanish. When the time came to leave France, Longfellow had been uncertain whether to go to Spain or to Germany, but finally decided on Spain, then Italy. Before he left Italy, he had already been abroad longer than he and his father had planned. However, he seems to have developed a growing sense of the importance of a stay in Germany; so in late December he started for Dresden by way of Trieste and Vienna. Trieste he found an enterprising city, "with little to interest any but a commercial man." Vienna was better: he viewed a large collection of antique armor; visited the castle of Greifenstein, prison of Richard of the Lion-heart; and was moved to comment on Richard as a representative of the medieval troubadours.

He was not happy in Dresden, though he had letters of introduction from Washington Irving and was invited to balls and concerts, going one evening with a Mr. Walther to a "beer-house, to see the world." In fact, his homesickness took an astonishing turn. He wrote Carey and Lea, the Philadelphia publishers who had printed some of his poems in the *Atlantic Souvenir* about the time of his going abroad, offering to write for their publication an American sketch-book, tentatively entitled *Sketches and Tales of New England Life*. He included a table of contents, and indicated that he was well along with his planning (*Life*, I, 165). This project, surprising for a prospective language professor preparing himself for his vocation while living abroad, did not materialize, but he did ultimately write and publish two of the thirteen tales he had projected.

After a month in Dresden, he was reunited with his college class-mate Edward Preble in Göttingen, where he was considerably happier. He attended lectures at the university and had an academic tutor, apparently for the only time in his foreign language studies. The university impressed him favorably, for its fine library was the largest in Germany. By February 27, his twenty-second birthday, he could write his father about his new elasticity of spirits. He was not even worried about Bowdoin, having convinced himself that "my friends can probably think of some other situation equally good as the professorship at Brunswick" (*Life*, I, 166). By now he was wanting to extend his stay, even suggesting to his father that he would like to spend a year in Germany, for he is "a little unwilling to give up what is now in my reach, as I shall never again be in Europe." Why he was so sure he would never be in Europe again is not apparent; it is not fully accounted for by the homesickness he experienced at first in each new country he entered.

In a letter of March 10 to his father (which Samuel Longfellow did not print), he suggested an alternative to the Bowdoin professorship. He proposed to supply leadership for the founding, presumably with his father's backing, of a real university in Portland, with Göttingen as the model. By now he had a low opinion of such American colleges as Bowdoin, which tried to fill up existing buildings instead of, as in Germany, clustering students around able professors "in whom the spirit moved" until the buildings were needed.[2]

In late March he wrote to his sister Elizabeth: "With Göttingen I am much delighted, though I have no other society than my books. My studies, you already know, are modern languages and modern literature" (*Life*, I, 168). Then with no transition, he continued, "My poetic career is finished. Since I left America I have hardly put two lines together." Perhaps he had got on the subject because he had thought of writing her an epithalamium because of her recent engagement. Instead of verse, however, he sent her best wishes and a quotation from Jeremy Taylor: "She that is loved is safe: and he that loves is joyful."

By May, he was tired enough of his studies to vary them with a visit to the Low Countries and to England, where he saw London for the first time. In a letter to his mother, he expressed delight in Holland, but he made no comment on his week in London, remarking that he did not know what to say. He returned to Göttingen partly by steamboat on the Rhine, "a noble river, but not so fine as the Hudson" (*Life*, I, 170). But his impressions of the town of Bingen and of the old castle at Vautsberg figure many years later in his poetry.

On May 15, the same day he wrote to his mother, he reported to his father that he was attending lectures three hours a day and devoting the remainder to the study of German under the guidance of an able professor. Having accounted for the whole day, he then added that he was also writing "a kind of Sketch-Book of scenes in France, Spain, and Italy." It is worth noting that he reported to his father this scheme but not the one for an American sketchbook; in fact, he had strictly enjoined Carey and Lea to keep that matter secret. Full of projects as he was, he added: "my fervent wish is to return home. I would not remain for a moment, were it not from the persuasion of its necessity. But the German language is beyond measure difficult; not to read,—that is not so hard,— but to write. And one must write, and write correctly, in order to teach" (*Life*, I, 171). Despite this expression of stern resolution, he did not confine himself to German studies but, as his notebooks show, varied them with readings in Spanish, French, and Old English. In fact, he seems to have experienced more confusion of purpose in Germany than anywhere else—beginning to think again about his literary ambitions, trying to concentrate on German, being diverted by other studies from time to time, and constantly harassed by the desire to be home. Perhaps he was not too disappointed, then, when his father urged him to hasten home, partly because of the grave illness of his sister Elizabeth—to whom he had so recently written best wishes for her approaching marriage. By June 18, he was in Paris, where he heard the sad news of his sister's death. After passing through London, he sailed on July 1 from Liverpool for New York. The "Certificate of Arrival" made out for him in England described him as "23 years old; height, 5 ft., 8 in.; 'chesnut' hair; fresh complexion; blue eyes; long nose; 'chesnut' eyebrows."[3] After three and a half eventful years, he was homeward bound. He was now less a Puritan New Englander and more a cosmopolitan, and he took home with him great enthusiasm for teaching the foreign cultures he had observed and experienced.

III *The Young Professor*

When Longfellow was reunited with his family in Portland, it was mid-August of 1829, nearly time for the fall term to start at Bowdoin, and his status there was still uncertain. The vote of the overseers to make him an instructor had not been altered, nor had he taken any official notice of it. However, the time for a show-down could not be long delayed. After conferring with his father, the young ex-traveler wrote the following letter to President Allen:

Dear Sir,

Your letter to my father dated Sept. 26, 1828, and enclosing a copy of the vote of the Trustees and Overseers of Bowdoin College, by which they have elected me Instructor of the Modern Languages in that institution, has been duly handed me.

I am sorry, that under existing circumstances, I cannot accept the appointment. The Professorship of Modern Languages, with a salary equal to that of the other Professors, would certainly not have been refused. But having at great expense, devoted four years to the acquisition of the French, Spanish, Italian, and German languages, I cannot accept a subordinate station with a salary so disproportionate to the duties required.

I have the honor to be, Sir,

Very respectfully
Your Ob' Ser'
HENRY W. LONGFELLOW
(Thompson, 147-48)

The letter was both tactful and firm, and it secured an approximation of the desired results, as the minutes of the meeting of the trustees show:

In the Board of Trustees of Bowdoin College, September 1, 1829:

Mr. Henry W. Longfellow having declined to accept the office of Instructor in Modern Languages,

Voted, That we now proceed to the choice of a Professor of Modern Languages.

And Mr. H. W. Longfellow was chosen.

Voted, That the salary of said professor be established at eight hundred dollars annually, until further order of the Board.

Voted, That H. W. Longfellow be appointed Librarian for one year, with a salary of one hundred dollars (*Life,* I, 174-75).

It was a good Yankee compromise. The library duty was for only one hour a day, and Longfellow soon found that he could spend most of that time reading. In effect, therefore, he had his professorship at only one hundred dollars less than the regular salary for professors. On the other hand, the trustees had saved face by requiring him to begin on a probationary basis, as they had decided was proper for such a young man. Actually, it was not long until his salary was raised to the regular rate for professors.

Longfellow had made his pilgrimage beyond the sea. An unforgettable experience, it had not only prepared him reasonably well for his professorial assignment; it had also contributed greatly to his store of subject matter, both factual and emotional, for later writing, though he did not draw heavily from that store for many years. He had had over four years of post-graduate study, one at home and more than three abroad, and he was only twenty-two and a half years old.

As he had expected, he found himself the entire Modern Language Department, which indeed he brought into being. The first year he had classes in French and Spanish without satisfactory text materials from which to teach them. He promptly set about preparing materials. His first published book, in 1830, was his translation of C. F. L'Homond's *Elements of French Grammar*. The same year he edited for his classes, with a long preface in French, *Manual de Proverbes Dramatiques,* a collection of popular stories; and, similarly, with a preface in Spanish, a small Spanish reader, *Novelas Españolas (Life,* I, 175; III, 421). By December, he wrote to his father about these text ventures, explaining that they were necessary because existing texts were much too stiff and formal for young minds. Previous text writers had seemed "to forget that the young mind is to be *interested* in order to be instructed" *(Life,* I, 177). Throughout his academic career, Longfellow was to be distinguished for making learning inviting to his students.

With his eagerness to interest his students, with his personal charm, and also "with the glow of foreign travel upon him," he promptly became a highly popular instructor. One of his early students, who later became president of Middlebury College, wrote in recollection: "He neither sought popularity nor repelled it. He always and evidently enjoyed having students come to him with any reasonable question about languages, authors, literature, mediaeval or modern history,—especially the former. They always left him not only with admiration, but guided, helped, and inspired" *(Life,* I, 178).

At Bowdoin it was customary for a new professor to give an inaugural address, though not immediately after entering upon his duties. Longfellow did not deliver his until the autumn commencement of 1830, a year after his appointment. His choice of subject, "Origin and Growth of the Languages of Southern Europe and of their Literature," can hardly have been surprising, unless for its breadth. Perhaps even that seemed natural to an audience being virtually introduced to foreign literature. The young professor thanked the institution for conferring upon him the favor of the professorship, no doubt sincerely, for he was finding the assignment most congenial: "I regard the profession of a teacher in a far more noble and elevated point of view than many do. I cannot help believing that he who bends in a right direction the pliant disposition of the young, and trains up the ductile mind to a vigorous and healthy growth does something for the welfare of his country and something for the great interests of humanity" (*Life*, I, 181).

Another quotation shows more specifically his rationale for language study: "I cannot regard the study of a language as the pastime of a listless hour. To trace the progress of the human mind through the progressive development of language; to learn how other nations thought and felt, and spake; to enrich the understanding by opening upon it new sources of knowledge; and by speaking many tongues to become a citizen of the world; these are objects worthy the exertion their attainment demands at our hands... it will be my aim, not only to teach the turns and idioms of a language, but... to direct the student in his researches into the literature of those nations whose language he is studying" (Thompson, p. 170).

However dated his poetry may seem to many readers, his theory of language teaching is remarkably modern. But in generalizing on his concept of literature, he could not forget his Puritan background: "It is this *religious* feeling,—this constant grasping after the invisible things of another and higher world,—which marks the spirit of modern literature" (*Life*, I, 182). The ancients had dreamed of immortality, "but their heaven was an earthly heaven. . . . But to the modern poet the world beyond the grave presents itself with all the force of reality, and yet with all the mystery of a dream." The situation hardly required this testimonial, but Longfellow was religious in outlook and purpose throughout his life—in an age when the religion of his forefathers had lost most of its terror and had not yet been buffeted by the skepticisms of the late nineteenth and the twentieth centuries.

Despite his youthful burning ambition to become an author, Longfellow was hardly distinguishable at this stage from any other ambitious young academic. He prepared necessary text materials; he went beyond the immediate line of duty to compose lectures for the upper classes, to write and deliver public lectures, and to contribute scholarly articles to the *North American Review*, the nearest equivalent in his time to modern scholarly journals. In a March 9, 1833, letter to his favorite correspondent, Greene, he listed his publications, exclusive of texts and translations, since returning from Europe:

1. Article on The French Language, in the North American Review.
2. Article on The Defence of Poetry; in the same.
3. Article on the Moral and Devotional Poetry of Spain; the same.
4. Article on the Italian Language and Dialects; the same.
5. Notice of an Italian Reading-book, in the Cambridge Monthly.
6. Sundry papers of prose and verse, in the New England Magazine.
7. In the Token for 1832, a story.
8. In the same, for 1833, a story.

(*Life*, I, 192)

Articles one to five come under the heading of scholarly writing, as does part of the sixth. To account more fully for his activity outside the classroom, he continued: "To these add, as delivered in public, though not published: One poem (by courtesy so called); one inaugural address; one address before a literary society in Portland; one address before the Benevolent Society in Portland; one address on Female Education... and sundry college lectures." The pattern is clearly that of a conscientious academic person; there is only a little evidence of special interest in imaginative writing.

IV *Romance at Home*

Longfellow did not quite follow the familiar New England Puritan pattern of marrying as soon as he was established vocationally. He was at the beginning of his third year at Bowdoin before he married. Although he had long been responsive to pretty women, as evidenced by numerous comments in his letters and journals, he seems not to have seriously considered marriage until about a year before he achieved it. Perhaps his continuing desire to be "eminent in something" persuaded him to give no hostages to fortune until well on his way. Also, he had been fortunate in the availability of feminine society without marriage: at home, sisters of whom he was fond; abroad, attractive young women at most of his residences. Even in Brunswick he could and frequently did drop in at the pleasant home of Professor Cleaveland to smoke a pipe with the professor and to sing around the piano with his three daughters (Thompson, 156).

By his second year at Bowdoin, however, he had abundant reason to turn his mind toward marriage. Pierre Irving wrote him an enthusiastic letter about setting up housekeeping with his new bride. George Greene, newly returned to Rhode Island, wrote him that he had brought home a bride, a sixteen-year-old Roman girl whom he had met in Florence. A dormitory room could seem quite lonely in comparison with such domestic felicity.

During one of his visits to Portland, he had been struck with the attractiveness of one of the three daughters of Judge Barrett Potter, a leading citizen of the town. Report has it that he followed her home from church one Sunday but did not speak to her.[4] Mary Potter was five years younger than Longfellow; so he was probably unaware of her before he went abroad. Once lovestruck, he began to court her, sending letters to her by way of his sister Anne. If somewhat devious, the courtship was nevertheless successful. In due course he wrote the customary letter to her formidable father, thanking him "for the confidence you have reposed in me in placing in my hands the happiness of a daughter" (Thompson, 158). They were married in September, 1831, when Longfellow was twenty-four.

Mary Potter Longfellow was an attractive girl in appearance, disposition, and intellectual accomplishments. As a judge's daughter, she was well educated and in sympathy with her husband's academic situation. While traveling with the Longfellow's in Europe in 1835, Clara Crowninshield wrote of her, "She is very *sweet* and amiable, but she is so absorbed in her husband that she only lives in him."[5] She was hardly in awe of her professor spouse, however, for she referred to him as "a good little dear," and she probably made him less fretful in his irritations than he otherwise would have been during his last years at Bowdoin.[6] Their married life, from all the evidence a perfectly happy one, was destined to be brief; it lasted only through three years at Bowdoin and the first few months of Longfellow's second visit to Europe. On November 28, 1835, in Rotterdam, she died of illness following a miscarriage.[7] Longfellow was to remember her as he described her years later in "Footsteps of Angels": "the Being Beauteous/Who unto my youth was given."

V Rumblings of Discontent

Despite the friction that had accompanied his appointment at Bowdoin, Longfellow was happy and content for a time. He was proving that he could make good in the most congenial vocation available to him, and he enjoyed the responsiveness of his students. It was pleasant to be consulted as an educator and gratifying to be published as a scholar in the *North American Review*. But the satisfaction hardly lasted through the two years which preceded his marriage. Three weeks before the marriage date, he wrote to his sister Anne in an aggrieved tone hardly to be expected of a young man about to take a bride to the college town where he had been establishing himself: "I do not believe that I was born for such a lot. I have aimed higher than this: and I cannot believe that all my aspirations are to terminate in the drudgery of a situation, which gives me no opportunity to distinguish myself, and in point of worldly gain, does not even pay me for my labor. Besides, one loses ground so fast in these out of the way places: the mind has no stimulus to exertion—grows sluggish in its movements and narrow in its sphere—and there's the end of a man. We will see" (Thompson, 183).

Perhaps this statement should not be taken at face value. Prospective bridegrooms are often harried, and Longfellow's attitude toward the academic life fluctuated throughout his career. But he was not a contented man at this juncture. How much the fretfulness was due to realization that scholarly activity and imaginative writing were not compatible must remain conjectural.

A number of things at Bowdoin were disquieting to the young professor who wanted to become eminent. The Maine Legislature continued to be niggardly with appropriations. The college library was too small for his research studies, and he had to borrow many books from Harvard through his friends (Thompson, 169). By 1832 he was writing to a friend that three years had been quite enough for "laboring on in this solitude," for "I now feel a strong desire to tread a stage on which I can take longer strides and speak to a larger audience" (*Life*, I, 200).

But probably the greatest single cause for his dissatisfaction was the controversy over the college presidency. President Allen was becoming increasingly unpopular, and, with the help of a law passed in 1831, the trustees ousted him. He brought suit in 1833 to recover his salary, and Stephen Longfellow was defendant for the trustees. Despite his brilliant handling of the defense, Allen won and returned to the presidency. The young professor, already restless, made strenuous efforts to find a new situation: "From 1832 on, in fact, so great was his desire to get away from Bowdoin that he seriously tried to secure several positions that were inferior to the one he was holding. First he thought of becoming secretary of legation at Madrid; then he sought a place at the University of Virginia; next he considered the Round Hill School at Northampton, Massachusetts. Finally, in 1834, he negotiated for a professorship of Spanish at the newly founded New York University."[8]

VI *Called to Harvard*

Once again, Longfellow's fortune hung on a slender thread. Just as the enthusiasm of a Bowdoin trustee who had been impressed by his Latin translations was the prime mover in securing for him his Bowdoin professorship, so now his old friendship with Professor George Ticknor of Harvard played a key role in his life. Ticknor had been one of his advisers before he went to Europe for the first time, and he had never lost track of him or his work. On June 18, 1834, Ticknor wrote a glowing recommendation of him when he was under consideration at New York University.[9] Soon afterward, Ticknor's own fortunes took a turn which caused him to resign. Thereupon he recommended Longfellow as his successor in the Smith Professorship.

By October, Harvard President Josiah Quincy had begun a cautious investigation of Longfellow's qualifications. The results were apparently satisfactory, for Quincy wrote Longfellow in December to ask whether he would be available for the position, assuring him that, if so, he would be nominated "under circumstances which render your appointment not doubtful."[10] The letter concluded with a suggestion (doubtless inspired by Ticknor, who had urged German studies on him when he first went abroad) that he would be allowed to reside in Europe for a year or eighteen months for "ye purpose of a more perfect attainment of ye German." Longfellow wrote at once to his father: "Good fortune comes at last; and I certainly shall not reject it. The last paragraph of the letter, though put in the form of a permission, seems to imply a request."

Despite his enthusiasm, Longfellow was much too good a Yankee trader to assure President Quincy of an eager acceptance. The day after he received the letter, he replied calmly that a position at Harvard "would be very acceptable to me," but, before making his decision, he wanted to know more about the duties "of that situation, in order to avoid any misunderstanding hereafter." He added that, if appointed, he would probably wish to avail himself of the permission to visit Europe. In replying, Quincy restated the salary, $1,500, and stipulated Cambridge residence. As to the duties, these would be somewhat different from Professor Ticknor's; a committee was working on the matter and would be happy to interview him. Longfellow met with the committee in late December, and negotiations followed. The corporation was unwilling to elect him before he went abroad, but it did vote to assure him that he would be elected upon his return. Longfellow would have preferred the status of Harvard professor while in Europe, but by February 3 he had apparently decided that he had accomplished all that he could by negotiation, for he wrote to President Quincy that he accepted the terms offered.[11]

It was now settled that Longfellow would be leaving Bowdoin, as soon as arrangements could be made, to accept the distinguished Smith Professorship at Harvard. Doubtless he began immediately to make plans for his second residence in Europe. This time he would go not as a callow young college graduate but as a seasoned professor and established family man.

CHAPTER *4*

Professor and Poet: Harvard, 1835-54

I *A Rising Young Scholar*

AUTHORITIES DO NOT AGREE on whether Longfellow
brought back from Europe in 1829 the language proficiency
he claimed in his letters to his father. One view (chiefly supported
by Lawrance Thompson) is that he was something of a playboy
and a dilettante during his three years abroad; much of the time
he was more intent on seeing and enjoying the wonderland of his
dreams than on serious study of the language and literature of the
several countries he visited. His brother's biography takes Longfellow's claims at face value, and most other biographers have
followed his lead. Probably young Longfellow had for the most part
followed his own best judgment by mixing study and mingling with
the people. In any case, only limited formal instruction was available
to him. His competence at Bowdoin must have been considerable
from the beginning; certainly it was enough to satisfy both the
students and the administration.

Whatever he had learned in Europe, he continued to build upon
it energetically during the Bowdoin years. In a letter to George
Greene (June 27, 1830), he described his scholar's day as beginning
at six in the morning and ending at midnight (*Life*, I, 183-84).
Thompson says: "During his first three years of teaching at Bowdoin, he built a remarkably large superstructure of literary and
linguistic study on the somewhat meagre foundations laid down in
France, Spain, Italy, and Germany.... The quantity and range of
his reading in European literature was phenomenal ... he put heart
and soul into his language study. The European experience flowered
into an idealistic concept of the wide opportunity to be found in
teaching and learning modern languages" (Thompson, 169-70).
Somehow Longfellow had diverted his earlier burning desire for
literary expression into scholarly activity. It was primarily as a
scholar that he set out in 1835 for Europe.

To be sure, even at Bowdoin he had done a small amount of
imaginative writing. In November, 1834, about the time the Harvard
negotiations were getting under way, "The Wondrous Tale of a

Little Man in Gosling Green," a short story, won a prize of fifty dollars and publication in Horace Greeley's *New Yorker* (Thompson, 200-1). More ambitious was the undertaking which finally took shape as his first "literary" book: *Outre-Mer*, begun as a magazine prose serial and published in two volumes in 1835 after he had left for Europe (*Life*, I, 193, 194, 203). His Phi Beta Kappa poem, "The Past and the Present," written first for delivery at Bowdoin and revised for a Harvard appearance in the fall of 1833, could have been a factor in his Harvard appointment. Nevertheless, the general pattern of his writing had been scholarly: "By 1835 he had definitely marked for himself a career as a literary scholar. Linguistic studies had replaced to a large extent his poetical ambitions during the course of his Bowdoin instructorship and the reputation which had earned him the Smith Professorship at Harvard had been achieved by means of articles and textbooks concerning the romantic languages."[1]

II *Second Visit to Europe*

Longfellow's father had financed, albeit not too cheerfully or too liberally, the first European sojourn. This time Longfellow had somehow to pay his own way, including his wife's expenses. President Quincy's letter had stipulated that the European study was to be "at your own expense." He was concerned, too, that Mary might be lonely during his long hours of study in libraries and in their rooms. But Yankee frugality and ingenuity, combined with a bit of luck, solved the problem. Two of his wife's best friends, Mary Goddard and Clara Crowninshield, both daughters of well-to-do men, had been wanting to visit Europe. Miss Goddard and Miss Crowninshield agreed to pay Longfellow for guide service, thus helping his financial situation and providing company for his wife.[2] Early in April, the party of four sailed for London.

Although his ostensible mission in Europe was to acquire "a more perfect attainment of the German," Longfellow did not proceed directly to Germany. He went first to London, which was natural enough since he had spent only a week there on his previous European stay and since he knew that the rest of the party would be eager to see its sights. Longfellow carried a letter from Emerson introducing him to Thomas Carlyle. Mary Longfellow recorded that Mr. Carlyle "passed a half-hour with us much to our delight," and she noted that his unpolished manner was combined with fine language and beautiful thoughts (*Life*, I, 205). Perhaps Longfellow was surprised to find that his fellow author from Portland, Nathaniel P. Willis, had a large London following. He met a number of celebrities, including members of the nobility, and there were visits with booksellers and publishers. Longfellow had been commissioned by Harvard College to buy books for the library while abroad, and he used this opportunity to arrange with the famous London publisher Bentley for an English edition of *Outre-Mer*.

After three weeks in London, the party journeyed to Stockholm by way of Hamburg and Copenhagen. It is not altogether clear why or when Longfellow decided to visit Scandinavia. Andrew R. Hilen, who has thrown considerable light on the subject in *Longfellow and Scandinavia,* traces the interest back to Portland Academy when Longfellow's interest in the North followed that of his admired Sir Walter Scott. His favorite poet during part of his college career was Thomas Gray, who was much interested in Scandinavia. But perhaps his interest had been whetted most of all by his friendship in Naples with the young Swedish poet Karl August Nicander. Moreover, Scandinavian literature was much discussed in the *North American Review* while Longfellow was contributing to it.[3] Other motivation probably included a poet's intuition that these legend-rich countries might supply literary materials and a scholar's realization that knowledge of other Germanic languages might be essential to "a more perfect attainment of the German." In any case, he left London with plans to spend the summer in Stockholm, the winter in Berlin, and the next summer in Copenhagen.

The Swedish part of the plan did not go well. The trip from Hamburg via Travemünde and Copenhagen to Gothenburg proved slow and difficult. The party missed its boat at Stockholm. Unwilling to wait for another, Longfellow bought a Russian carriage and proceeded overland. Arriving in Stockholm, he found that his friend Nicander was not there to show him around. Despite this disappointment, he arranged for a course in Swedish with a competent instructor, who taught him to read the language proficiently. But he did not progress to his own satisfaction, nor did he like the Swedish climate. Indeed, the whole experience was disappointing.[4]

The delays in Sweden apparently caused him to change his itinerary. Instead of going to Berlin, the party returned to Copenhagen and took rooms in the elegant Hotel Royal as a reward for having endured hardship in Sweden. In Copenhagen he found that he was in the center of research in Icelandic philology, and presently he was enjoying the stimulating society of other scholars. He also enjoyed searching old bookshops for "curious books" wanted by the Harvard Library. A visit to the Copenhagen Museum provided inspiration later for "The Skeleton in Armor" and for "The Saga of King Olaf." He would gladly have stayed longer, but left in late September. While they were at Copenhagen, Mary Goddard received word that her father had died, and she immediately left for home, reducing the party to three (Thompson, 220).

Mary Longfellow had not been in good health on the Swedish and Danish travels. She complained of ague, and Longfellow planned to go by water from Copenhagen to Holland to make travel easier for her. She was pregnant but none of the letters or journals indicate that either she or her young husband was aware that pregnancy could be causing her illness. For some reason, Longfellow had decided to study Dutch briefly before going to Heidelberg, the Berlin part of the itinerary having been abandoned. When they arrived in Amsterdam after a rough passage from Hamburg, Mary was very ill. She suffered a miscarriage that night and almost died, but presently began to recover.

Longfellow was aware that Dr. Joseph Bosworth, the famous Anglo-Saxon scholar, was in Rotterdam. He wanted to make his acquaintance; so as soon as Mary could travel they proceeded there. Mary took a turn for the worse, and, although Longfellow got two physicians and a nurse to attend her, and he and Clara Crowninshield cared for her tenderly, she grew worse. On November 29, 1835, with Dr. Bosworth, who was an Episcopalian clergyman, present, she died. Longfellow was the more grieved because he knew that she had not been eager for the European venture and that, in her condition, much of the traveling had been very hard for her.

Longfellow was devastated. In anguish he confided to his journal: "This morning between one and two o'clock, my Mary—my beloved Mary—ceased to breathe. She is now, I trust, a Saint in Heaven. Would that I were with her. This morning I have knelt beside her, and kissed her cold lips, and prayed to God, that hereafter in moments of temptation, I might recall that solemn hour, and be delivered from evil" (Thompson, 223). It was a crucial moment for him: he had loved his young wife, and his natural impulse must have been to accompany her body home and to call off the whole enterprise, even if it meant the loss of the Smith Professorship. But he was descended from a long line of Puritan Calvinists, and apparently he was soon able to convince himself that Mary's fate had been predestined. Moreover, he had not even begun to study German, the main purpose of his coming. He decided to have her body embalmed, placed on a ship due to sail soon for Boston, and buried where "hereafter we may lie side by side in the peaceful shades of Mount Auburn" (Thompson, 226, 396). The second day after her death, he wrote his father-in-law a long letter, narrating the events preceding her death, praising her, and describing the last hours of her life and her resignation to death (224-26).

The day after he wrote to Judge Potter, Longfellow, with only Clara Crowninshield and himself left of his party of four, proceeded to Heidelberg. Possibly, Puritan-like, he had interpreted his loss of Mary as punishment for his delays in getting to his main business. In any case, he could not have endured a longer stay in Holland after the anxiety and grief he had suffered there. Arriving in Heidelberg, he found rooms for Clara at Frau Hepp's home—where he was to form lasting friendships—and for himself not far away.[5] In this historic, picturesque old university city, he settled down to his studies, though for a time he doubtless devoted much of his thought to a past of mingled triumphs and difficulties, of happiness and grievous loss. He must have pondered about a future which had so recently seemed settled and secure but now looked forlorn.

On the last day of the year, a little over a month after his bereavement, he wrote in his journal: "Thus closes another year—everyway the most important year of my life. I pause to look back, like one awaking from a sorrowful dream. How strangely it moves before me—and how dark. Far back stands the peaceful home I have left—and the friends I love are there—and there is a painful parting, and leave-taking of those that are never to meet again on earth—and from that far distance my father's face still looks toward me sorrowfully and beseechingly. Thus the year began in sadness. It has closed in utter sorrow."[6] It is curious that this entry mentions his father rather than his lost wife; perhaps even at this moment personal loss was less in his mind than his determination to live up to his father's expectations for him.

Despite his probably having more than average emotional responsiveness, Longfellow had great natural resiliency. The first fruit of his year-end inventory was evidently the Carlylean resolve to put work above all: he would get on with his studies. Again he resolutely pushed aside literary ambition, which had shown signs of revival before he left Bowdoin, and his persisting passion for eminence. In late January he wrote to Greene: "For my own part, I feel at this moment more than ever, that fame must be looked upon only as an accessory. If it ever has been a principal object with me—which I doubt—it is now no more so" (Thompson, 228). In his journal entry for the same day he thanked heaven that he was free of the "corroding ambition" Greene had complained of, and he continued: "Literary ambition! away with this destroyer of peace and quietude and the soul's self-possession! The scholar should have a higher and holier aim than this. He should struggle after truth; he should forget himself in communion with the great minds of all ages; and when he writes it should be not to immortalize himself, but to make a salutary and lasting impression on the minds of others" (229). It is apparent that, perhaps partly because of his new friendship with the scholarly Bosworth, Longfellow began his Heidelberg residence determined to be a scholar rather than an author. But this resolution was destined to waver before he left, for he made much progress toward developing his literary career while there.

By fortunate chance, his readings in the sentimental German Romantic literature, which naturally occupied much of his study in Heidelberg, proved particularly suitable for his mood. He read Uhland and especially Novalis, the young German poet "who had wept alone over a grave in the twilight and had fashioned 'Hymns to the Night' in his grief" (229). Reading Novalis, he could feel the spirit of Mary who, as she lay dying, had promised, "I will be with you" (230). Soon he discovered that, "The strange weird sentiment of *Sturm und Drang* literature was palatable food for his hunger." From Novalis he went on to Goethe's *Sorrows of Werther*, *Faust*, and *Wilhelm Meister* and to the writings of Jean Paul Richter and Schiller. Ticknor had written him that his salvation lay in "constant and interesting intellectual labor." Ultimately it did, but not in quite the way he and Ticknor contemplated. The combination of his own sorrow and his readings in the great German poets gave him a new depth of emotional comprehension, and it led him within a few years to an even greater conflict between literary creativity and scholarship, a conflict destined to be resolved by his emergence as a significant author.

Although, as the winter wore on, he had recurrent moods of deep grief—"at night I cry myself to sleep like a child"—some happiness reentered his life. Occasionally he turned from his studies to play cards in the evening with Clara Crowninshield and Julie Hepp. The American poet Bryant had arrived in Heidelberg a few months earlier, and Longfellow became well acquainted with him and his family, even serving as a guide for Mrs. Bryant, her daughter Fanny, and Clara Crowninshield on an excursion down the Rhine to Coblenz.[7] His German was improving, for Clara recorded in her diary (p. 283): "At table a gentleman began to talk with Mr. Long-fellow and praised his German, as all foreigners do when we speak." In Heidelberg he made another acquaintance of even more lasting importance than Bryant—George Greene's cousin Sam Ward, an urbane and witty young man who was thereafter to be one of Long-fellow's close friends. Besides his relationship with the Hepps, his most important foreign friendship on this tour was formed with Baron Jacques von Ramm, who was the inspiration for a character in *Hyperion*.

Longfellow's way of working was always somewhat fitful. Apparently he read and studied with passionate intensity for days and even weeks until a reaction set in. In Heidelberg, spring brought restlessness, and by the end of June he had developed an irresistible urge to leave his studies to travel through the Austrian Tyrol and parts of Switzerland. This visit was memorable in many ways. His meeting with new friends, including the Appleton family, changed the entire course of his life. Nathan Appleton, perhaps the wealthiest man in Boston, was touring Europe with his wife; his son Tom, wit and friend of authors and artists; and his daughters Mary and Frances, or Fanny, as she was commonly known. Longfellow seems to have been charmed by the entire family; his courtship of Fanny will be discussed later.

In mid-August he was still on tour, with no indication of when he might return to Heidelberg. But on August 17 he received a letter from Clara Crowninshield, for whom he was still responsible, informing him that she was "out of patience waiting for an escort to America" (Thompson, 237). Reminded of his duty, he returned immediately to Heidelberg to make plans for his return. Clara's diary for this period has a human-interest entry: "At two Mr. Longfellow went to call on his friend and see his father's wine cellar and order a quantity to be sent to America." About 6:15 "he came in and said he had been tasting 20 different sorts of wine. His face was flushed, and our laughing at him, or really the effects of the wine, confused him so much that he could not count the money straight to pay the bill."[8] For the return voyage, Longfellow found himself the escort not only of Clara but also of Mrs. Bryant and her daughter, for Bryant had been called home earlier. The party sailed from Le Havre for New York early in October, 1836. Longfellow had been gone just about a year and a half, the maximum time suggested by President Quincy.

III   *The Harvard Professor*

By November Longfellow was back in the United States. He established residence in Cambridge in December, being fortunate enough to find rooms in the same house with Cornelius C. Felton (*Life*, I, 243), whom Dickens was to call "heartiest of Greek Professors," and who was to prove a steadfast friend to Longfellow by helping him later with an editorial project that was too time-consuming and too taxing on his eyes. Longfellow had been formally elected Smith Professor on November 17, 1836, by the Harvard Corporation, and the election was confirmed by the Board of Overseers on February 1, 1837.[9] On March 22 he wrote to his father that his first quarter's salary had been paid although he had not begun classroom duties. However, he kept busy with social activities and with preparing lectures, the first of which he delivered on May 23.[10]

The committee for ascertaining the duties of the "Smith Professor of Modern Languages, and of Belles Lettres" was still in existence. Longfellow met with the committee, and shortly afterward President Quincy gave him a tentative outline of his duties; he was to superintend, instruct, and lecture. The department gave instruction in French, Spanish, Italian, and German, but there was to be a native instructor (hired by Ticknor) for each. Longfellow had expected to supervise and to lecture, but not to give basic instruction. His forthright request for revision of his assignment brought some adjustment, but there was periodic friction throughout his Harvard tenure. He was to become all too familiar with this phrasing in reports about action taken on his requests: "Voted—That it is inexpedient to make such alteration, or such provision."

All in all, Longfellow was a very successful Smith Professor, which means that he was also an effective departmental chairman. He successfully, apparently with just the right measure of courtesy and firmness, supervised his team of foreign instructors, which he described as "this *four-in-hand* of outlandish animals, all pulling the wrong way except one" (*Life,* I, 267). He wrote his father that "my occupations are of the most delightful kind." Some time later his father expressed obvious pleasure in his son's new situation: "I rejoice, my dear son, that you are at length established in so very eligible a situation . . . I think your ambition must be satisfied, and your only object now will be to fill with eminence and distinction the office in which you are placed, and to become distinguished among the literary men of the age" (Thompson, 241).

Longfellow had already developed at Bowdoin the principal academic theories and procedures he used at Harvard. His chief innovation was his "doctrine of interest." Other professors looked upon knowledge as discipline more than as something important in itself, and they made little effort to make their presentations interesting. Even at Bowdoin he had produced new text materials with appeal to the students as his objective. At Harvard he lectured from notes—the method favored in Germany and by Ticknor—instead of reading perfunctorily from completely written lectures.[11] Edward Everett Hale, who was in a German class of Longfellow's during his first term, describes his teaching methods thus: "He began with familiar ballads,—read them to us, and made us read them to him. Of course, we soon committed them to memory without meaning to, and I think this was probably part of his theory."[12]

It is apparent that Longfellow was able to create a lively, pleasant classroom atmosphere. His students liked him, but he also won their respect: "Once when there were very threatening indications of a rebellion among the students, and the other professors were unable to get a hearing from the angry and excited mob, Mr. Longfellow began to speak, and instantly the students became quiet, saying, 'Let's hear Longfellow, for he always treats us as gentlemen.' "[13] It also did not take the charming young professor long to win acceptance in the somewhat liberalized but still rather strait-laced Boston-Cambridge community. By March, 1837, he could write his father: "There is such a social spirit here and in Boston, that I seldom see a book by candle-light. Indeed, I pass half of my evenings, at least, in society . . . People here are too agreeable to let a man kill himself with study" (*Life*, I, 250).

He was inclined to dress rather gaily, being fond of the figured waistcoats, the highly-colored cravats, and the light-colored gloves favored in European society; but apparently his dress was always in good taste and "not the elaborate dandyism of his popular contemporary, N. P. Willis."[14] Soon he had an opportunity to secure rooms in the more attractive and comfortable Craigie House, an old mansion made famous by George Washington's use of it as headquarters for nine months during the Revolution. It was now kept by Mrs. Craigie, an eccentric widow, who tried to turn her would-be tenant away with the remark that she did not intend to take any more students as roomers (*Life*, I, 263ff.). When she learned that her caller was not only a professor but also the author of *Outre-Mer*, of which she had a copy, she lodged him sumptuously. They got along famously, except that they could never agree about the cankerworms in the elms outside the house. Longfellow wanted them destroyed, but she protested, "Why, sir, they are our fellow-worms; they have as good a right to live as we have." So the worms lived, the elms died, and Longfellow had to replace them with surplus trees from the Harvard Yard when he became the owner.[15]

IV Back to Authorship

While Longfellow was in Heidelberg mourning the loss of his wife, he resolved to forego his literary ambitions and to devote himself rigorously to scholarly studies. This resolution proved unrealistic, however, for the experiences he underwent at this very time brought an intellectual maturity and emotional fervor that sooner or later inevitably sought literary expression. It is significant that, although he had won his appointment partly through scholarly writing, he published only one learned article while at Harvard.[16]

During his eighteen years there it was his literary output that made him world famous.

Engrossing as he found his Harvard duties, in less than a year he was again writing poetry, practically the first in a dozen years. On his thirty-first birthday, February 27, 1838, he copied into his journal "Evening Shadows" (*Life*, I, 276-77), later to be expanded and published as "Footsteps of Angels," commemorating Mary Longfellow and his brother-in-law, George W. Pierce, news of whose death had reached him in Heidelberg less than a month after Mary died. A few months later, he wrote what was to become the best known, as well as the most controversial, of all his short poems, "A Psalm of Life." Appropriately, he first read the poem to a class at the close of a lecture on Goethe, for it had obviously been influenced by Goethe and Schiller. The inspiration of this poem, so greatly loved in the nineteenth century but more misunderstood than appreciated in the twentieth, is apparent to anyone who has mourned. He was writing to assuage his own despondency and discouragement, to tell himself that one can live victoriously even with loneliness and grief. He had learned from Carlyle, from the German writers, and from his own experience that one can find both solace and courage in work. He who is "up and doing, with a heart for any fate" can find happiness. This, then, was the genesis of a poem that was to hearten thousands of readers who never knew that the poet had written from the depths of his own despair.

Somehow Longfellow managed to do a great deal of writing in the late 1830's. He was full of work and enterprises. In 1838 he was planning a book of fairy tales in collaboration with his classmate Hawthorne, whose first successful book, *Twice-Told Tales* (1837), he had reviewed favorably, much to Hawthorne's gratification. Later in 1838 Longfellow "Talked with Felton and Cleveland about setting up a newspaper in Boston, devoted to literature and general intelligence" (*Life*, I, 304). Neither of these projects worked out—in fact, Longfellow was never to do much collaboration; he was too busy with successful projects of his own.

The only important literary result of Longfellow's first stay in Europe had been *Outre-Mer*. Soon after "A Psalm of Life," he turned again to prose, partly to commemorate his second period of residence in Europe, but perhaps even more to embody, in another way, and more fully, the message of "A Psalm." From his study of German literature, he had come to believe that there was in composition something of rehabilitation: it could bring the past into proper perspective. Although he had expressed this idea in "A Psalm," a prose romance would permit expressing it more fully. The result was *Hyperion*, published as "By the author of *Outre-Mer*," in July,

1839. He had written it around a German motto which he had resolved to adopt as a watchword for his life henceforth: "Look not mournfully into the Past. It comes not back again. Wisely improve the Present. It is thine. Go forth to meet the shadowy Future, without fear, and with a manly heart" (*Works*, II, 6).

Although Longfellow is known today almost exclusively as a poet, it was not until he was well into his Harvard period that he was convinced that his forte was not prose but poetry. By the late 1830's, despite his investment of time in and his hopes for *Hyperion*, he was already beginning to veer toward poetry. By the time *Hyperion* was published, he had managed to write enough respectable poetry for a slender volume. On September 12, 1839, he recorded in his journal that he meant to publish such a work, and *Voices of the Night* appeared that autumn. Its success must have been heartening to the author, for a third edition appeared in 1840 (*Life*, I, 310n.). This volume contained the musical "Prelude" written especially for it, with its closing injunction, "Look, then, into thine heart, and write!" Also included were several of his most successful sentimental lyrics: "Hymn to the Night," to which Poe gave high praise; the controversial "A Psalm of Life"; the autobiographical "Footsteps of Angels"; and others, besides a selected group of "Earlier Poems" that included "The Spirit of Poetry" and "Burial of the Minnesink."

After *Voices of the Night* appeared, Longfellow could no longer be ignored as a poet. The warm reception accorded the volume and many individual poems encouraged him to write poetry at an accelerated pace. The very next year he published a second notable volume, *Ballads and Other Poems*. In it he proved his skill as a balladist with "The Skeleton in Armor" and with the once popular but excessively sentimental "The Wreck of the Hesperus." The volume also included "The Village Blacksmith," which he had described as "another psalm of life," and such once popular lyrics as "The Rainy Day," "Maidenhood," and "Excelsior."

Longfellow was by now indeed well launched as a poet. It might seem that his cup would be overflowing with satisfaction, but it was not. There was some friction with the Harvard authorities; his health had become bad enough to worry him; but, probably what depressed him most of all was discouragement over his fruitless courtship, in person and with his pen, of Fanny Appleton. In view of these circumstances, perhaps it should not be surprising that he requested early in 1842 a leave of absence to begin May 1 and to last six months in order for him to visit Germany and try the effects of the baths on his health. The Harvard Corporation granted Professor Longfellow his leave "for the benefit of his health."[17]

V *The Lady Is Unwilling*

There is evidence that both Henry Longfellow and Fanny Appleton were romantically interested in each other from the time of their meeting and subsequent association in Switzerland in the late summer of 1836. They were not married until July 13, 1843, nearly seven years later, but they were extraordinarily happy afterward. Although she was more than ten years younger than Longfellow, Fanny was nearly nineteen when they met. Why was the marriage of two such well-suited persons so long delayed? Perhaps the question can never be answered fully, but the recent publication of selections from Fanny's letters and journals[18] throws considerable light on the matter.

For one thing, neither was quite ready to fall in love when they met. Although Longfellow was emerging from the emotional trauma that followed the death of his first wife, the event was still little more than half a year behind him. Fanny, for her part, had formed an erroneous image of him, especially with respect to his age. Before they met, she wrote to a friend: "Prof. Longfellow sends up his card to Father. Hope the venerable gentleman won't pop in on us, though I did like his *Outre-Mer*."[19] Perhaps she had wished that he were an eligible young man. A little after their Interlaken meeting she wrote of him, as though puzzled: "a young man after all, or else the son of the poet." A few days later she could record "Have a nice walk in the P. M. with Mr. L. to the old bridge." Shortly he was giving her and her sister lessons in German and reading to them the "pretty ballads of Uhland." By August 6, she had concluded "Mr. L very inquisitive." For a little over two weeks they were together a great deal; then Longfellow received on August 17 the letter from Clara Crowninshield which necessitated his immediate return to Heidelberg and shortly thereafter to America. On August 19 Fanny made a laconic but significant entry in her journal, "Miss Mr. L considerably."[20]

Back in America, the Smith Professor was busy with his new duties, but he was not too busy to meet the Appleton sisters frequently for walks on the Boston Common or to call at the Appleton home on Beacon Street. Apparently Longfellow was enough in love and rash enough to propose to his lady before the end of his first year at Harvard—and to be rejected by her, to his probable surprise and certain hurt.[21] One can only conjecture why she turned him down. She may still have been worried about the disparity in age, though this was less than she had anticipated. It could be that the young Smith Professor did not seem a very good match to Fanny or to her Boston family. He may also have been too precipitate for her; she was ready for friendship but not yet for marriage.

Longfellow did not give up easily. He and Fanny's sister Mary continued friends; he wrote December 10, 1837, to Mary, partly in German, of his disappointment (Thompson, 256). He also confided to his friend Greene from time to time (259ff.). By May 12, 1838, he and Fanny's sisters were on friendly terms again. It must have been about this time that Longfellow decided (frugal Yankee that he still was) to court his lady in roundabout fashion and at the same time to achieve his ambition to write a novel.

The characters Paul Flemming and Mary Ashburton of *Hyperion* could not fail to suggest to their friends, as well as to all the Appletons, that they were based on Henry Longfellow and Fanny Appleton. To be sure, in the novel, Paul renounces his love for Mary and resolves to go on with his career without her, whereas Long-fellow clearly had no notion of continuing to live without Fanny Appleton if he could help it. On March 23, while still working on *Hyperion*, he described "A delightful day with the Appletons" and spoke of the brother and sisters, "They are dear children, notwithstanding they have no talent for matrimony" (Thompson, 278). Shortly before publication of the book, he expressed the hope that he had so painted the lady "as to make her fall in love with her own sweet image in the book" (282). But when the book appeared there was no word from the person he had most wanted to impress. Several months afterward, he met her on the streets of Boston—and she did not speak. His journal entry is plaintive: "Met the stately dark ladie in the street. I *looked* and *passed*, as Dante prescribes. It is ended."[22]

It was not permanently ended, although both parties had reason to think so at the time. Fanny's letters and diary show that she was not pleased to be portrayed in *Hyperion*, or with her professor-suitor generally. On August 9, 1839, shortly after the book appeared, she wrote to a woman friend: "met the Professor in New York, who civilly sent us a copy of his *Hyperion*, and a rank Swiss cheese! which Mr. Charles S says testifies his admiration, as strong and as disagreeable! There are really some exquisite things in this book, though it is desultory, objectless, a thing of shreds and patches like the author's mind. . . . The heroine is wooed (like some persons I know have been) by the reading of German ballads in her unwilling ears, and the result is equally natural in both cases."[23] It is not easy to imagine just what sort of suitor Fanny wanted at this time, but it was evidently not Longfellow.

Subsequent observations in her letters or journals tell their own story. On November 4 of the same year she wrote: "I . . . have already been hoisted into such a public notoriety by a certain impertinent friend of mine you wot of that I am entirely disgusted with the honor." But she had not lost interest in his literary activity. On December 29 she wrote to another correspondent: "The Prof has collected all his vagrant poems into a neat little volume christened mournfully *Voices of the Night.* He does not look like a night-bird and is more of a mocking-bird than a nightingale, though he has some sweetly plaintive notes. All the Psalms are fine but the rest *peu de chose.*" Her criticisms of Longfellow's publications suggest that Fanny would have considered a first-rate author an eligible suitor but was still unconvinced that Longfellow was one. Nearly a year later, on November 8, 1840, she wrote: "Have you seen the Prof's last attempt, 'The Country [sic] Blacksmith? *very* good, especially the children looking in and the daughter singing." After *Ballads and Other Poems,* containing "The Village Blacksmith," appeared, she wrote on December 24, 1841: "The Professor has a creamy new volume of verses out—rather meagre—*selon moi,* the cream of thought being somewhat thinner than that of the binding."

In December, 1838, Mary Appleton, who was almost four years older than Fanny, was married to an Englishman Robert Mackintosh, son of Sir James Mackintosh—despite the lack of "talent for matrimony" in the Appleton family. The occasion was a great wrench to Fanny, who had been very close to her sister. The fact that Mary had not liked MacKintosh at first but was obviously enthralled to be his bride[24] may have given her sister cause for sober thought; but, if so, this was slow in affecting her relationship with Longfellow. Apparently they both still considered the courtship ended when he went on leave in 1842 to take the baths at Marienburg.

VI *Some Happy Years*

All is grist that comes to a good mill. Longfellow seems to have been sincere in his reason for requesting leave from Harvard, but improved health was by no means the only dividend he got from his six-month (and last) residence in Germany. His absence evidently gave Fanny Appleton the opportunity to realize that he had come to occupy a larger place in her heart than she had supposed. Abroad, he had experiences and made new contacts that had much influence on his subsequent writing.

The Marienburg baths at Boppard on the Rhine offered a rigorous program of bathing and exercising to which Longfellow gave credit for marked improvement in his health. Probably more important, however, was the availability of a congenial social-literary circle which he could and did join, at nearby St. Goar. This group consisted centrally of the poet Ferdinand Freiligrath, an important German writer of about his own age; Freiligrath's charming wife; and an attractive young German poet and singer, Louise von Gall.[25] Longfellow must have envied the obvious domestic felicity of the Freiligraths, and apparently they were mystified because he and Louise von Gall did not make a match; they, of course, did not realize the extent to which his affections had been preempted by Fanny Appleton. Freiligrath later translated *Hiawatha* and several of Longfellow's other poems into German; with his pronounced political interests, he was doubtless an influence on the anti-slavery poems Longfellow wrote on his return voyage. They remained life-long friends, and Freiligrath was one of the persons considered to succeed Longfellow in the Smith Professorship. Shortly before leaving Boppard on the Rhine, Longfellow wrote "Mezzo Cammin," the fine sonnet in which he laments his lack of significant poetic accomplishment and expresses a hope that he may yet build a tower of song with lofty parapet before the cataract of death already thundering from the heights descends upon him. This poem, not published until his brother included it in his *Life* in 1886, is important enough to be quoted in full:

MEZZO CAMMIN
Boppard on the Rhine. August 25, 1842.

Half of my life is gone, and I have let
   The years slip from me and have not fulfilled
   The aspiration of my youth, to build
   Some tower of song with lofty parapet.
Not indolence, nor pleasure, nor the fret
   Of restless passions that would not be stilled,
   But sorrow, and a care that almost killed,
   Kept me from what I may accomplish yet;
Though, half-way up the hill, I see the Past
   Lying beneath me with its sounds and sights,—
   A city in the twilight dim and vast,
With smoking roofs, soft bells, and gleaming lights,—
   And hear above me on the autumnal blast
   The cataract of Death far thundering from the heights.
                   (*Life*, I, 404)

On the stormy homeward voyage, he wrote the little group of poems published later in 1842 as *Poems on Slavery*. Whittier was so gratified that he not only tried to get Longfellow to be a candidate for Congress but assured him of election. In the poems Longfellow had made his bow to Freiligrath, to the sober thoughts induced by the stormy voyage and the general state of his life, and to his awareness of the condition of this country. He would have none of Whittier's offer; instead he resumed his Harvard duties and his mounting literary projects. Amidst all this busyness he must have been surprised to discover that his absence had indeed made his lady's heart fonder. But it was a few months after his return before this became apparent.

When they met again at the home of the Andrews Nortons, shortly before Tom Appleton was to leave for Europe, Fanny told Longfellow of her prospective loneliness and added: "You must come and comfort me, Mr. Longfellow."[26] This was more encouragement than he had expected—or needed. Within a month, the new relationship had so prospered that he proposed again. She formally accepted, in a note of May 10, whereupon he rushed immediately from the Craigie House to Beacon Street "too restless to sit in a carriage," walking "amid the blossoms and sunshine and song of birds, with my heart full of gladness and my eyes full of tears!— Oh, Day forever blessed; that ushered in this *Vita Nova* of happiness!" (Thompson, 337).

All of the turbulence in their relationship preceded their engagement. Fanny wrote rapturously soon afterward to her Aunt Martha, to her brother Tom, and to Longfellow's sister Anne Pierce and his mother. They were married on July 13, and Fanny's millionaire father gave them the Craigie House as a wedding present (*Life*, II, 3). Fanny must have had some difficulty reconciling her long hesitation with her new-found happiness. On May 28, 1844, "when she was looking forward to the birth of her first child, Fanny sat at a window in the Craigie House and watched her husband rowing in the sunset on the river: '[I] longed to be with him.... How completely my life is bound up in this love—how broken and incomplete when he is absent a moment, what infinite peace and fulfilment when he is present. And he loves me to the uttermost desire of my heart.' "[27]

Fanny proved an ideal wife. She served as her husband's "eyes" during the period of near blindness in the early years of their marriage, reading to him and transcribing his scrawled writings. She was the direct instigator of a number of poems, including "The Arsenal at Springfield" and "The Old Clock on the Stairs." An able and willing letter writer, she took much of the burden of correspondence off his hands and also proved a steadying influence for his Harvard relationship and for his compositions during his productive middle years. In addition, she was the efficient, charming hostess of Craigie House, where European literary and artistic celebrities were entertained as a matter of course.

Their happiness continued through the birth of two sons, the birth and early death of their first daughter, and the birth of three other daughters. It was doomed to end tragically, but Fanny was her husband's sweetheart to the end. A month after her death, he wrote to her sister Mary: "I never looked at her without a thrill of pleasure; she never came into a room where I was without my heart beating quicker, nor went out without my feeling that something of the light went with her."[28]

During the early years of their marriage, Longfellow made his great bid for, and won, literary recognition. To be sure, he was still the Smith Professor at Harvard, but even the college showed signs of recognizing that his writings might be more important than his obligations to the language department. Fanny was as intent about his poetic efforts as he was himself. At first she was a little worried about the effect of their marriage on them, for on January 31, 1844, she wrote to her brother Tom: "Henry thinks happiness does not inspire his muse; perhaps she is jealous and sulks."[29] But a week later, she could note that a reviewer called Henry "'unquestionably the first of American poets!' How I love to hear him praised!" By April she could write to his mother: "Henry continues very well, and very busy, having resumed his lectures, from which he reaps golden opinions among the students, I hear, but he wishes he had a little more leisure to indulge his poetical vein, which struggles to free itself from the bonds of these more practical duties. I am a pretty active spur upon his Pegasus." There can be no doubt of the bride's sympathy with her husband's literary aspirations, especially in poetry.

The large flow of literary work which Longfellow had begun before marriage continued unabated. In 1843, the year of the marriage, *The Spanish Student,* a "closet drama," was published. With it, Longfellow came perhaps the closest to an actable play that he would ever come. Before his marriage, he had been working on a most ambitious editorial project, *The Poets and Poetry of Europe,* a huge work designed to help familiarize Americans with the non-English poetry of Europe, and a natural outgrowth of his teaching. He himself supplied a good many of the translations; he labored on the project prodigiously, and this work, more than anything else, was probably responsible for the eye trouble he had before and following his marriage and intermittently for the rest of his life. Had it not been for Fanny's help and for his friend Professor Felton's writing many of the biographical sketches, he probably could not have finished it. However, it was published in 1845 and, in spite of poor print, did much to introduce modern foreign literature into the United States.

In 1846, he published a new volume of short poems, *The Seaside and the Fireside,* in which the most important poem was "The Building of the Ship." It stirred Lincoln, and it has been ever since a central document in American patriotic literature. But the work destined to become most famous was *Evangeline,* published in 1847. It has been called the first important long poem in American litera- ture, and was perhaps the most widely read, certainly the most wept-over, poem of the century. His friends, including Holmes and the historian J. L. Motley, were lavish in their praise. Hawthorne was so impressed that he was nearly tempted to write a history of Acadie: "You have made the subject so popular that a history could hardly fail of circulation" (*Life,* III, 24). The decade ended with *Kavanagh,* another attempt to write a novel; and, as events proved, it was practically his leavetaking of imaginative prose writing.

By 1851, Longfellow was finally launched on the work which he hoped would be the loftiest part of that "tower of song" he had long been trying to build. The authors he most admired and emphasized in his literature classes wrote in the epic strain—Dante, Cervantes, Goethe—and he was also a great admirer of Milton and *Paradise Lost.* Perhaps he himself could write a religious epic—a work in which he could blend the experiences of his residence and studies abroad with his feelings for the American Adam and his life in the New World Eden into one great religious poem, or rather a series of poems. In 1851 he published *The Golden Legend,* the middle part of a projected three-part dramatic work which was to embody the Christian virtues of Hope, Faith, and Charity. The *Legend* was ranked by *Blackwood's* with "the celebrated drama of Goethe," and Ruskin praised Longfellow's portrait of "the temper of the monk." The poem sold well, and was to prove the most success- ful part of the venture. This poem was the last major work he completed while a college professor, though he conceived the idea for *Hiawatha* before he retired.

It was partly his vexation at being unable to get on with *Hiawatha* which induced him to act upon his long-cherished inclination to give up his academic position in favor of full-time authorship. Also, he was again having trouble with his eyes. His wife was willing, if not even anxious, for him to be free of the fret of the campus and able to concentrate more on his writing. He began making pre- liminary gestures toward retirement early in 1854. On April 19, he delivered his last college lecture and on July 19 took part in his last commencement: "The whole crowded church looked ghostly and unreal, as a thing in which I had no part" (*Life,* II, 248). Twenty-five years after he had become a professor to escape being a lawyer, he took leave of the academic life to realize, if possible, his boyhood dream of becoming an eminent poet.

What was Longfellow's attitude toward the academic life? Wagenknecht doubts that he ever truly enjoyed it,[30] but there is considerable evidence that he did like at least the sense of accomplishment it gave him. But while still at Bowdoin he had fretted at its interference with his creative impulses, and the interference had been even greater at Harvard. Too, he doubted at times that an academic person could achieve the intellectual growth he still hoped for. On September 10, 1838, he wrote: "Perhaps the worst thing in a college life is this having your mind constantly a playmate for boys,—constantly adapting itself to them, instead of stretching out and grappling with *men's* minds" (*Life*, I, 296).

How much his friction with college administrations had to do with his turning away from the campus is problematic. He had started out with a battle at Bowdoin over his rank, and President Allen's difficulties with the trustees was certainly a factor in his decision to leave. At Harvard he had to battle the Corporation from time to time over his duties and the regulations governing his department. For example, early in his career he asked for the use of the Chapel or the Philosophical Room to make his course of public lectures more attractive, but the Corporation voted "it is inexpedient" to grant the request.[31] When the French teacher was released, he was required to take over on an emergency basis the basic instruction in French. The Corporation tried to force him to continue this instruction, which he was unwilling to do without more extra pay than was offered.

However, it seems to have been the intoxication of literary success more than friction with the Corporation which made him discontented at Harvard. There is even some evidence that he rather liked matching wits and strategy with the somewhat niggardly and ultra-conservative administration. But after the considerable fanfare which attended the publication of *Hyperion* and *Voices of the Night* in 1839, he ridiculed his future as a professor: "I could live very happily here if I could chain myself down to college duties and be nothing but a professor .... But I am too restless for this. What should I be at fifty? A fat mill-horse, grinding round with blinkers on" (*Life*, I, 331). About this time, a crisis involving his duties made him consider resigning and did result in his proposing radically decreased duties at a lower salary. Rather to his surprise, the Corporation was enough impressed to give him most of what he asked for.

But other crises developed. The next year, a committee reported that the popularity of languages was provoking "a distaste for severer and more disciplining studies," [32] and it recommended that study of only one language be allowed. The report was accepted by the faculty in February, and Longfellow had a new battle on his hands, which he also won. But it was a lonely and wearing struggle, for he had the only faculty vote for his entire department. When the Italian instructor had to be discharged in 1846, Longfellow took over the instruction in that language and continued it under protest to 1853. In 1850 he was asked to do a series of seventy lectures on "Modern Literature," and at the same time to meet and instruct the classes of the German teacher, who was on leave. Since he was eager to work on *The Golden Legend* at the time, it is no wonder that he felt both resentment and frustration.

Written evidence relating directly to the resignation is rather scanty. In a February 22, 1854, letter to Samuel Longfellow, Mrs. Longfellow wrote: "Henry, as you have doubtless heard, is weary after twenty-five years teaching, and has resigned his Professorship— to have time for other things and to feel free."[33] In March, 1854, Longfellow wrote his sister: "My reason for leaving the College is in part the helpless state of my eyes; and in part the weariness of doing the same things over and over again for so many, many years."[34] It is interesting that he did not mention either a particular grievance against the college or fretfulness to get on with his writing. His letter of resignation gave no reasons (he apparently had talked the matter over orally with the president), nor did President Walker's letter of acceptance. The president did, how-ever, express regret at the retirement "of one whose reputation has, for so long a time, made part of the reputation of the College."

All that seems certain is that Longfellow and the college parted on good terms, as was proper, for it had been a rewarding rela-tionship for both. Longfellow had been on the whole a good academic person, if at times a little lax in routine matters. According to Johnson, "He left the Department of Modern Languages firm in every branch."[35] Johnson thinks that, with Ticknor, he pioneered instruction in the modern languages and thus paved the way for the development of graduate study in the languages, an area in which Harvard has long been proud of its leadership. Longfellow, on his side, had profited immeasurably from his studies in the great modern writers and from the enthusiasm of the classroom. Not only had he made Dante, Goethe, and Cervantes vital and memorable to class after class of students, but his own literary aspirations had been lifted through his study of their writings. However, he was probably right in concluding that he had already made his best contribution to the classroom and would do better for the future to husband his eyesight and his energies for the books he still wanted to write.

CHAPTER 5

Poet and Patron of Letters, 1855-82

I *Family Man and Writer*

LONGFELLOW'S FAMILY INTERESTS were well centered in the Craigie House by the time he resigned from Harvard. His father had died in 1849, his ne'er-do-well older brother Stephen in 1850, and his mother in 1851. Now his children made a lively fireside: two boys, Charles and Ernest; two girls, Alice Mary and Edith; Annie Allegra would be born the next year.[1] Longfellow's journals record walks with his boys from time to time, and Fanny mentions his having to punish Charles. His fondness for his daughters became nationally known after the publication of "The Childrens' Hour" in 1859.

It was indeed a happy household, with the obvious affection of the parents for each other and for their attractive children; but with the deaths of four close relatives within five years (including infant daughter Fanny in 1848), the supposed emotional tranquillity of the early years of Longfellow's family life must have been at some variance with reality. However, sitting all night alone with his dead mother, he seems to have lost much of his quarrel with death: "A sense of peace came over me, as if there had been no shock or jar in nature, but a harmonious close to a long life" (*Life*, II, 191). With this experience, death took a holiday for Longfellow, though it was not through with him. His home life for the next decade seems to have been as happy as all of it is popularly supposed to have been, and he undoubtedly counted himself especially blessed because he realized that only those who have been acquainted with grief can know true felicity.

Now at last his lines had fallen unto him in pleasant places—domestically, professionally, and financially. His income from his writings, meager at first, had risen enough to assure him a competence for his family, and he was sufficiently shrewd to see that it would continue to rise. Craigie House, surrounded by elms, was pleasant for most of the year, but, with his brother-in-law Tom Appleton, Longfellow purchased a cottage at the seaside resort of Nahant, farther up the coast, and spent a great deal of time there with his family during the summers. He did not find the summer house very conducive to writing, but he loved to live within sound of the sea.

By happy chance, two events which had considerable influence upon Longfellow's literary life took place soon after his retirement from Harvard. The first was the founding of the Saturday Club, which consisted of a monthly dinner meeting of kindred spirits, mostly literary, at the still famous Parker House in Boston. It had been foreshadowed in the late 1830's, when the Transcendental Club, with Emerson and Alcott as moving spirits, functioned briefly. There were other preliminaries, but the Saturday Club itself did not get organized before 1855 or possibly 1856; since it was so informal, details of its origin are lacking. Longfellow seems not to have been technically a charter member, but a comment in a letter of May 14, 1857, to Tom Appleton shows that he considered himself a founder: "We have formed a Dinner Club, once a month, at Parker's. Agassiz, Motley, Emerson, Pierce, Lowell, Whipple, Sam Ward, Holmes, Dwight... Woodman... myself, and yourself. We sit from three o'clock till nine, generally, which proves it to be pleasant."[2] Closely related to the Saturday Club was the Atlantic Club, founded soon after the beginning of the *Atlantic Monthly* in 1857. The Atlantic Club included several of the same persons as the Saturday Club. Longfellow's journals contain many references to attendance at both clubs, where he, like Hawthorne though to a lesser extent, was more a listening than a talking participant. In the long sessions of the Saturday Club, much literary stimulus must have been derived by Longfellow and his fellow authors and friends of literature.

As has been mentioned, the project on Longfellow's mind when he resigned from Harvard was *Hiawatha*. It is not known just when he conceived the idea for this famous poem, but he began writing it on June 25, 1854, shortly after delivering his last college lecture, and he finished it on March 21, not quite a year later. It was published on November 10, 1855, by Ticknor and Fields, and was an immediate success—more successful, in fact, than anything he had yet published.

Longfellow must have been pleased with the reception of *Hiawatha*. Probably the sprinkling of adverse criticism did not disturb him greatly, for he was shrewd enough to accept the idea of the modern advertising axiom, "There is no such thing as *bad* publicity"; and he must have derived great satisfaction from proving to himself, as well as to others, that, freed from academic toil and worry, he could produce a major work, together with some shorter poems, within a single year. On March 12, 1856, he was pleased to note in his journal. " 'Grace Darling' is reading Hiawatha to crowded houses in Philadelphia; and last night Mrs. Barrow, at the Boston Theatre, after the play, read 'Hiawatha's Wooing' in costume" (*Life*, II, 275).

Of the shorter poetry for 1854-55, two reminiscent poems are noteworthy: "The Rope Walk" and "My Lost Youth," both going back to recollections of childhood that had been revived by some recent visiting in Portland. "My Lost Youth," using a verse from a Lapland song for its refrain, like *Hiawatha* shows an indebtedness to his Scandinavian visit, almost twenty years earlier. But reminiscences doubtless came easy to Longfellow at this time: retirement from his professorship so soon after a series of family deaths would be bound to induce the backward look.

It is of particular interest that in this period Longfellow concentrated heavily upon American subject matter. After *Hiawatha*, for which he had gone with the help of sourcebooks into the heartland of America, he returned to his own New England. He seems to have decided early that his epic drama *Christus* would properly have America as the setting of its third and final part; an unanticipated result of this decision was the writing of the highly successful "The Courtship of Miles Standish." By March 25, 1856, he was looking over books on the Puritans and Quakers, both at home and in the college library; and on April 2 he recorded: "Wrote a scene in my new drama, 'The Old Colony,' just to break ground." On May 1 he was "At home all day pondering the New England Tragedy, and writing notes and bits of scenes." The next day he was "Snug by the fireside, meditating the Tragedy. It is delightful to resolve in one's mind a new conception. It is only the writing down which fatigues" (*Life*, II, 276-78).

Work on this project was briefly interrupted by plans for a fourth visit to Europe, this time with Fanny and the children. The plans had to be abandoned, however, when Longfellow injured his leg so severely that traveling was out of the question. However the family may have felt, Longfellow himself was not disappointed, for "The undertaking was too formidable. If I had gone at all, I should have gone very reluctantly" (*Life*, II, 283). Probably, too, he was relieved not to have his full-time writing interrupted so soon.

Before he had finished the "New England Tragedy," as he was calling it by then, he recorded on December 2, 1856, "In the evening, wrote the first scene in "The Courtship of Miles Standish," then intended as a prose drama. The entry preceding this one recorded, "I have lying on my table more than sixty requests for autographs." The author of *Hiawatha* was rapidly becoming famous! On January 29, 1857, he wrote to Freiligrath thanking him for so admirably translating *Hiawatha* into German. By 1857, the enterprising publishing firm of Ticknor and Fields was issuing selections from Longfellow in its famous "Blue and Gold" editions. These little volumes of notable American authors were to become familiar and treasured American household possessions in the late nineteenth century (*Works*, III, 211).

On April 29, he recorded, "Lowell was here last evening to interest me in a new Magazine.... I told him I would write for it if I wrote for any Magazine" (*Life*, II, 297-98). This was of course the *Atlantic Monthly*. By May 5, he was dining at the Parker House with Emerson, Lowell, Motley, Holmes, Cabot, Underwood, and the publisher Phillips to talk more about it. He concluded, "It will no doubt be done; though I am not so eager about it as the rest." On June 20: "Had an offer of one thousand dollars for ten poems, of any length, from the New York Ledger. Declined. I do not wish to write for any newspaper." He did later publish in the *Ledger*, however, and very profitably. Apparently the *New England Tragedy* merited no further mention in his journal for some time. But on August 17, 1857, he recorded hearing a Quakeress from England speak in church, and ten days later, "Finished this morning the first rough draft of Wenlock Christison" (*Life*, II, 304). Evidently he had settled by now on his final scheme of basing the first of two Colonial plays on the Puritan persecutions of the Quakers and the second on the Salem witchcraft affair, but he could not make progress with either; they were not to appear until 1868.

On November 5, 1857, he wrote his good friend Sumner that he had contributed "Santa Filomena" to the first issue of the *Atlantic Monthly*, a new magazine just established by Phillips & Sampson (*Life*, II, 308). He made no comment about the magazine. On December 4 he made a short entry: "Met Whittier at the publisher's. He grows milder and mellower, as does his poetry." His journal and letters about this time have many references to contemporary English and American authors, nearly all of whom he seems to have liked. Fanny Longfellow was also commenting freely on authors: about Emerson with enthusiasm; about Margaret Fuller with obvious dislike. Longfellow was somewhat disparaging of the popular dandy Nathaniel P. Willis and of J. R. Ingraham, the prolific writer of cheap novels; both, like him, were from Portland. On December 29 he made a final entry for 1857: "Work a little at 'Priscilla.' Toward evening, walk in a gently falling snow, under the shaded lamp of the moon" (*Life*, II, 311). Obviously, Longfellow was enjoying being a poet.

By March 1, "Priscilla" had again become "The Courtship of Miles Standish." A week later, ill with a cold, he did not write but instead read *Wuthering Heights*, " a fierce and wonderful novel, by Emily

Brontë . . . . Written by one so young, it is a miracle." On October 16, 1858, *The Courtship of Miles Standish* was published, with the print order doubled from ten thousand to twenty thousand copies (*Life*, II, 326). For this poem, success seems to be measured chiefly in terms of sales; we are not given comments by other writers or critics as for *Hiawatha*. By December 13, he was back working on "Wenlock Christison," as he was now calling his Quaker play. He was still not content to rest on his achievement, but he was finding it hard to handle the stern part of the Colonial material.

Meanwhile in Craigie House the life of a growing family went busily on. On January 2, 1859, he recorded going in the evening to hear *Hiawatha* as set to music by Herr Stoepel. On January 29 he recorded the death of his friend the historian Prescott: "So departs out of our circle one of the most kindly and genial men: a man without an enemy; beloved by all and mourned by all" (*Life*, II, 331). In praising Prescott, Longfellow was possibly expressing a wish that he might himself be so remembered; actually, he could have been quoting from his own obituary. On February 25, he noted that "a very good poem might be written on the Saga of King Olaf, who converted the North to Christianity."

Even without the professorship, he was enjoying a full life. On April 26, 1859, he wrote to Sumner: "What you quote about the père de familee is pretty true. It is a difficult *rôle* to play; particularly when, as in my case, it is united with that of *oncle d'Amérique* and general superintendent of all the dilapidated and tumble-down foreigners who pass this way!" (*Life*, III, 64). The same letter contained a reference to the notorious Webster murder case.[3] On June 3, he wrote to Sumner that the artist-poet Thomas Buchanan Read had been painting his portrait, "standing at my desk, with the clock behind. He is now doing my three girls in one group, a charming picture" (*Life*, II, 337). On January 17, 1860, "Went with F. and the boys to hear Rossini's 'Barber of Seville,' with young Adelina Patti as Rosina."

His freedom to do more reading must have been a great source of satisfaction to him. He noted on July 19, 1859, that he had received from the publisher "Tennyson's new poem, Four Idyls of the King. Eagerly devour the first of them, which is charming,— reminding one of Chaucer's 'Griselda.'" The next day he had finished all of them: "The first and third could have come only from a great poet. The second and fourth do not seem to me so good." He was also following the work of his American contemporaries. On July 25 he noted receiving the current *Atlantic*, in which "Mrs. Stowe's Minister's Wooing continues very charmingly" (*Life*, II, 339). By March 1, 1860, he had received a copy of Hawthorne's

The Marble Faun and noted, "A soft rain falling all day long, and all day long I read The Marble Faun. A wonderful book; but with the old, dull pain in it that runs through all Hawthorne's writings" (*Life*, II, 351). Later in the month he was reading a new novel by George Sand and Dickens' *Barnaby Rudge:* "Dickens is always prodigal and ample, but what a set of vagabonds he contrives to introduce us to."

His fame was growing. On August 4, 1859, he enclosed with a letter to Sumner a clipping announcing that Harvard had conferred the honorary LL.D. on him—no doubt a most pleasing recognition to the Smith Professor five years after his retirement. By November, Thackeray was writing him from London soliciting contributions to the *Cornhill Magazine:* "Has Hiawatha ever a spare shaft in his quiver, which he can shoot across the Atlantic?" (*Life*, II, 346). On March 17, 1860, he noted with obvious satisfaction his publisher's announcement of a new edition of *Hiawatha:* "He sells two thousand a year; which is a great sale for an old book, of which fifty thousand have already been sold."

On May 30, he attended an anti-slavery meeting at which he heard Wendell Phillips and two "colored men" speak (*Life*, II, 354). On August 2, he "Rowed and walked, and read Goldoni." Three days later he heard John Ware of Cambridge preach "a good sermon from the text, "While I was busy here and there, he was gone.' I applied it to myself." Longfellow, still a son of the Puritans, continually lamented the loss of "God's precious time." At the end of the month, he paid another of his rather frequent visits to Portland, which by now "has become to me a land of ghosts and shadows." Life was going along very smoothly for the Cambridge poet, if not so productively as he could have wished, with only the gentle sorrows of the death of a friend or other changes in Cambridge, Nahant, or Portland. Mercifully, he had no premonition that tragedy was stalking him, that he was on the eve of suffering the most devastating of the several personal losses which formed an undercurrent of sorrow in his superficially tranquil and happy life.

II *Death Intrudes*

The entries in Longfellow's journal for the first half of 1861 show less concern with family matters than usual. Despite the popular belief that he was not much involved in the trouble over slavery and the outbreak of the Civil War, there are numerous references to the impending conflict and then to its outbreak. He had no patience with President Buchanan, "an antedeluvian," who cared nothing for the future "if he gets safely through his term." The ringing of bells for Washington's birthday had for him "a sad sound, reminding me of the wretched treason in the land" (*Life*, II, 361). The slow dissolution of the Union reminded him of a Greek tragedy. He was favorably impressed, however, by President Lincoln's Inaugural Address, "conciliatory, and yet firm." On April 30, eighteen days after the firing on Fort Sumter, he recorded: "When the times have such a gunpowder flavor, all literature loses its taste," an observation which explains much of his own loss of favor in twentieth-century America. Concerned as he was about the war, however, he wrote on June 20 to G. W. Curtis that he would not enter a prize contest for "a National Song or Hymn . . . . Such arenas I never enter."

On July 8, he noted that the weather was very hot. There would be no more dated journal entries until September; instead a blank space is followed by a quotation from Tennyson:

> Sleep sweetly, tender heart, in peace!
> Sleep, holy spirit, blessed soul!
> While the stars burn, the moons increase,
> And the great ages onward roll.
>
> (*Life*, II, 368)

On June 19 he had written in his journal, "If one could only foresee one's fate!"[4] Apparently it was about this time that Holmes made his too prophetic remark about the Longfellow domestic felicity. According to W. D. Howells, "Curtis once told me that a little while before Mrs. Longfellow's death he was driving by Craigie House with Holmes, who said he trembled to look at it, for those who lived there had their happiness so perfect that no change, of all the changes which must come to them, could fail to be for the worse."[5]

Samuel Longfellow gives only a laconic account of the tragic event: "On the ninth of July his wife was sitting in the library, with her two little girls, engaged in sealing up some small packages of their curls which she had just cut off. From a match fallen upon the floor, her light summer dress caught fire. The shock was too great, and she died the next morning. Three days later, her burial took place at Mount Auburn. It was the anniversary of her marriage-day; and on her beautiful head, lovely and unmarred in death, some hand had placed a wreath of orange blossoms. Her husband was not there,—confined to his chamber by the severe burns which he had himself received" (*Life*, II, 369).

Longfellow, who had been in an adjoining room at the time, tried valiantly to save his wife's life by enfolding her in a rug and in his arms. He did protect her face, but his own face and arms were

HENRY WADSWORTH LONGFELLOW

terribly burned before he extinguished the fire. Although he was in shock himself, or very near it, he survived, but was never to be quite the same again. Had it not been for the severe illness of Fanny's father, who died the day after her funeral, the Longfellows would already have been at their summer home in Nahant.

Early in life Longfellow had written, "With me all deep feelings are silent ones" (*Life*, II, 372). Although sorely stricken by his loss, he never said a great deal about it. His son Ernest was to remember, "My father was badly burned while trying to save her, and I remember his lying in bed and holding up his poor bandaged hands and murmuring, 'Oh, why could I not save her?' "[6] His brother wrote of a visit to him soon after her death: "To a visitor, who expressed the hope that he might be enabled to 'bear his cross' with patience, he replied: '*Bear* the cross, yes; but what if one is stretched upon it!'" (*Life*, II, 369). A month after her death, however, he could write to her sister Mary: "I am at least patient, if not resigned; and thank God hourly ... for the beautiful life we led together, and that I loved her more and more to the end." At the close of the letter, his thoughts were on his children: "My heart aches and bleeds sorely for the poor children. To lose *such* a mother, and all the divine influences of her character and care. They do not know how great this loss is, but I do. God will provide. His will be done!"[7]

With the light of his life so suddenly and cruelly extinguished, it was the children whose trusting hands guided him through the blackness of despair. He has, he says in his letter to Mary, only one question: "What will be best for them?" The answer to that question was that he must be both father and mother, and this double burden he bore with strength and sensitive understanding. It was partly, no doubt, this love and sympathy for his own that made him the friend of children all over the world.

Sooner or later he was bound to express in verse something of what the loss of his wife meant to him. However, it was not until eighteen years afterward—on the anniversary of her death and within three years of his own—that he wrote a sonnet tribute to her not published until four years after he died. It is one of his finest poems:

THE CROSS OF SNOW

In the long sleepless watches of the night,
  A gentle face—the face of one long dead—
  Looks at me from the wall, where round its head
  The night-lamp casts a halo of pale light.
Here in this room she died; and soul more white
  Never through martyrdom of fire was led
  To its repose; nor can in books be read
  The legend of a life more benedight.

> There is a mountain in the distant West
> That, sun-defying, in its deep ravines
> Displays a cross of snow upon its side.
> Such is the cross I wear upon my breast
> These eighteen years, through all the changing scenes
> And seasons, changeless since the day she died.
>
> (*Life*, II, 373)

III *Comfort in Labor*

When his wife died, Longfellow was already well along with another major work, *Tales of a Wayside Inn.* Knowing that he must find solace in labor, if anywhere, and being too disturbed to do original writing, he resumed translating the *Divine Comedy,* which he had begun as part of his preparation for teaching Dante at Harvard twenty years earlier. Longfellow reported in a letter to Freiligrath in 1843 that he had translated sixteen cantos,[8] but had laid it aside in favor of creative projects. However, he never lost his interest in translating and took justifiable pride in his ability as a translator.[9] Now, according to his brother, he translated a canto from Dante daily (*Life*, II, 372). He kept at the task as a major part of his activity until the whole blank verse version, still considered one of the best, was completed. His journal for 1862, after he had resumed fairly regular entries, is full of references to his work and to progress with it.

His journal records also show that the Civil War continued to touch him very closely. His son Charles, despite his mother's avowed and his father's alleged pacificism, insisted on volunteering. On March 6, 1862, Longfellow noted: "C. has been asked to go to Ship Island. Drive to town with him to see him on board. It is a great tug at the heartstrings, this parting with a son for the first time" (*Life*, II, 377). By the end of April he was lamenting the death of his good friend Felton. In June he "joined a party of friends in a visit to Niagara Falls, which he had never seen—taking his boys with him." This was to be his deepest penetration into Western America; he who had become so well traveled in Europe and who had written and was to write so much about his native land was content to live on the Eastern seaboard. He did not even like Niagara, a tremendously popular resort at the time, observing, "Niagara is too much for me; my nerves shake like a bridge of wire." By late June he was preparing to go to Nahant, but this time with a sense of "utter loneliness!"

However, by the end of 1862 he had recovered enough tranquillity to resume work on the *Tales of a Wayside Inn.* On November 25, 1863, the first edition of fifteen thousand copies was published, and he invited his publishers, together with his friends Sumner and Greene, to dine with him (*Life*, II, 395). This first part of a work that was to become Longfellow's longest book contained several popular favorites: "Paul Revere's Ride," "The Falcon of Sir Federigo," "King Robert of Sicily," and "The Saga of King Olaf." It was highly successful, no doubt partly because the poet's following, already large, had been increased by sympathetic interest in his domestic tragedy.

His troubles were not over. On December 1 he received a telegram from Washington informing him that Charles had been badly wounded, and he and Ernest left for Washington the same day (*Life*, II, 395). While he was waiting for the wounded to be brought to the dressing station, a man in military overcoat introduced himself: "I am Dr. B— of Riga; have translated your Hiawatha into Russian." Charles' injury proved to be not as severe as feared, and Longfellow took him home without incident.

His extensive and growing correspondence must have been a considerable satisfaction to him. On January 2, 1864, Hawthorne, now in the last year of his life, wrote him: "I have read the Wayside Inn with great comfort and delight. I take vast satisfaction in your poetry, and take very little in most other men's, except it be the grand old strains that have been sounding on through all my life" (*Life*, II, 399). On February 24, Emerson wrote him, "When will you come back to the Saturdays, which want their ancient lustre?" By May 23 he was writing to Sumner lamenting the news of Hawthorne's death. For the funeral, he composed a fine poem, sending a copy to Mrs. Hawthorne, who wrote him a beautiful letter in response (*Life*, II, 409-11).

In October, 1864, a new edition of *Hyperion* appeared in London. While working on the new edition, in January of the same year, Longfellow had written: "Read over a part of Hyperion, to prepare for a new edition. Ah, me! how many graves I dug open! When it is once revised, I shall never dare look into the book again" (*Life*, II, 402). Early in 1865, the beautifully bound first volume of his translation of the *Divine Comedy* appeared, to his great satisfaction. He was by now famous enough for his publishers to think of collected editions of his poems as a good risk. On March 14 he noted: "Fields comes out, with the proposition to publish a selection from my poems, in a cheap form. Begins with twenty thousand." The book was published as *Household Poems*. Looking over the poems to make the selections was not a happy experience: "They remind me almost too keenly of the days that are no more. 'There is no greater grief than to be mindful of the happy days in misery,' so says

Boethius... and one Dante, in a curious book, so tragic that he calls it a comedy" (*Life*, II, 426).

On October 25, 1865, he noted the first meeting "of our Dante Club" (*Life*, II, 428). This was a group of Dante scholars whom he had assembled for critical advice while the completed translation was being seen through the press. The most important members were Lowell, who succeeded him in offering courses in Dante at Harvard, and Professor Charles Eliot Norton, who later made a prose translation of the *Comedy*. One of the historians of the Club and also a member of some importance was the young William Dean Howells, then in Cambridge to work on the *Atlantic Monthly* and recently returned from four years as U. S. Consul at Venice. The weekly meetings, ending with "a little supper," seem to have been very pleasant, as well as profitable, occasions. Longfellow always had the ability to make his guests feel welcome, as Norton's comment shows: "Mr. Longfellow had a special charm as a host, the charm of social grace and humor, by which his guests were brought into congenial disposition" (*Life*, II, 430).

The Dante Club meetings continued through 1866. This year he wrote Numbers V and VI of the sonnets he composed to preface (two for each) the three parts of his *Divine Comedy*. On June 1 his entry was simply "A lovely, sad day." But he did more than translate and meditate sadly. On December 18, in a letter to Sumner, he urged the senator to introduce an international copyright bill in the Senate. About this time Longfellow received a letter bringing him from Italy a Diploma and Cross of the Order of SS. Maurizio and Lazzaro. Though grateful, he refused them; he felt that it would not be proper for him, "as an American Citizen, a Protestant, and Republican," to accept a Catholic Order of Knighthood (*Life*, III, 90).

On February 27, 1867, he observed his sixtieth birthday, with "Sundry bouquets, and presents from the children. Ernest presented me with his charming portrait of his sister, reading" (*Life*, II, 433). Ernest had by this time shown signs of developing into a portrait painter of some fame, a promise to remain largely unfulfilled. Longfellow also noted the arrival of the poetic tribute by Lowell quoted in the first chapter of this book. On June 1, his old mentor George Ticknor wrote him a eulogistic letter about his Dante translation (*Life*, II, 436-37). In 1867 also appeared the first new volume of poems in several years, *Flower-De-Luce*, a collection of twelve poems, including the tribute to Hawthorne, the war poems "Christmas Bells" and "Killed at the Ford," and the group of six Dante sonnets.

On April 6, 1868, Longfellow noted that the printers were progressing slowly with the *New England Tragedies*. His literary career was still making gratifying, if somewhat painful, progress; the sadness of his bereavement continued; his health was only intermittently good. On April 16 he reported: "A whole week of aches and pains and influenza." But he could respond a month later to a favorable turn in the weather with something of his old enthusiasm: "Suddenly, with a gush of song and sunshine, after long days of rain and dreary weather, spring and summer come together, bride and bridegroom,—blush of youth, and heat of passion" (*Life*, II, 438).

IV   *The White Mr. Longfellow*

By 1868, although still little past sixty, Longfellow was becoming the grand old man of American letters. This year he decided to make another visit abroad, a journey destined to be very different from all the others—not a residence for language study and not a lonely time. He was accompanied by an amazingly large party of relatives—his son Ernest and his new bride, all three of his daughters, plus two sisters, a brother, and his brother-in-law Tom Appleton—and the whole affair took on the nature of a triumphal tour. Before the party sailed, Publisher Fields gave the poet a parting dinner, with Agassiz, Dana, Greene, Holmes, Lowell, Norton, and Whipple as guests. Longfellow recorded: "Holmes read a charming poem, and we enjoyed ourselves extremely" (*Life*, II, 438). In New York the group embarked on a steamship bound for Liverpool.

In England, the visit turned into a triumphal progress. They first toured the Lake Country briefly, and then left for Cambridge, where Longfellow received the LL.D. degree amid numerous tributes. A spectator wrote this impression: "Long, white, silken hair and a beard of patriarchal whiteness enclosed a fresh-colored countenance, with fine-cut feature and deep-sunken eyes, overshadowed by massive eyebrows" (*Life*, II, 442). In London he breakfasted with William Gladstone and lunched with Lord John Russell at Richmond. The Queen received him at Windsor Castle, and he called by request on the Prince of Wales. With his daughters, he spent a day visiting Dickens at Gadshill, and later there was a visit with the Archbishop of Canterbury. Before crossing the Channel, he also visited Tennyson on the Isle of Wight.

The party went up the Rhine to Switzerland and then visited in northern Italy and Paris, where they heard Molière at the Theatre Français. Returning to Italy, they spent a few weeks in Florence and then settled down for the winter in Rome, where Longfellow was the center of a group of American visitors and resident artists.

Spring took them to Naples and Sorrento, then northward through Venice, Innsbruck, Munich, Nuremberg, and Dresden. Back in England, before the party returned to America, Oxford conferred an honorary degree upon "the most distinguished of American poets."

This eighteen-month excursion was Longfellow's farewell to Europe, and the only one of his visits which was primarily a sightseeing tour and a gathering of literary laurels. The recognition and adulation accorded him in Europe must have helped console him for the failure of *The New England Tragedies,* which Ticknor and Fields had brought out in his absence. Despite his growing popularity, the American public did not respond to them: "They fell flat on the market, the books remaining largely unsold."[10]

Nevertheless, during the fourteen years of life remaining to him, Longfellow was one of the most famous men in the world. "Surely," wrote Greene, "no poet was ever so fully recognized in his lifetime."[11] High and low, European and American, an unbreakable bond seemed to exist between the poet and his readers. Whittier, sending greetings on his friend's seventy-fifth birthday, wrote: "I would not add to the overwhelming burden of congratulation and grateful appreciation which thy birthday must bring, but I cannot let the occasion pass without expressing my gratitude for the happy hours spent over thy writings, and the pride which I share with all Americans in thy success as a writer and thy character as a man. It is permitted to but few in this world to reach a position so honorable or to enjoy so widely the love of their fellow men."[12]

Unlike Emerson, who was four years older and was to die the same year, Longfellow retained his intellectual and poetic powers to the last. But he realized that the strenuous part of his life was over and that he had done whatever he would do to "become eminent in something." Indeed, although he was not altogether satisfied with his career, he was already eminent throughout Western civilization. From this time on, he lived quietly at the Craigie House with his family and friends, still writing a good deal, willingly helping younger writers when they came to him, and even making himself courteously accessible to complete strangers. Part of the imposition he probably accepted in recognition of the price a celebrity must pay for his prominence; most of it he allowed from pure generosity.

A listing of some of his famous foreign visitors in these closing years is impressive: from England came James Anthony Froude, Anthony Trollope, Wilkie Collins, William Black, Charles Kingsley, Dean Stanley, Lord Houghton, Lord and Lady Dufferin, and the Duke of Argyll. Others were his good friend the violinist Ole Bull from Norway and the Emperor Don Pedro of Brazil (*Life,* II,

454-55). Humbler ones included an old Italian woman who brought him a Christmas tree as a present and an Irishwoman with a petition to the governor to pardon her son, in prison for theft. Correspondents included "a gentleman in Maine" who wanted him to read and criticize an epic poem which covered the six days' work of the Creation in about six hundred lines. Requests for autographs became more and more numerous, including one from Chattanooga for a hundred to be used in a fair to raise money for Southern sufferers (*Life*, III, 276). He granted this request. One autograph seeker added a request that he copy his "Break, break, break!" also! (*Ibid.*, 318). Another, from Ohio, sent him one hundred blank cards "with the request that I write my name on each, as she wishes to distribute them among her guests at a party she is to give on my birthday" (*Ibid.*, 298).

From about the time of his return from Europe, Longfellow became for his publisher, James T. Fields, a valuable piece of literary property to be shrewdly merchandised; it is only fair to observe also that Fields held him in high personal regard. But new publications, some made up of old works combined with new, appeared with remarkable frequency throughout the remainder of his life. The three parts of his translation of Dante's *Divine Comedy* were published in 1867-70, and this brought him much honor and doubtless a good deal of money. A revised and greatly enlarged edition of *The Poets and Poetry of Europe* also appeared in 1871. This was followed the same year by *The Divine Tragedy*, the final part of his religious epic, though it is first of the three parts in chronological content. It sold better than *The New England Tragedies*, and it might have had even more success except that it is hard for anyone to improve on the simple beauty of the Christ story as told in the Bible. Moreover, Longfellow had done little more than render it into verse. All three parts of the epic were published the next year as *Christus: A Mystery*. Longfellow had had his misgivings about this work, though he was more ambitious for it than for anything else he wrote; hence he was more disappointed than surprised when his public proved unenthusiastic.

Another publication of 1872 was *Three Books of Song*, containing the second part of *Tales of a Wayside Inn*; an ambitious new dramatic poem, *Judas Maccabaeus*; and eleven translations. In 1874 came *Aftermath*, containing the third part of *Tales of a Wayside Inn*, and some shorter poems grouped as *Birds of Passage*. The next year *The Masque of Pandora, and Other Poems* appeared. More important than the title poem are "The Hanging of the Crane," not so much for its quality as for the price paid for its serial publication; and "Morituri Salutamus," the poem he wrote to commemorate the fiftieth anniversary of the graduation of his Bowdoin College class—one of the few "occasional" poems he ever wrote, and a truly fine utterance. For the next few years he was engaged on a tremendous editorial project, *Poems of Places,* published in 1876-79, in thirty-one volumes. He had probably been talked into this undertaking by Fields. Despite Longfellow's qualifications for such a venture, he must have found it burdensome at his age. On January 18, 1879, he noted: "Send the last copy of Poems of Places to the printer. That stone is rolled over the hill" (*Life,* III, 283). Despite the prestige of Longfellow's name and the "dainty" format, the work did not sell well, and the publishers lost money.[13]

In 1878 came a volume of new poetry: *Kéramos: And Other Poems.* The title poem, one of his best, contains pleasing reminiscences of his Portland boyhood and states his theories of art perhaps better than any other of his works. In 1879-80 appeared a great testimonial to his popularity: the elaborate two-volume set of his works described in Chapter 1 of this book. *Ultima Thule,* published in 1880, contained, among other poems, his tribute to Bayard Taylor; the beautiful lyric, "The Tide Rises, The Tide Falls"; some additional sonnets; and the credo poem, "L'Envoi. The Poet and His Song." Doubtless he intended this to be his last volume and it was the last published during his lifetime, though *In the Harbor* appeared the year of his death. Its most noteworthy inclusion is "The Bells of San Blas," a noble utterance composed only a few days before his death, which occurred on March 24, 1882, about a month after his seventy-fifth birthday. Also published posthumously, in 1883, was *Michael Angelo,* a long fragment of a poem which he had very much wanted to complete as another commentary, added to his Dante, on his reactions to Italian Renaissance culture and his views on art.

Everything seemed to conspire to make the image of the aging Longfellow the one that would endure for posterity. The serenity of his last years and the accumulation of honors made a great impression on a nation in which brotherly good feeling was gradually replacing the bitterness over slavery and the Civil War. Europe also was enjoying a period of cultural progress. The Russian serfs had finally won a measure of freedom; Tennyson and Kipling had made the expansion of the British Empire seem a great boon to the world. Doubtless the popularity of Tennyson and Longfellow brought reciprocal benefits. The presence in the same community with Longfellow of such literary lights as Whittier, Holmes, Lowell, and Emerson also cannot have failed to bring recognition to American culture. It was an age when decorum and formality on the one hand were matched with uninhibited expressions of sentiment on the other. Women followed the tragic figure of Evangeline through a mist of tears; children who knew little of actual travel could vicariously glide with Hiawatha in his birch bark canoe; even the men could enjoy some of the short lyrics for their homely philosophy and the *Tales of a Wayside Inn* for their narrative interest.

Financial success went hand in hand with rising fame. Aside from what he inherited from his wife, Longfellow had come a long way from his family's hard situation in the panic year of 1857 when, according to his son Ernest, they had to give up the horses "which we had always had, and our butler."[14] By 1868 his annual income had risen to over $48,000, a princely sum in those days. He liked to live well, lamenting his lack of thrift: "gold turns to charcoal in my hands," but he nevertheless left an estate valued at $356,320 at his death.[15] His final years were as comfortable as money could make them.

A few events of the tranquil closing years invite mention. In July, 1875, he went to Brunswick to deliver "Morituri Salutamus," the anniversary poem he had written the previous autumn. He read it in his "low and mellow tones" to a hushed audience.[16] The next year he attended the Centennial Exhibition in Philadelphia, spending a week there. To Boston he went less and less, much as he enjoyed the meetings of the Saturday Club and of the Atlantic Club.

In 1879 he was especially pleased when the schoolchildren of Cambridge presented him with an armchair made from "the spreading chestnut tree," which had had to be cut down. Seven hundred children contributed dimes for the purpose (*Life,* II, 465-66). In 1880 his seventy-third birthday was celebrated in all the public schools of Cincinnati; by 1881 the idea had spread far and wide. In December, 1881, the rising Hoosier poet, James Whitcomb Riley, and a friend paid him a visit, only one of countless visits by writers and nonwriters—in 1877 he had recorded "This forenoon fourteen callers; thirteen of them English" (*Life* III, 290). But he was always especially interested in new poets, and, against doctor's orders, he gave Riley and his friend an audience. The young Hoosier was unforgettably impressed by his visit with "Longfellow—poet and patriot."[17]

It is difficult to appreciate today the veneration in which Longfellow was held at the end of his life. His friend Norton wrote in 1878: "Longfellow was here the other day, more truly delightful than ever in the sweet mellowing of his old age." Another friend "tells the impressive story of how when the poet stepped into a horse-car, every man in the vehicle rose as a matter of course to offer a seat, and 'every head was uncovered!'"[18] William Winter, by then "the Great Cham" of the New York Theater, wrote after

Longfellow's death of his boyhood admiration: "I had read every line he had then published; and such was the affection he inspired, even in a boyish mind, that on many a summer night I have walked several miles to his house, only to put my hand upon the latch of his gate, which he himself had touched" (*Life*, III, 308). All his life he had about him the indefinable quality called personal magnetism. Readers admired him from afar; he charmed all those who came in personal contact with him.

At his death, however, praise was mingled with reservations. One of the most discerning comments, in the light of later reactions, was a long editorial in the London *Times*, which said in part: "He himself well knew that he was not in the first rank . . . poetry at its best is a fabric spun only by the strongest brains . . . . The author of that poem [*The Golden Legend*] does not belong to the same strong, swift-souled race as Byron or Shelley." But he was nevertheless accorded a substantial place: "Mr. Longfellow has left no enemies behind him; he had many warm friends and admirers; and his reputation as a poet may survive much longer than those who vaunt 'the poetry of realism' care to admit."[19]

Some were already beginning to see that he might be more a phenomenon of literary history than a truly great literary artist. Most, however, lamented his death as a great loss both to art and to humanity. Perhaps the most judicious estimate was in an address to the Massachusetts Historical Society by his friend and fellow Dante scholar, Charles Eliot Norton. It makes an appropriate ending for the first part of this book:

> He was fortunate in the time of his birth. He grew up in the morning of our Republic. He shared in the cheerfulness of the early hour, in its hopefulness, its confidence. The years of his youth and early manhood coincided with an exceptional moment of national life, in which a prosperous and unembarrassed democracy was learning its own capacities and was beginning to realize its large and novel resources; in which the order of society was still simple and humane. He became, more than any one else, the voice of this epoch of national progress,—an epoch of unexampled prosperity for the masses of mankind in our New World, prosperity from which sprang a sense, more general and deeper than had ever before been felt, of human kindness and brotherhood (*Life*, III, 368-69).

CHAPTER 6

Longfellow as a Prose Writer

I *Finding a Medium*

SINCE NEARLY ALL of Longfellow's literary reputation rests on his poetry, the reader may be surprised to learn that he was over thirty before he was certain that his best medium was verse and past forty when he published his final attempt to write a novel. Washington Irving, the idol of Longfellow's boyhood and the model for much of his early writing, was a prose writer. In college the debate speech on the Indian versus the Colonist and his commencement oration (both discussed above in Chapter 2) brought Longfellow more notice than did his college poems. He admired the prose writings of Hawthorne, Emerson (with qualifications), and other prose writers of his day. His letters to members of his family, to friends, and to college administrators show a considerable facility in writing clear, interesting prose. For various reasons, therefore, it is appropriate to devote a chapter to his prose writings before proceeding to detailed commentary on his verse.

II *Essays, Scholarly Writing, and Short Stories*

That his college commencement oration was not an isolated performance is proved by the existence of a series of five Addisonian essays which Longfellow published during his senior year in the *United States Literary Gazette*. On March 2, 1825, he wrote to his mother: "If you choose to read some of my prose writing, look into the U. S. Literary Gazette for March 1, No. 22, under the title of 'The Lay Monastery,' and you will find the first number of a series of essays, which I am writing occasionally, for your amusement and my own profit" (*Life*, I, 61-62). The other four numbers were published on March 15, April 1, June 1, and October 1 of the same year.[1] All are signed "The Lay Monk," and Longfellow obviously wished his readers to picture a writer considerably older than his eighteen years.

Perhaps the most remarkable thing about "The Lay Monk" essays is that Longfellow wrote them and published them while a college undergraduate. Some preciousness in the style might betray a young author, but on the whole they are surprisingly mature, in both form and content. The first, "The Author," describes the writer as "a wayfaring man in the literary world," "a truant from society," and "a child of wayward fancy." A great lover of nature, he has a special fondness for rambling in the woods; at this point, Longfellow seems to be imagining himself an, as yet, less poetic Bryant. The second, "Winter Months," is also contemplative nature rhapsody. Winter he especially likes because of its suitability to the studies of the poet.

By all odds the most important of the five essays is the third, "The Literary Spirit of Our Country." He probably composed it about the same time as his commencement oration. It resembles both the oration and some of his senior year letters to his father. He expresses pride in his native land and in "the star of mental light" which looks "cheerfully upon New England." Then he surveys the place and time in relation to literary outlook, and concludes: "Perhaps there never was a better field for the exercise of talent than our own country exhibits at the present day." He gives several reasons, which may be summarized briefly. Where only a few great minds are devoted to letters, the chances for distinction are far greater. If the American Homer and Shakespeare are ever to appear, it must be in the early days. Climate and natural scenery are favorable too. It does not matter that America is not classic ground—classic Greece and Italy are not affording inspiration to Greece and Italy today. Indian material is promising. All that is needed for "the progress of poetry in America" is cultivation through proper patronage. And Americans should learn form and taste from England, but develop their literature independently.

When he wrote this essay, Longfellow had already come far in forming definite opinions about poetry and American literature. No. IV, "Poets and Common-Sense Men," shows further thinking by the young poet: "True poets embody and give form to the fine thoughts which are passing through their own minds; but these men, like mere painters, only animate those forms, which have long existed in every one's fancy." No. V, the final essay, "Valentine Writing," is the slightest of the five. It shows a playfully romantic attitude toward what the college senior obviously regarded as a pleasant custom.

Although the first of the five essays was not published until October, Longfellow probably discontinued working on the series by the date of his graduation. For a time after this, he was evidently too excited about the prospect of going to Europe to do any more writing for publication. With his plans made, however, and with nothing to do until departure several months hence (except read law without a taskmaster), he again began to divert himself. This time he and several of his college friends wrote a number of *Salmagundi*-type essays, supposedly emanating from a hypothetical but ancient social club called Brazen Nose College; they published several of these pseudonymously in the *Portland Advertiser* (Thompson, 80-81). Apparently they have not been reprinted. They are interesting chiefly as evidence of Longfellow's recurrent playfulness and his literary restlessness at the time.

His earliest piece of scholarly prose was "Defense of Poetry" (*Works*, I, 353-93), which appeared in the April, 1832, *North American Review* in response to a new edition of Sir Philip Sidney's essay. Included not very appropriately in the first edition of *Outre-Mer*, it was later omitted. The essay, written when Longfellow was twenty-five or younger, contains a number of interesting observations. He gives high praise to Sidney as a poet and a gentleman-scholar. He also includes quotations not only from Sidney's poetry and prose but from several other English poets. He comments on Byron as an overrated and too-much imitated literary figure. The most significant part is probably his remarks, late in the essay, about poetry in America. He makes a plea for more and better American poets, commenting that there were already three or four good ones and three or four hundred bad ones. The essay shows a somewhat youthful outlook, but it also proves that Longfellow very early began to think seriously about American literature in general, as well as of his own possible contribution to it.

Lamenting the lack of such a work as Sidney's "Defense" in America, he wrote:

> O that in our country it might be the harbinger of as bright an intellectual day as it was in his own;—with us, the spirit of the age, is clamorous for utility, for visible, tangible utility,—for bare, brawny, muscular utility. We . . . are swallowed up in schemes for gain, and engrossed with contrivances for bodily enjoyments, as if this particle of dust were immortal,—as if the soul needed no aliment, and the mind no raiment. . . . Yet the true glory of a nation consists not in the extent of its territory, the pomp of its forests, the majesty of its rivers, the height of its mountains, and the beauty of its sky; but in the extent of its mental powers—the majesty of its intellect,—the heights and depth and purity of its moral nature. . . . True greatness is the greatness of the mind:— the true glory of a nation is a moral and intellectual preeminence (*Works*, I, 360-61).

He lamented the "Gothic" fear in America of a love of letters and the fine arts, especially poetry, and he praised the manliness and participation in affairs of Homer, Dante, Milton, Cervantes, and

Sidney. He presented a lofty concept of the nature and mission of poetry: "poetry is but the warm expression of the thoughts and feelings of a people ... the spirit of the age itself,:—embodied in the forms of language, and speaking in a voice that is audible to the external as well as the internal sense" (*Works*, I, 375-76). He ends with a plea for a national outlook in American poetry: "whilst we are forming our literature, we should make it as original, character- istic, and national as possible .... let us have no more skylarks and nightingales. For us they only warble in books. A painter might as well introduce an elephant or a rhinoceros into a New England landscape. We would not restrict our poets in the choice of their subjects, or the scenes of their story; but when they sing under an American sky, and describe a native landscape, let the description be graphic, as if it had been seen and not imagined" (*Works*, I, 378, 387). He concludes with a warning to poets and their followers against overestimating the early efforts of a fledgling culture: "We hope, however, that ere long, some of our most gifted bards will ... bring up rich pearls from the secret depths of thought" (*Works*, I, 392).

His second European tour interrupted his writing. Apparently the next periodical publication was another short piece, "The Great Metropolis" (*Works*, III, 310-15), which appeared in the *North American Review* (April, 1837). This is an Irvingesque descriptive sketch of London, which he had recently visited for the second time. A mood piece, it is reminiscent of Addison as well as of Irving. Some quotations are interesting: "I have an affection for a great city .... I feel that life is not a dream, but a reality .... in great cities we learn to look the world in the face .... We become ac- quainted with the motley, many-sided life of man .... Its population is estimated at two millions. The vast living tide goes thundering through its ten thousand streets in one unbroken roar." He seems to have been interested in London more as a phenomenon of concen- trated population than as the place where great poets and other celebrities had lived.

Longfellow's next noteworthy scholarly publication is his review of Hawthorne's *Twice-Told Tales* (*Works*, III, 303-9). Apparently it was easy for Longfellow to give high praise to the work of his former Bowdoin classmate—so high, in fact, as to seem fulsome to the modern reader: "This star is but newly risen; and ere long the observations of numerous star-gazers, perched upon arm-chairs and editors' tables, will inform the world of its magnitude and its place in the heaven of poetry .... This book, though in prose, is written, nevertheless by a poet." He is especially pleased that *Twice-Told Tales* seems to signal a new discovery of the literary potential of

American material: "The truth is, the heaven of poetry and romance still lies around us and within us .... One of the prominent characteristics of these tales is, that they are national in their character. The author has chosen his themes among the traditions of New England.... The dreary, old Puritanical times begin to look romantic in the distance .... Truly, many quaint and quiet customs, many comic scenes and strange-adventures, many wild and wondrous things, fit for humorous tale, and soft, pathetic story, lie all about us here in New England" (306-7). He compares Hawthorne's use of New England materials in these stories to the use of German, Dutch, and English legends by European writers, and he thinks Hawthorne stands up well in the comparison. Longfellow displays sincere interest in his classmate's book but perhaps less in the work itself than in its role as a harbinger of a maturing American literature.

A long article published the same year as the Hawthorne review was "Frithiof's Saga" (*Works*, III, 260-302). This first appeared, like the review, in the July, 1837, number of the *North American Review*. During his visit to Sweden in 1835, Longfellow developed a great interest in the famous Swedish poet Esaias Tegnér (1782-1846). In 1837 he translated some passages from Tegnér's magnum opus, *Frithiof's Saga,* and in 1841 he translated and published all of a shorter religious poem, *The Children of the Lord's Supper.* When Tegnér died, Longfellow wrote a memorial poem, published in 1847 as "Tegnér's Drapa." The essay shows a detailed knowledge of Swedish literature, and it quotes extensively from the poems of Tegnér. Longfellow begins by calling Tegnér "a man of a grand and gorgeous imagination,—a poetic genius of high order," and he concludes, "And here endeth the Legend of Frithiof the Valiant, the noblest poetic contribution which Sweden has yet made to the literary history of the world."[2]

The next year "Anglo-Saxon Literature," another long piece of scholarly writing, appeared in the *North American Review*, in July, 1838 (*Works*, III, 316-44). At first glance, Longfellow's interest in Anglo-Saxon language and literature may seem surprising since his responsibility, at both Bowdoin and Harvard, was for modern languages only. But he had been engaged in studying comparative language and literature for several years, and some of the languages were Germanic, as is Anglo-Saxon. Moreover, he had been befriended in Holland by Joseph Bosworth, perhaps the most distinguished Anglo-Saxon scholar of the time.

This essay exhibits a considerable acquaintance with Old English writings; apparently Longfellow had learned to read Anglo-Saxon with ease. It points out the peculiar position of Anglo-Saxon literature as a fossil rather than an earlier form of a modern language: "A national literature is a subject which should always be approached with reverence. It is difficult to comprehend fully the mind of a nation; even when that nation still lives, and we can visit it, and its present history, and the lives of men we know, help us to a comment on the written text. But here the dead alone speak" (*Works*, III, 322). Longfellow quotes with approval from the unidentified Saxon Ealdorman who compared human life to the flitting of a sparrow through a room. He also comments in detail on the characteristics of Anglo-Saxon poetry. He especially admires the prose of King "Alfred, the Truth-teller." Modestly, he claims for his essay only exploratory value: "I cannot close this sketch of Anglo-Saxon Literature without expressing the hope, that what I have written may 'stir up riper wits than mine to the perfection of this rough-hewn work.' The history of this literature still remains to be written. How strange it is that so interesting a subject should wait so long for its historians!" (*Works*, III, 344).

A shorter essay of 1838, not listed in the bibliography in Kennedy's life of Longfellow, is "Paris in the Seventeenth Century" (*Works*, III, 345-52). Longfellow was periodically infatuated with the age of Louis XIV. In this essay he quotes extensively, especially from Voltaire, to present a picture of the grand monarch as "a strange mixture of magnanimity and littleness." He describes with affection the old city of Paris, which can still give the sympathetic traveler the illusion of being "in the center of the Paris of the seventeenth century; the gay, the witty, the licentious city, which in Louis the Fourteenth's time was like Athens in the age of Pericles."

Kennedy does list a later essay, "The French Language in England," published in the *North American Review* (October, 1840), but it is not reprinted in the edition of Longfellow's works used for this book. It is worth mentioning as the only extensive piece of scholarly writing Longfellow seems to have done while at Harvard; he had been much more productive at Bowdoin, where his creative urges seem to have been largely submerged in the ambition to achieve academic distinction.

It is of interest that, in 1852, near the end of his academic career, Longfellow was considering publication of his various periodical contributions in a volume of prose to be called *Drift Wood* (*Works*, III, 211). The project was dropped. Had it materialized, more of his early prose, known to include many other essays and reviews, would likely be available today. One other article of a later date may be mentioned: his "Washington Irving" (*Works*, II, 403-5), excerpted from the funeral address he delivered December 15, 1859, at a meeting of the Massachusetts Historical Society in Boston. One of the few public addresses Longfellow gave, it is interesting also for its middle-life praise for the idol of his youth. He praised the *Sketch-Book* for arousing his imagination and exciting his youthful mind, and he expressed pleasure in having found the man as charming as his writings. It was Irving who had made the Hudson as romantic as the Rhine; it was Irving who had shown the way for other American writers.

Although nearly all of Longfellow's early prose was nonfiction, he followed Irving in making occasional ventures into the field of the short story. Mention was made in Chapter 4 of the prize he won with his story, "The Wondrous Tale of a Little Man in Gosling Green," published pseudonymously in *The New Yorker* (November 1, 1834). Apparently this story has not been reprinted. Somewhat earlier he had written anonymously at least two other stories which have been reprinted. Both of these appeared in *The Token,* the giftbook in which a number of Hawthorne's early stories were first published.

"The Indian Summer" (*Works,* III, 175-88) came first in 1832. An Irving-like sketch, it is held together by a slender narrative thread. Longfellow pulls out all the stops of sentimentality, especially in his portrait of the unnamed heroine, a young girl cut off in the bloom of life, a paragon of goodness left alone by a wandering dissolute brother, who, however, returns to her deathbed. The setting is "In the melancholy month of October." Pauses at the funeral are "interrupted by sobs of the mother." The author observes: "There is something so patient and enduring in the love of a mother!" "The mother watched her dying child with an anguish, that none but a mother's heart can feel." The story, far too sentimental for modern taste, is even more maudlin than Irving's "The Broken Heart."

"The Bald Eagle" (*Works, III,* 189-208), published in 1833, is considerably better—or less bad. It has its setting in the Bald Eagle tavern. Lafayette is visiting America in his old age, and a group awaits him in the tavern. But a Negro slave accidentally fires a musket, the agreed-upon signal, ahead of time and with confusing results. Finally it becomes apparent that Lafayette is not coming, and everyone is cruelly disappointed. The ending is a good specimen of Longfellow's style and attitude toward his material: "It was a gloomy night at The Bald Eagle. A few boon companions sat late over their bottle, drank hard, and tried to be merry; but it would not do. Good humor flagged, the jokes were bad, the laughter forced, and one after another slunk away to bed, full of bad liquor, and reeling with the fumes of brandy and beer." Longfellow undoubtedly wrote the story partly out of his recollections of

Lafayette's visit to Portland in 1824 when his father served on the welcoming committee.

Had Longfellow continued with his attempts at story writing, he might have achieved a skill approaching Irving's, but nothing he wrote in this genre compares with the contemporary work of Poe or his classmate Hawthorne. He lacked Poe's skill in unifying his material to achieve a clear story line and Hawthorne's ability to meditate about his characters until he could devise a story that emerged naturally from their problems and what they symbolized.

II Outre-Mer: *A Pilgrimage Beyond the Sea*

During his first stay in Europe, the young Longfellow kept a journal, apparently rather irregularly. He must have had some thought at the time of making literary use of it sooner or later. At Bowdoin he was too busy with his new duties to do anything with it immediately, but by 1831 he undertook to find out how the public would react to it. In 1831 he began anonymous serial publication in the Boston *New England Magazine* of installments of "The Schoolmaster," ostensibly an account by a New England schoolmaster of his wanderings through Europe. By 1833 several numbers had appeared, but for some reason Longfellow discontinued the magazine publication, dropped the schoolmaster guise, and began issuing anonymously parts of *Outre-Mer* in pamphlet form (*Life*, I, 193-94). In 1835, after he had sailed for his second European study tour, the complete work was published in two volumes by Harpers(203). While Longfellow was in London, he arranged for an English edition (205). The American one was anonymous; the English one was ascribed to "An American." Although he had published several textbooks and translations before 1835, *Outre-Mer* was his first belletristic book, and there is evidence that he was very anxious about its reception.

It is easy to see that Longfellow was patterning his book on the early books of Washington Irving. It is the same sort of medley of descriptive sketches, local tales, and observations on people and places. Although his name was not on the title page, his friends could not have failed to recognize it as his work, for the travels he recounts were exactly those that he himself made from his arrival in France in 1826 until his departure from Germany in 1829.

Although the work was not fully published until six years after its author's return, it is still a young man's book—and a very bookish young man at that. At the beginnings of chapters and elsewhere, Longfellow quotes from a wide variety of literature in several languages. He gives a great many incidental Irvingesque musings. It is evident, however, that he was very open-eyed and open-eared, not only for the languages and literature he was studying, but also for the life of the people; he constantly exhibits a lively curiosity and one not always so Puritanical as his popular image might lead the reader to expect. There is not, however, any inkling of moral obliquities on his part; he is simply an intelligent young man looking upon a wider slice of life than he had known at home. He is particularly ambivalent about the Catholic religion he encountered everywhere; he obviously admired the devotion it evoked and the respect for art it included, but he was skeptical of the morality of some of its practices. Apparently the country he admired most was the one he was in at the time. He found much charm in France, a rich variety in Spain with its Moorish heritage, and a tradition of grandeur in Italy. The horseback riding and stage travel over bad roads seem not to have troubled him, despite his supposed lack of robustness.

The "Epistle Dedicatory" to the "Worthy and Gentle Reader" dedicates the book with misgivings, fearing "it is little in accordance with the stirring spirit of the present age."[3] In the first chapter, devoted to "The Pilgrim of Outre-Mer," he explains that he has named his book for the phrase, "Pays d'Outre Mer," which is "a name by which the pilgrims and crusaders of old usually designated the Holy Land" (28). He is himself a pilgrim of Outre-Mer, "for to my youthful imagination the Old World was a kind of Holy Land, lying afar off beyond the blue horizon of the ocean; and when its shores first rose upon my sight, looming through the hazy atmosphere of the sea, my heart swelled with the deep emotions of the pilgrim, when he sees afar the spire which rises above the shrine of his devotion" (28-29).

In retrospect, the young traveler could feel quite blasé about his travel experiences: "I have traversed France from Normandy to Navarre; smoked my pipe in a Flemish inn: floated through Holland in a Trek-schuit; trimmed my midnight lamp in a German university; wandered and mused amid the classic scenes of Italy; and listened to the gay guitar and merry castanet on the borders of the blue Guadalquivir" (29). He writes partly because he wants to "call back the shadowy past." Surprisingly, when he writes in this way, Longfellow seems to anticipate Thomas Wolfe; different as they are, they were both young men intoxicated with new experiences.

He notes: "As France was the first foreign country I visited, every thing wore an air of freshness and novelty which pleased my eye and kept my fancy constantly busy. Life was like a dream"(33). A little later, he remarked: "When I enter a new city, I cannot rest till I have satisfied the first cravings of curiosity by rambling through its streets. I... prefer a thousand times to find my own way(41). Presently he shifts from his travel observations to tell a long story of a tradesman and a friar. The tradesman and his wife, whom a fat friar covets, trick the friar by making him think he has an assignation with the wife in the absence of her husband, who is actually present. When the husband attempts to chastise the friar, he accidentally kills him instead. There follows a weird account of how the friar's body goes back and forth—an account almost worthy of Faulkner—but finally the body tied on horseback disappears in the river, and the tradesman and his wife escape suspicion.

Soon the traveler is again making general observations. He says he enjoys seeing the rustic swain and the village maiden enjoying the carrousel; he also enjoys the village dances. From comments on amusements, he shifts to remark that "The cemetery of Père la Chaise is the Westminster Abbey of Paris" (91) and to make melancholy reflections about Heloise and Abelard. October, his favorite month, seems to have been especially enjoyable in France: "In the beautiful month of October, I made a foot excursion along the banks of the Loire, from Orléans to Tours" (103). Despite his supposed dislike for exercise, he praises foot travel, calling it superior to any other form except horseback. His Puritan background does not often reveal itself, but he does comment that "The ancient historic romances of the land have, for the most part, been left to slumber unnoticed; while the obscene and tiresome Fabliaux have been ushered into the world as fair specimens of the ancient poetry of France" (121). He laments the poor judgment evident in this trend and commends the birth of "a more discerning judgment." He seemed a little surprised to discover that "The French are prëeminently a talking people; and every new object afforded a topic for light and animated discussion" (147). Another observation which may then have had an element of novelty is, "French fashions are known and imitated all the world over" (150).

In the middle of the book he devotes attention to another embellishment of a local story. The chapter called "The Notary of Perigueux" is the tale of a notary who was frightened by an apothecary into believing he had fatal scarlet fever—when he had only burned himself by putting a hot pipe next to his skin. This jesting story ends the section on France.

Just as Longfellow himself did, the "Pilgrim of Outre-Mer" goes from France to Spain, where he continues his observations. Early in his description of Spain, he makes some general comments:

Of the national character of Spain I have brought away this impression; that its prominent traits are a generous pride of birth, a superstitious devotion to the dogmas of the Church, and an innate dignity, which exhibits itself even in the common and every-day employments of life. Castilian pride is proverbial. A beggar wraps his tattered cloak around him with all the dignity of a Roman senator; and a muleteer bestrides his beast of burden with the air of a grandee.

I have thought, too, that there was a tinge of sadness in the Spanish character. The national music of the land is remarkable for its melancholy tone. . . . Even a Spanish holiday wears a look of sadness (181).

He comments at some length on the Spanish "favorite national sport,—the bull-fight." He declines to describe it, not because he disapproves but because it has already been so well described by many writers, from one of whom he quotes a twenty-line verse description. He was obviously intrigued by the beauty of the Spanish women. The image of a Basque girl haunted him years afterward; he describes an Andalusian girl thus: "A beautiful girl, with flaxen hair, blue eyes, and the form of a fairy in a midsummer night's dream, has just stepped out on the balcony beneath us!" (189). But the tone is bantering; he goes on to mention her brother, a bold dragoon who wears a long sword—"so beware!"— and her mother, a vulgar woman who eats garlic in her salad and smokes cigars. But again, at Cadiz, he returns to the subject: "The women of Cadiz are world-renowned for their loveliness. Surely earth has none more dazzling than a daughter of that bright, burning clime. What a faultless figure! what a dainty foot! what dignity! what matchless grace!" (275).

He is also preoccupied from time to time with observations about religious observances in Spain. He describes a group of children around a priest, singing a hymn to the Virgin, and observes:: "Why perplex the spirit of a child with these metaphysical subtleties, these dark, mysterious speculations, which man in all his pride of intellect cannot fathom or explain?" (228-29). But he admired the Spanish religious poetry: "The prevailing characteristics of Spanish devotional poetry are warmth of imagination, and depth and sincerity of feeling" (257). But he could not forgive Catholic behavior in the Middle Ages: "During the Middle Ages, there was corruption in the church—foul, shameful corruption; and now also hypocrisy may scourge itself in feigned repentance, and ambition hide its face beneath a hood; yet all is not therefore rottenness that wears a cowl" (259). Actually, there is much to admire: "I have always listened with feelings of solemn pleasure to the bell that sounded forth the Ave Maria.... There is something beautiful in thus measuring the march of time.... though I may differ from the Catholic in regard to the object of his supplication, yet it seems to me a beautiful and appropriate solemnity" (277).

He devotes considerable space to the effect of the Moors on Spain: "The Goth sat at the Arab's feet; and athwart the cloud and storm of war, streamed the light of Oriental learning upon the Western world.... Such is the Alhambra of Granada; a fortress,— a palace—an earthly paradise,—a ruin, wonderful in its fallen greatness!" (284-86).

Obviously Longfellow was so intrigued by Spain that he left it only reluctantly to proceed to Italy. Homesick at first, he soon fell in love with Italy too. However, realizing perhaps that his book was growing long, he devoted much less space to Italy than to France or Spain. In Rome he wrote a sarcastic description of an Englishman: "The principal object he seemed to have in view was to complete the grand tour" (297). At one point he observes, "Life is short, and art is long" (298) without source ascription, to plead for slower and more reverent traveling. Evidently, as he was supposed to do, he spent more time studying the language than sightseeing: "I retire to my chamber, and poring over the gloomy pages of Dante, or 'Bandello's laughing tale,' protract my nightly vigil till the morning star is in the sky" (303). But he did not pass up the customary moonlight visit to the Coliseum: "I have just returned from the Coliseum, whose ruins are so marvelously beautiful by moonlight. No stranger at Rome omits this midnight visit" (317). He ends his Italian section with a sententious description of a sick monk: "I saw the sick monk no more; but a day or two afterward I heard in the village that he had departed,—not for an earthly, but for a heavenly home" (336).

Apparently Longfellow decided to conclude *Outre-Mer* with his unrevised notebook for the rest of his travels, a sketchy account of his proceeding to Germany by way of Rimini, Bologna, Ferrara, Padua, and Venice, which seemed to him "visionary and fairy-like." From there he went on to Trieste and Vienna and afterward down the Rhine, but he did not describe what he saw. He made a bow to Holland, and then commented on home: "Let us wander where we may, the heart looks back with secret longing to the paternal roof" (347). This statement seems to indicate that, during all his stay abroad, mingled with his excited enjoyment of most of what he saw and did was a continuing homesickness.

Of particular interest is the one-page colophon, beginning, "My pilgrimage is ended. I have come home to rest" (349). He explains that he has written the book as it came to his mind, "for the most part, when the duties of the day were over, and the world around me was hushed in sleep," for "The pen wherewith I write most easily is a feather stolen from the sable wing of night." Now, as he sits with his completed manuscript long past midnight, "the melancholy thought intrudes upon me,—To what end is all this toil? . . . Dost thou covet fame? . . . Alas! this little book is but a bubble on the stream; and although it may catch the sunshine for a moment, yet it will soon float down the swift-rushing current and be seen no more!" It was obviously a very romantic young man, one with a somewhat Byronic outlook, who completed his writing of *Outre-Mer* on the eve of visiting Europe for the second time.

III *A Traveler's Romance:* Hyperion

The indifferent success of *Outre-Mer*, combined with time-consuming duties at Harvard during his first years as Smith Professor, apparently prevented Longfellow from attempting another prose volume, or much other literary work, for several years. However, in 1838, soon after he had utilized his German studies to write "A Psalm of Life" as an inspiriting bit of counsel for himself, he resolved to embody in an extensive prose work his fond recollections of his life in Germany and his researches in German literature for the Harvard lectures. This was *Hyperion*, begun in the summer of 1838, probably at Portland after a summer course of lectures. His brother says, "Considerable portions of these lectures were afterwards woven into Hyperion, and may be read there" (*Life*, I, 273. Also Thompson, 272-76). By September 13, Longfellow could record in his journal, "Looked over my notes and papers for Hyperion. Long for leisure to begin once more." He continued work on it through the winter months, and it was published in the summer of 1839.

Hyperion embodies much of Longfellow's reaction to his studies in German literature. Mention should also be made of his visit with the Carlyles in London in 1835 and the probability that Longfellow had been intrigued by Carlyle's exposition of the doctrine of the "Everlasting Yea" in *Sartor Resartus* a few years before he set to work on his book. The work devotes space to Jean Paul, Uhland, and Hoffman, besides Goethe, thus showing that Longfellow had been reading extensively in German literature. But Thompson is probably right in observing that it reflects most of all his recent studies in Goethe, included in his Harvard lectures for the summer of 1838. In his Goethe lecture, he had called attention to "Goethe's passionate youth, his romantic yet strong manhood, and his serene, sublime old age" (Thompson, 272). He had been especially impressed by Goethe's emphasis in *Wilhelm Meister* on "the ennobling power gained through suffering."

He named his book *Hyperion* because "He would show how the soul of youth, lifted up by high-reaching aspirations, could surmount all suffering with a victory bolder than Werther's suicide" (Thompson, 275). He had considered other names for it—*St. Clair* and *Paul Flemming*—but he decided that his original choice of *Hyperion* was most appropriate.[4] A year after it was published, he wrote to his friend Greene: "I called it Hyperion, because it *moves on high,* among clouds and stars, and expresses the various aspirations of the soul of man .... It contains my cherished thoughts for three years" (*Life,* I, 342).

Although Longfellow was sanguine about the success of *Hyperion* when it was published and excited about the favorable—and unfavorable—attention immediately afterward (*Life,* I, 325, 330), the publisher failed within a few months, and twelve hundred copies, half the edition, were locked up, thus taking the book off the market for four months. But Longfellow could nevertheless observe: "No matter, I had the glorious satisfaction of writing it" (*Life,* I, 342). However, it was destined to do reasonably well in sales, better than either of his other prose volumes, though nowhere nearly as well as his volumes of verse. His brother gives the sales as of 1857 at 14,550 copies (*Life,* II, 295).

Longfellow called *Hyperion* a romance, the term used by Hawthorne and others for long imaginative narratives which we today call novels. Possibly it can be classified as a novel; if so, it is certainly one of the loosest-structured novels in existence. To be sure, there is a more or less central character, Paul Flemming, who at the beginning is still mourning the loss of "the friend of my youth." At the end he has renounced a seemingly hopeless new love in favor of a life of high resolve and noble accomplishment. Between we have mostly travel descriptions, including a "beer scandal" and references to student dueling, none of which, however, is on stage; and there are long philosophical discourses on the nature of university life, art and literature, and life and death.

The romance as a whole is prefaced by the inscription from the graveyard of St. Gilgen, quoted in Chapter 4 of this book. The work is divided into four books. Book I is prefaced by this quotation from Goethe's *Wilhelm Meister:*

> Who ne'er his bread in sorrow ate,
>> Who ne'er the mournful midnight hours
> Weeping upon his bed has sate,
>> He knows you not, ye Heavenly Powers.

The quotation keynotes a somber, contemplative book, as does the stylized language of the first page: "The setting of a great hope is like the setting of the the sun. The brightness of our life is gone. . . . The soul withdraws into itself. Then stars arise, and the night is holy. Paul Flemming had experienced this, though still young. The friend of his youth was dead. . . . And when, after a season, he looked up again from the blindness of his sorrow, all things seemed unreal."[5]

Most of the second chapter is devoted to a legendary tale about the Christ of Andernach. Throughout there are quaint references to "my hero," and "gentle reader," and use of archaic expressions such as "thou art." Chapter IV is again a story, or really a story within a story. The inside story is of the Lady of Lichtenstein Castle, whose lover—one of two brothers, both of whom love her—went away to the Crusades and returned not to her but to his Greek bride in the castle; she tires and leaves him, whereupon he and his brother follow their sister into holy orders. As Paul Flemming's girl guide told him this story, she forgot to steer their boat and let it drift downstream. After they got back to the little village, she "pointed up the romantic, lonely valley which leads to the Liebenstein, and even offered to go with him. But Flemming patted her cheek and shook his head. He went up the valley alone" (37). But obviously the young hero was recovering from the loss of the friend of his youth.

One whole chapter is devoted to "Jean Paul, The Only-One." Longfellow was excitedly interested in the vapory romanticism of this popular German writer, and the style of his own book was much influenced by Jean Paul. Presently Flemming meets one of his two chief interlocutors, the Baron of Hohenfels; the other is an Englishman named Berkley. The Baron was based on Baron Jacques von Ramm, a German-speaking Russian from Esthonia whom Longfellow had known in his student days in 1835-36;[6] no original seems to have been discovered for Berkley. The Baron of Hohenfels made a very satisfactory conversational counterpart for young Flemming: "He pursued all things with eagerness, but for a short time only; music, poetry, painting, pleasure. . . . His feelings were keenly alive to the enjoyment of life" (51). One interchange finds Flemming describing his concept of university life: "What a strange picture a university presents to the imagination! The lives of scholars in their cloistered stillness;—literary men of retired habits, and professors who study sixteen hours a day, and never see the world but on a Sunday" (58). Later, when they are discussing genius, the Baron says, "We must pardon much to men of genius." Flemming is skeptical, but the Baron insists, "The world loves a spice of wickedness" (66).

Chapter VIII is devoted to "Literary Fame." Flemming reflects that men ought not to seek fame; instead "they should be constantly and quietly at work, each in his own sphere, regardless of effects, and leaving their fame to take care of itself" (69). The Baron is more concerned with achievement of expression than with fame. Life provides the coarse materials of the poet's song: "Glorious, indeed, is the world of God around us, but more glorious the world of God within us. There lies the Land of Song; there lies the poet's native land. . . . If he would describe the world, he should live in the world. . . . A ruined character is as picturesque as a ruined castle . . . wherever the scholar lives, he must never forget his high vocation" (74-76). Flemming adds: "perhaps the greatest lesson which the lives of literary men teach us, is told in a single word: Wait!—Every man must patiently bide his time" (78). By the end of the chapter, he is back to his starting point: "the talent of success is nothing more than doing what you can do well; and doing well whatever you do,—without a thought of fame. If it comes at all, it will come because it is deserved, not because it is sought after" (80). Doubtless Longfellow in his own reflections on success and fame had by now arrived at this conclusion.

Part I ends with a listing of Paul Flemming's readings, which probably represents rather closely what Longfellow read in 1835-36 at Heidelberg: "the ancient poetic lore of Germany, from Frankish Legends of Saint George, and Saxon Rhyme-Chronicles, and Nibele-lungen-Lieds, and Helden-Buchs, and Songs of the Minnesingers and Mastersingers, and Ships of Fools, and Reynard the Foxes, and Death-Dances, and Lamentations of Damned Souls . . . and . . . the modern bards." The young scholar must have been up to his ears in German literature.

Book II starts with a rhapsody on spring. Presently Flemming and the Baron resume their dialogues, concentrating first on Goethe and his writings. An interesting interlude is a description of old Frau Himmelauen, who sits in her "owltower" and views the populace. The Baron says to Flemming: "Do you know she has nearly ruined your character in town? She says you have a rakish look, because you carry a cane, and your hair curls. Your gloves, also, are a shade too light for a strictly virtuous man" (94). The young Longfellow himself was always something of a dandy, even when abroad.

Book II also introduces Fräulein Emma von Ilmenau, the pale sixteen-year-old girl whose tragic romance is a featured episode of the novel. Her introduction serves to launch the Baron and Flemming on a discussion of love and passion. Emma's suitor is a Polish count who already has a young and beautiful wife. The Baron maintains that "people do not die of love now-a-days." Flemming grants that death may seldom come in such circumstances, but "yet it is folly to pretend that one ever wholly recovers from a disappointed passion. Such wounds always leave a scar" (99).

One whole chapter is devoted to "A Beer-Scandal." On their way home one night, the Baron and Flemming stop at a students' tavern, apparently just in time to get in on the fun. Older students are heckling younger ones, and there is much lusty singing. One student challenges another to a beer-drinking contest and wins by downing three "mighty goblets" without a pause. The affair is climaxed by the great duelist Von Kleist, who leaps upon and strides down a long table, wreaks havoc, and winds up with six duels on his hands: "He fought them all out in as many days; and came off with only a gash through his upper lip and another through his right eyelid from a dexterous Suabian Schläger" (112).

Many pages are filled with what now seems windy rhetoric about such somber subjects as death and eternity, but this material may have been very effective as lectures to Harvard undergraduates, for whom it was probably prepared. Longfellow did not publish his class lectures as literary essays as Lowell was to do, but he was not above drawing this sort of extra dividend from them. At one point he says: "in order fully to understand and feel the popular poetry of Germany, one must be familiar with the German landscape" (138). But he considers the people important too. He continues with a rather sensual description of the miller's daughter, who "comes down to bathe her face in its stream, and her bosom is so full and white, that it kindles the glow of love in the cool waters."

At Frankfort, the two friends hear "the glorious Don Giovanni of Mozart," which is Flemming's favorite opera (141). They are delighted with the ballet and "amused with the countenance of an old prude in the next box." But Flemming is interested in Frankfort most of all as the birthplace of Goethe, and the entire next chapter is devoted to the great German poet: "with all his errors and shortcomings, he was a glorious specimen of a man" (148).

Book III takes the traveler into summertime—the pleasant summertime which the old German Minnesingers sang about so well. The great event is Flemming's visit to Switzerland, including Interlachen, where he meets Mary Ashburton, who is modeled on Fanny Appleton. He falls in love with her voice before he sees her face: "the few words she said were spoken in a voice so musical and full of soul, that it moved the soul of Flemming, like a whisper from heaven" (193). He gives Fanny a thin disguise; Mary is the daughter of a recently deceased English officer. Flemming concludes, with an allusion to Froissart, that there is "no lady in the world so worthy to be beloved as she" (198). In his description of his heroine,

Longfellow pulled out all the stops: "Her form arose, like a tremulous evening star, in the firmament of his soul" (203). Flemming and Mary go sketching together, and he commends her skill. They discuss the nature of art at great length, and he reads from her verbal description of an artist's life in Rome—making her appear much more like a Bluestocking than Fanny Appleton probably wanted to seem. Then he reads Uhland's ballads to her; she insists that he render them only in English; she does not care for the harsh-sounding German which he regards so highly. As we have noted, Fanny's letters show that she also did not much relish being courted by ballad reading.

In the midst of his courting, Flemming receives a letter from Heidelberg informing him that the poor, seduced Emma von Ilmenau is dead. "She was one of those gentle beings who seem created to love and to be loved" (113), he had said of her earlier and subsequently had written a sentimental description of the perfect beauty of that night when "there fell a star from heaven!" (164). Now he wonders, "Why was the lot of this weak and erring child so hard?" (230).

Then he returns to his courtship, which seems to prosper. But he proposes too precipitately and is decisively rejected (249ff.). It is interesting to speculate whether Longfellow had temporarily given up hope of winning Fanny Appleton when he wrote this. The situation is odd, for, as noted in Chapter 4 above, he seems to have hoped the book would help his suit; the conclusive ending of the Flemming-Ashburton romance hardly points this way. However, perhaps in the long run it did help. At any rate, when Longfellow and Fanny were finally married, her wedding present to him was the sketch book she had made while they were together in Switzerland, with the inscription, "Mary Ashburton to Paul Flemming" (Thompson, 342).

Once the romance is broken off, there is not much left of the plot of *Hyperion,* even though all of Book IV remains. Soon Flemming sets out traveling with Berkley, and they talk interminably. Berkley gives Flemming a division of men into three classes: Happy Men, Lucky Dogs, and Miserable Wretches. Now that Flemming has missed being a Happy Man, he can still be a Lucky Dog; he does not have to be a Miserable Wretch—a derelict. A hint is found in Suckling's song beginning, "Why so pale and wan, fond lover?" but this Flemming rejects: "Why quote the songs of that witty and licentious age? Have you no better consolation to offer me?" (271). Travel seems a better remedy; so they visit Innsbruck, Salzburg, Munich, and other places.

One chapter is largely devoted to discussion of Hoffman and his writings, another to the "Musical Sufferings of John Kreisler." But it is in St. Gilgen's churchyard that the stricken lover finally receives solace: "A holy calm stole over him. The fever of his heart was allayed" (304-5). Several chapters later he reads the marble tablet in the chapel wall with its appropriate inscription, quoted as the book's frontispiece. Now Flemming "resolved that he would no longer veer with every shifting wind of circumstance . . . no longer to waste his years in vain regrets . . . but to live in the Present wisely, alike forgetful of the Past, and careless of what the mysterious Future might bring. . . . Henceforth be mine a life of action and reality" (335). The language sounds very much like Carlyle. Later there is one more sob scene, when Flemming by chance overhears Mary Ashburton saying her English prayers in an adjoining room at an inn, but he is up betimes the next morning to resume his way, and with only a glance at the window of "the Dark Ladie" he "had left her forever!"

Obviously, although Longfellow was well into his Harvard career when he wrote *Hyperion,* the romance is a young man's book. Much of it, especially the episode concerning Emma von Ilmeneau, is so sentimental as to seem bathos today; but it was no more sentimental than other American novels of its own time and even later. Structurally, it cannot be called a good novel, if indeed the definition of a novel can be stretched to include it. It lacks story unity; it is, as Fanny called it, "desultory, objectless, a thing of shreds and patches." But it is important, not only in revealing Longfellow's development as man and author, but also for "the new atmosphere of German life and literature which it opened to Americans."[7]

IV *An Essay in the form of a Novel:* Kavanagh

Despite the fact that Longfellow was pleased, on the whole, with the reception accorded *Hyperion,* he did not attempt another novel for a full decade, and then only a slender one, half the length of the romance on his life in Germany. *Kavanagh,* published in 1849, two years after *Evangeline,* is said to have been "undertaken by Longfellow as a relief and a change from the work of writing the poem."[8] It seems likely, however, that at this late stage in his Harvard career, he was more intent on utilizing the simpler form of prose to try out some of his ideas on his reading public.

Although the novel was criticized for its brevity and its lack of fidelity to actual New England life, it drew many favorable comments. Emerson expressed much pleasure in reading it, and called it "the best sketch we have seen in the direction of the American Novel" (*Life,* II, 140). Hawthorne called it "a most precious and

rare book. . . entirely original, a book by itself, a true work of genius,
if ever there was one."[9] Howells said, much later, "It seems to us
as yet quite unapproached by the multitude of New England
romances that have followed it in a certain delicate truthfulness, as
it is likely to remain unsurpassed in its light humor and pensive
grace."[10] Fanny Longfellow, no mean critic, thought it would be
less successful than *Hyperion,* but for a special reason: "I doubt if it
will be as popular as *Hyperion,* for Germany is Henry's native
country."[11]

Longfellow seems to have written *Kavanagh* with a twofold purpose: (1) to produce an appealing Irvingesque tale; (2) to ration-
alize his own failure to achieve the literary distinction he had
envisioned for himself. The second point emerges most clearly from
the book. Mr. Churchill, the schoolmaster who is easily recognizable
as Longfellow himself, fritters away his creative energies in his
teaching, his marking of student exercises, and his criticizing of the
literary effusions of others. Constantly deferring his own great American Romance, he observes from time to time that others with
whom he has discussed them are appropriating his literary projects.

The title of the book is perhaps not a fortunate one, though it has
some exotic appeal. It led Emerson to believe that he would read
a story about a family legend. Actually, the book is named for the
Reverend Arthur Kavanagh, a minister who has the last speech in
the book and is the hero of the sentimental love story, but who
certainly cannot be considered the principal character. This is clearly
Mr. Churchill, the New England schoolmaster whose given name
we never learn. In the style of early American fiction, a more
suitable title for the book would be something like "Literary Frustration; or, The Thwarted Professor-Poet Presented in the Guise of a
Village Schoolmaster, Together with Assorted Portraits of Village
Characters, Including the Customary Romance between Two
of Them."

The actual story of *Kavanagh* is a very slight one, although a
number of characters—too many—are introduced. Mr. Churchill and
his wife, who are introduced first, are present throughout. As the
story opens, Mr. Pendexter, a venerable Calvinistic divine, is about
to give up his pulpit. We are introduced to Churchill's household,
consisting of his attractive wife, his son Alfred, the baby girl, and
Lucy, the fifteen-year-old maid of all work. Other characters of
some importance are the schoolmates Alice Archer and Cecilia
Vaughan, both destined to fall in love with Arthur Kavanagh, who
succeeds Pendexter as pastor. Kavanagh and Cecilia meet in a pet
shop where Cecilia is buying a carrier pigeon to transmit messages
she and Alice send to each other. Later, by tragic accident, the

pigeon carries the message of Arthur's love for Cecilia to Alice instead of to Cecilia, and the knowledge thus gained hastens the (apparently consumptive) girl's melancholy death.

An interlude brings in Mr. Hathaway, who enlists Mr. Churchill as one of the contributors to a new national magazine to be called *The Niagara*. Longfellow probably had in mind *The Pioneer*, the short-lived magazine edited by Lowell in 1843. Churchill is to contribute a series of papers on obscure martyrs—actually on the "unrecorded and life-long sufferings of women." *The Niagara* never gets started, but does provoke a significant discussion between Hathaway and Churchill about the proper characteristics for American literature. Churchill is somewhat disturbed, though apparently not surprised, when Hathaway later publishes papers on "Obscure Martyrs."

The secondary love story of the maid Lucy, the counterpart of that of Emma von Ilmenau in *Hyperion*, comes to its tragic conclusion some pages before the end of the book. Lucy runs away with a foreign boot peddler and comes back, presumably "ruined," to drown herself in the river. The main love story fares better. Cecilia and Arthur Kavanagh are very happy, despite the death of Cecilia's friend Alice, who had become superfluous since she also loved Arthur, and the story ends on a quiet note with Churchill still bemoaning the dissipation of his creative energies and the lack of significant accomplishments.

Obviously, the little book is not important as a novel or as entertainment for the modern reader. It does, however, invite quotation, especially for the light various passages throw on Longfellow's domestic life, his attitude toward religion, his views on nationalism in American literature, and his literary ambitions and frustrations.

A number of passages seem to mirror Longfellow's happy married life with Fanny Appleton, a marriage about five years old when he wrote the book. In an early chapter, he pictures Churchill wishing to have his wife beside him as he writes, so he can read passages to her. But this night she is sleepy; so he sends her off to bed: "He watched his wife as she went up stairs with the light. It was a picture always new and always beautiful, and like a painting of Gherardo della Notte. As he followed her, he paused to look at the stars. The beauty of the heavens made his soul overflow" (30). There are passages in his journals and letters which suggest that Longfellow idolized Fanny in much this way. Near the end of the book, after receiving Kavanagh's avowal, Cecilia wrote: "Come to Me." This probably reflects something in the still unpublished note of Fanny to Longfellow which brought him to her in such urgency of joy. In his novel Longfellow writes: "The magic syllables brought Kavanagh to her side. The full soul is silent. Only the rising and falling tides rush murmuring through their channels. So sat the lovers, hand in hand; but for a long time neither spake,—neither had need of speech" (141). Such utterances seem sentimental to us, but they probably did not seem so to Longfellow since they were so close to his own experience.

It has been noted above in connection with *Outre-Mer* that Longfellow made many comments on religious attitudes and practices, especially Catholic, which he had observed abroad. There are numerous hints at his religious beliefs throughout his poetry, but perhaps his most forthright treatment of religion is in *Kavanagh*. He introduces the Reverend Arthur Kavanagh as a descendant of an ancient Catholic family which had settled in Maine. Arthur had attended a Jesuit college, but his search for truth and freedom had converted him to Protestantism. However, "He had but passed from one chapel to another in the same vast cathedral" (90-91), bringing from the old faith what was holy and pure but leaving behind its bigotry, fanaticism, and intolerance. Kavanagh does not have the bigotry of his Calvinistic predecessor, Mr. Pendexter. Longfellow describes Kavanagh in his study: "The study in the tower was delightful. There sat the young apostle, and meditated the great design and purpose of his life, the removal of all prejudice, and uncharitableness, and persecution, and the union of all sects into one church universal" (97). Apparently Longfellow regarded Arthur Kavanagh with approval; if so, he was at this time clearly a liberal Unitarian.

Chapter XX, in the middle of the book, is devoted largely to a discussion of nationalism versus universalism in literature; Mr. Hathaway, the prospective editor of the proposed new magazine, upholds nationalism, and Mr. Churchill, partly representing Longfellow, argues for the importance of universalism. Hathaway says: "We want a national epic that shall correspond to the size of the country; that shall be to all other epics what Banvard's Panorama of the Mississippi is to all other paintings,—the largest in the World!" (105). Churchill's only rejoinder to this is "Ah!" Hathaway continues: "we want a national literature altogether shaggy and unshorn, that shall shake the earth, like a herd of buffaloes thundering over the prairies!" But Churchill is unconvinced: "Great has a very different meaning when applied to a river, and when applied to a literature.... A man will not necessarily be a great poet because he lives near a great mountain. Nor, being a poet, will he necessarily write better poems than another because he lives nearer Niagara." Hathaway gets him to agree that scenery can have some effect on genius and then Hathaway continues "let us have our literature national. If it is not national, it is nothing."

Churchill does not agree: "Nationality is a good thing to a certain extent, but universality is better. All that is best in the great poets of all countries is not what is national in them, but what is universal. Their roots are in their native soil; but their branches wave in the patriotic air, that speaks the same language unto all men." Hathaway gets Churchill to admit that nationality can be a good thing up to a point, but "Mere nationality is often ridiculous." He insists that "a national literature is not the growth of a day. Centuries must contribute their dew and sunshine to it" (108). Genius is not enough; for genius must employ art to achieve expression. America, however, has rich literary·potential: "As the blood of all nations is mingling with our own, so will their thoughts and feelings finally mingle in our literature. We shall draw from the Germans, tenderness; from the Spanish, passion; from the French, vivacity, to mingle more and more with our English solid sense. And this will give us universality, so much to be desired." It would probably be a mistake to conclude that all of Churchill's views represent Longfellow. It is clear that he wanted both sides of the debate to be expressed, but the idea that the national becomes great only as it portrays universal values was a favorite of his, and it anticipated the views of modern writers on literary regionalism.

Kavanagh is actually a potpourri, but apparently what concerned Longfellow himself the most was Mr. Churchill's ambitions and frustrations as an author. If the novel is read together with Longfellow's journal and letters of about the same time, it is easy to see that he is writing primarily about himself. Early in the book he has Churchill wanting to begin "the Romance," but, before he can do so, he must write a letter about the cottage bedstead, criticize a young lady's poetry, and see about the cooking-range (28). Presently the narrator is commenting on Churchill's fate as a schoolmaster: "a dreary, weary life it would have been, had not poetry from within gushed through every crack and crevice in it" (51). But it seems literally impossible to find the blocks of time needed for creative work on large projects. Once he faces "a whole leisure Saturday afternoon ... pure gold, without alloy" for work on the great Romance. But "an unknown damsel" brought a sheaf of poems and enlisted him as a critic-reader and as author of a preface. She is a poetess named Clarissa Cartwright, author of "Symphonies of the Soul, and other Poems" (129ff.). This title seems faintly humorous in intent, but the episode could express Longfellow's resentment of some of the "literary" visitors who imposed on him.

Near the end of the book, Longfellow lets his narrator comment on Churchill in a manner hardly, by implication, very complimentary to himself:

> The rest of his leisure hours were employed in anything and everything save in writing his Romance . . . still the vision of the great Romance moved before his mind, august and glorious, a beautiful mirage of the desert. . . . His imagination seemed still to exhaust itself in running, before it tried to leap the ditch. . . . He freely used his good ideas in conversation, and in letters; and they were straightway wrought into the texture of other men's books, and so lost to him forever. . . . All his defects and mortifications he attributed to the outward circumstances of his life, the exigencies of his profession, the accidents of chance. But, in reality, they lay much deeper than this. They were within himself. He wanted the all-controlling, all-subduing will (154, 162-65).

Here it seems certain that Longfellow was remarking on a defect he often sensed in himself; he realized that he did not have the "all-subduing will" of such writers as Dante and Goethe. But he lets Churchill excuse himself to Kavanagh: "I now despair of writing anything excellent. . . . My life is given to others, and to this destiny I submit without a murmur; for I have the satisfaction of having labored faithfully in my calling, and of having perhaps trained and incited others to do what I shall never do" (167). Longfellow seems to have come far from his youthful resolve to become eminent in literature; like Churchill, he apparently justifies continuing to give his best energies to the teaching of students.

Though slender, *Kavanagh* is a more mature book than *Outre-Mer* or *Hyperion*. It shows little progress in the craft of novel writing, but it is an interesting and significant indication of what was on Longfellow's mind at the time. It also reveals that he was canny enough to include the kind of sentimental love story that would help it to sell.

V *Miscellaneous Prose: Letters, Journals, "Table Talk"*

Although Longfellow made no further effort to write serious prose after *Kavanagh,* he did considerable prose writing all his life. In those days of limited communication facilities, he and his family and friends all relied heavily on letters to keep in touch with each other. Longfellow complained a great deal about writing letters, apparently because letter writing kept him from literary production. Nevertheless, he composed thousands of letters that were sparkling and lively. His correspondence with his father or with either of his best friends, George Greene and Charles Sumner, would make an interesting book.

While he was married to Fanny Appleton, he was relieved of a considerable part of the burden, if it was that, of writing to relatives, for she was a gifted correspondent and seems to have written letters more easily than he did. Or perhaps she deliberately took care of correspondence to leave him freer for creative writing. In 1851 he noted, "Wrote letters and a few lines in the Legend," and the next year: "Letters, letters, letters! I shall have to be uncivil and leave half of them unanswered" (*Life*, II, 203). "More and more the little things of life shut out the great. Innumerable interruptions—letters of application for this and that." During the latter part of his life he often recorded in the journal his annoyance at the demands of letter writing, but his letters are indispensable to a biography, both for revelations of personality and for references to his literary ideas and writings.

From the time he first went to Europe, Longfellow kept a journal, which is also a rich source of information on his personality, thoughts, and activities. Both the letters and the journal would be even more informative if they were fully available or if the available parts were more representative. We have them chiefly in the *Life* written by his brother, who used them very selectively, and, for the earlier years, in Thompson's *Young Longfellow*. Thompson, who had full access to the Longfellow materials, indicates that much of the most revealing material is still unavailable; first, because Samuel Longfellow did not elect to use it; second, because the Longfellow heirs still refuse to permit publication of vital parts of it (Thompson, xviii-xxi). Perhaps the journals will be published, with an index, eventually. Meanwhile, the available material, though without the intrinsic literary interest of Thoreau's journals, throws considerable light on a sensitive, reflective personality.

Free use has been made of available journal material in the first part of this book. Here a few additional bits will be introduced to give a fuller idea of the type of material Longfellow thought worth recording. During his first stay abroad, he noted: "Left Florence for the warmer sun of Southern Italy, with a vetturino, by way of Siena. . . . A fat priest entertained us with merry tales" (*Life*, I, 142). And a little later: "I left my letter last night to go to a conversazione at Madame Benzon's, at half past eleven o'clock. It is the house where Lord Byron visited constantly" (158). And in Germany, shortly before his return: "Evening at the Baron Löwenstein's. Tea, music, and supper. The French minister's wife a very graceful and fascinating woman. After all, the French ladies bear away the palm from all Europeans, as far as grace and gentility go" (164).

Sometimes he would merely note his enjoyment of the weather, as in this entry for 1838: "A most lovely, lovely day! Spring begins again. The air is soft, the sunshine warm and bright, the turf under foot like a saturated sponge. A happy, happy day!" (277). This was written during a difficult Harvard year when his courtship of Fanny Appleton was not prospering. There are many entries on lectures by Emerson which he attended; this one is representative: "This evening Emerson lectured on the Affections; a good lecture. He mistakes his power somewhat, and at times speaks in oracles, darkly. He is vastly more of a poet than a philosopher. He has a brilliant mind" (277). He completed the entry with an anecdote: a man had been asked if he could understand Mr. Emerson and replied, "No, I can't, but my daughters can." Even then, Emerson seems to have been more satisfying to the young reader or listener. There are many notes on authors. In 1871, he recorded a Saturday Club dinner, where, "We had among our guests Mr. Bret Harte, from California, who has made his mark in literature by tales and poems." A week later, he noted, "Bret Harte dined with me; the other guests Lowell, Howells, Henry James; S. and A." (*Life,* III, 155-56).

Perhaps with Franklin's *Poor Richard's Almanack* in mind or inspired by the same *Zeitgeist* which produced Holmes's *Autocrat* papers, Longfellow made an extensive collection of pithy sayings. He called them "Table Talk," and he included them with some essays in his collection *Drift Wood,* mentioned in the first section of this chapter. Samuel Longfellow prints a number in Chapter XIX of *Final Memorials.* Many of these have considerable interest; here are some specimens:

> He who carries bricks to the building of every one's house, will never build one for himself.
>
> Many critics are like woodpeckers, who, instead of enjoying the fruit and shadow of a tree, hop incessantly around the trunk, pecking holes in the bark to discover some little worm or other.
>
> A young critic is like a boy with a gun; he fires at every living thing he sees. He thinks only of his own skill, not of the pain he is giving.
>
> Sometimes a single felicitous expression or line in a poem saves it from oblivion.
>
> The utility of many useful things is not at first very manifest,— as poetry, for instance. Yet its uses are as many and as sweet as those of adversity.
>
> Every man is in some sort a failure to himself. No one ever reaches the heights to which he aspires.
>
> "It is not enough to be a great man," says the French proverb,

"but you must come at the right time." This is particularly true of authors.

Some sorrows are but footprints in the snow, which the genial sun effaces, or, if it does not wholly efface, changes into dimples.

Those poets who make vice beautiful with the beauty of their song are like the Byzantine artists who painted the Devil with a nimbus.

A story or a poem should be neither too short nor too long; it should be enough to satisfy, but not enough to satiate. I have always aimed to have my books small.

Style is the gait of the mind, and is as much a part of the man as his bodily gait is.

These aphorisms reveal, if not a particularly deep thinker, at least a somewhat more thoughtful Longfellow than the popular image of him.

Except when he was reflecting the style of Jean Paul or other romantic lovers of an inflated rhetoric, or was carried away by excessive sentimentality, Longfellow wrote a clear, pleasing, and effective prose. However, there is no point in claiming for him great stature as a prose writer. His philosophical prose lacks the stylistic distinction of Emerson's or of Thoreau's and certainly he never developed Hawthorne's ability to put impact and significance into a narrative presentation. In a literary sense, then, Longfellow's prose is of minor interest compared to his poetry, but it does have considerable importance to a reader who wishes to understand him.

CHAPTER 7

Household Lyrics, Ballads, Odes, Elegies, Sonnets

The land of Song within thee lies,
 Watered by living springs;
The lids of Fancy's sleepless eyes
Are gates unto that Paradise;
Holy thoughts, like stars arise;
 Its clouds are angels' wings.

. . . .

Look, then, into thine heart, and write!
 Yes, into Life's deep stream!
All forms of sorrow and delight,
All solemn Voices of the Night
That can soothe thee, or affright,—
 Be these henceforth thy theme.
 —"Prelude"

I General Observations about Longfellow as a Poet

WE HAVE SEEN that from early boyhood Longfellow wanted to be a poet and that by the time he had graduated from college the desire had intensified into a burning ambition. Just what qualifications, beyond the desire, did he have? He had a genuine poetic imagination, if not one of the most sublime; he had at an early age accumulated sufficient experience and had read enough to nourish a poetic imagination; he had an excellent ear for meter and rhyme; and, partly through translating from eighteen languages, he had become acquainted with a sufficient variety of prosodic forms to be able to choose with considerable success the one most suitable for a particular poem. His technical endowment was considerably better than average; it was, in fact, the best of any American poet of his time, and it was approached by only Bryant and Lowell. He was equipped to become a first-rate poet. Indeed, he may have been too well qualified and relied too much on mere facility. But he also had a good deal of rugged strength.

Perhaps Longfellow's natural gift for versification was too great to permit him to become a very systematic student of prosody. Indeed he seems to have been little interested in the techniques of poetry except on a pragmatic basis. He did not prepare lectures on the nature and forms of poetry as Bryant did; he did not absorb Coleridge's *Biographia Literaria* and other works of critical theory as did Poe. His Yankee thrift was apparent even here. If he had an idea for a poem, he brooded and researched until he came upon what he thought was the right form, but he exhibited little interest in prosody as such.[1]

It appears that Longfellow's attitude toward poetic techniques was of a piece with his general approach to life; he was always more intuitive than intellectual. In his "Table Talk" he said: "I have many opinions in Art and Literature which constantly recur to me in the tender guise of a sentiment. A clever dialectician can prove to me that I am wrong. I cannot answer him. I let the waves of argument roll on: but all the lilies rise again, and are beautiful as before" (*Life*, III, 381). This no doubt partly explains his impatience and unhappiness in the presence of criticism; he seems to have anticipated William James in concluding that we cease to thrill when we dissect. He believed that "the chief end of poetry is to give delight, to build an ideal world of 'escape' from a realistic world, and, finally, to honor God"[2] And the poet achieves poetry through sympathetic living and good intentions. Like Dorothea Brande in our own time, he believed that the writer is two persons: "the workaday man who walks, and the genius who flies."[3] On November 14, 1845, about the time he began work on *Evangeline*, he wrote in his journal: "Felt more than ever to-day the difference between my ideal home-world of Poetry, and the outer, actual, tangible Prose world. When I go out of the precincts of my study, down the village street to college, how the scaffoldings about the Palace of Song come rattling and clattering down!" (*Life*, II, 24). He looked on the ability to write poetry as a gift, and believed that one so gifted had a duty—to God—to develop to the best of his abilities and opportunities.

His poetry displays a great variety of form, a truly remarkable versatility. First and last, he wrote iambic verse in all its usual variations of four-stress lines and in blank verse, heroic couplet, and ballad meter; he was exceptionally adept in trochaic verse in *Hiawatha* and elsewhere; he used anapestic forms in "Paul Revere's Ride" and other narrative poems; he was notably successful with the refractory dactyllic hexameter in *Evangeline* and in *The Courtship of Miles Standish*. He was highly skilled in writing the Italian or Petrarchan sonnet also, but rather oddly he apparently

never attempted the English Shakespearean or Spenserian types.
But he could not only handle the basic forms; he could also modify
them successfully through various techniques, including occasional
use of a foot other than the basic form, changing the caesura, or
syncopating in the long lines by alternating heavy and light stresses.
Perhaps most surprising is his occasional use of a form so free as to
suggest modern "free verse."[4]

But he was not only extraordinarily versatile in his prosody; he
was equally venturesome in *types* of poetry. His works include
simple homely lyrics, ballads of varying lengths, odes and elegies,
epics, both religious and secular, plays, a variety of saga-type poems
employing legends and other folk material, and, as already mentioned, sonnets, in which he was more successful than any other poet
of his time. And all of his poetry has a certain sweetness of sound
and tone peculiarly his own. His versatility extended to his imagery
and diction; he had an unusual mastery of metaphor, and his large
vocabulary no doubt aided his meter and rhyme, and thus the
smoothness and the melody of his verse. He was, however, not so
much an innovator as a refiner; he sought, and with considerable
success, to do better what others had already done well. G. W.
Allen's conclusion is: "Longfellow's greatest contribution ... was not
specifically any new theory or practice but a general, broad, and
deep influence toward the search for new forms, based on a wide
acquaintance with the chief poetic techniques of the world."[5]

II *Simple Lyrics and Psalms*

On March 26, 1838, when he was thirty-one, Longfellow wrote in
his journal: "Human life is made up mostly of a series of little
disappointments and little pleasures" (*Life,* I, 282). When one leafs
through his collected poems in search of the source of his fame, one
is tempted to paraphrase: "Longfellow won most of his reputation
through writing a series of little poems." Such a statement is not
fully warranted, of course, for several of his long poems were
enormously and lastingly popular; yet the number of famous short
poems is indeed impressive. In the space available here, only a
fraction of them, and not even all the important ones, can be discussed, but an attempt will be made to give some impression of the
nature and variety of the short poems which a generation grew up
on, largely through memorizing them and meeting them constantly
in spelling books and readers.

One of the earliest was "Hymn to the Night," which even Poe
admired, especially for its beginning: "I heard the trailing garments
of the Night/Sweep through her marble halls!" Longfellow had a

life-long affection for the quiet hours of night. He loved to read and write at night. He may have paid for this devotion with the eye trouble which plagued him from his early Harvard years, but even at this cost he probably would not willingly have relinquished his night vigils with the muses:

> From the cool cisterns of the midnight air
> My Spirit drank repose;
> The fountain of perpetual peace flows there,—
> From those deep cisterns flows.

Another very early poem was perhaps his most controversial one, "A Psalm of Life," already mentioned several times. Burlesqued and ridiculed in modern times, it was extravagantly praised when it was published and long afterward. However, even as early as 1886, when he wrote the biography, Samuel Longfellow felt called on to defend it: "It has perhaps grown too familiar for us to read it as it was first read. But if the ideas have become commonplace, it has well been said that it is this poem that has made them so" (*Life*, I, 271). It is a little hard today to take seriously such phrasing as "Heart within, and God o'erhead!" and the imagery can never have been fully satisfactory: for example, the juxtaposition of "dumb, driven cattle" and "hero in the strife." But the poem inspired multitudes in its own day, and even now the reader who realizes that it reflects a harassed and lovelorn young professor's reaction to Goethe and to his own deep thoughts may not find it entirely bad. To say that it is trite is only as if to say *Hamlet* is too full of familiar quotations.

Longfellow had intended "A Psalm of Life" to be merely the first of a number of psalms—philosophic comments he would make from time to time, perhaps on the model of William Blake's "Songs of Innocence" and "Songs of Experience." Apparently it was Longfellow's failure to provide this first poem with a suitable alternative title which caused it to pre-empt the title of an intended series. A few months after he wrote "A Psalm of Life," he followed it with "The Reaper and the Flowers, a Psalm of Death." This is not known, however, as "A Psalm of Death," but as "The Reaper and the Flowers." It is a smoothly flowing series of quatrains on the idea that early death for some is part of the Divine scheme; and, though it doubtless solaced many bereft parents and relatives in those days of higher infant and child mortality, it is too "sticky" for the modern taste. The same is true of "Footsteps of Angels," but this poem is more important to the student, for it directly commemorates two deaths Longfellow had recently experienced: that of his first wife at Rotterdam and that of his friend and brother-in-law George Pierce, news of which followed within a month of his wife's death. Another "Psalm" of which Longfellow himself thought highly was his "Midnight Mass for the Dying Year." The poem is interesting structurally for its introduction of a new five-line stanza form and for the use of a short final line giving the effect of a refrain; but it has little to say to a modern reader.

"The Rainy Day" is one of Longfellow's best-known short lyrics—too well known for the good of his reputation, especially such self-pitying lines as "My life is cold, and dark, and dreary" and the cheery counterpart, "Behind the clouds is the sun still shining." Longfellow could not know, conditioned as he was by the Atlantic Coast's excessive rain, how his poem would sound to other Americans in "the land of little rain"! Another sentimental poem, popular in the nineteenth century but not in the twentieth, is "Maidenhood," written in rhymed triplets, ingeniously done, but presenting a concept of femininity equally inappropriate to the nineteenth-century pioneer woman and to today's young lady with her auto driver's license at age sixteen:

> Standing with reluctant feet,
> Where the brook and river meet,
> Womanhood and childhood fleet!
>
> . . . .
>
> Bear a lily in thy hand;
> Gates of brass cannot withstand
> One touch of that magic wand.

It is impossible today to imagine Longfellow writing the short poem "Excelsior" in the belief that it was important, or to understand his contemporaries' admiring enthusiasm for it. His editor says he was inspired to write it by finding in a scrap of newspaper the seal of the state of New York bearing the motto. He recorded finishing the poem at half-past three in the morning on September 28, 1841. He said his purpose was "to display, in a series of pictures, the life of a man of genius, resisting all temptations, laying aside all fears, heedless of all warnings, and pressing right on to accomplish his purpose" (*Poems,* 19). Written about the same time as Emerson's "Self-Reliance," it was in the *Zeitgeist.* It was a time when Americans were spurring each other on to all sorts of achievements, but probably a considerable part of the appeal of this poem, as is true of much of Longfellow's work, came from its exotic setting. I myself remember being much affected by the poem when I found it in one of my grade school readers, but more, as I recall, by its Alpine setting and the hint of thwarted romance than by the embodiment of lofty aspiration which climbs a mountain "because it is there."

It is interesting that Longfellow should have written in the same year of Tennyson's "Locksley Hall" (1842) "The Belfry of Bruges," a poem in the same trochaic eight-stress, fifteen-syllable meter. "The Belfry" and "Nuremberg," written two years later, show Longfellow capitalizing further on his knowledge of Europe and his readers' curiosity about it. Indeed these two poems are said to be "part of a plan which the poet had designed of a series of travel-sketches in verse" (*Poems*, 53). Both were very popular, presumably because of their swinging meter and the historical-traditional subject which Longfellow was able to present in a moving pageant. "Nuremberg" has the extra appeal of moving characters representing important ideals: Albrecht Dürer, "the Evangelist of Art" when "Art was still religion"; Hans Sachs, the cobbler-poet, who showed that art could be for the laboring people as well as for the intellectual aristocracy.

Two other much-read poems which form a natural pair are "The Arsenal at Springfield" and "The Old Clock on the Stairs." The chief reason for linking them is that Fanny Longfellow was at least partly responsible for Longfellow's writing both. "The Arsenal" is Longfellow's most pacifistic poem. Fanny seems to have been even more a pacifist than he was, but his lifelong belief in the biblical "faith, hope, and charity" made him readily responsive. On their wedding journey in 1843, they visited, among other places, the arsenal at Springfield, Massachusetts, with the result, Fanny said, that "I urged H. to write a peace poem." Perhaps the best stanza, expressing an oft-repeated thought, is

> Were half the power that fills the world with terror,
> Were half the wealth bestowed on camps and courts,
> Given to redeem the human mind from error,
> There were no need of arsenals or forts.

On the same journey, the newlyweds visited the homestead of Fanny's maternal grandfather in Pittsfield, Massachusetts, and saw the old clock which inspired the poem. Longfellow's more immediate inspiration was the writings of an early French missionary, who said of eternity that it is a balance of *toujours* and *jamais*. Longfellow managed in this medium-length poem, with effective refrain of "Forever—never! / Never—forever!" to give something of the pageantry of human life marching through time.

The poems Longfellow wrote in the mid-1840's after his marriage to Fanny were naturally full of sentiment, compounded of recollected sadness and present joys. "The Day Is Done" and "The Bridge" are the best known. "The Day Is Done" was written in 1844 as the proem to *The Waif,* a volume of selections from Longfellow's poems published at Christmas time. A plea for gentle happiness, it contains this revealing stanza:

> A feeling of sadness and longing,
> That is not akin to pain,
> And resembles sorrow only
> As the mist resembles the rain.

Something of the Puritan distrust of happiness and of satisfaction in somber feeling came out in Longfellow from time to time; like other Puritans, he seems to have been able to achieve the paradox of being happiest when not happy.

"The Bridge" is almost Byronic in parading poetic melancholy. The poet, looking on the River Charles at midnight as he had done countless times before, sees the moon's reflection and continues to stand musing on the days past when

> I had wished that the ebbing tide
> Would bear me away on its bosom
> O'er the ocean wild and wide!

> For my heart was hot and restless,
> And my life was full of care,
> And the burden laid upon me
> Seemed greater than I could bear.

He is happy now, but he still thinks of the long procession of others less fortunate: "The young heart hot and restless, / And the old subdued and slow!" The prosody of both poems is interesting. In quatrains close in form to ballad meter, Longfellow achieves remarkably smooth, melodious verse by simple variations in his meter, mainly occasional anapests and feminine endings.

In 1848 Longfellow wrote the "Hymn for My Brother's Ordination." His brother Samuel, twelve years his junior and destined to be his biographer, was being ordained in the Unitarian Church in Portland. A devoutly religious utterance, the poem was sung as part of the ordination service. It is odd that Longfellow, a flute player with an excellent ear for music, wrote so few songs and that Whittier, who was tone deaf, wrote so many.

In 1855 came the poem which many readers consider Longfellow's finest lyric, "My Lost Youth." He made frequent visits to Portland, especially until his parents died. On one of these, in 1846, he took a long walk around Munjoy's hill and to Old Fort Lawrence, listening to the sea and turning over in his mind a poem on the Old Fort (*Poems,* 193). But it was not until after he had retired from Harvard and was in an especially nostalgic mood that he wrote the lovely poem with its series of pictures of the boy and man in relation to the old seaport and with its haunting refrain, admittedly taken from an old Lapland song: "A boy's will is the wind's will, / And the thoughts of youth are long, long thoughts."

The late 1850's saw the composition of several more of the popular sentimental poems, including "Santa Filomena," "Daybreak," and "The Childrens' Hour." "Santa Filomena" was his eloquent tribute to Florence Nightingale, "Saint Nightingale," for her heroic work in the hospitals during the Crimean War:

> A Lady with a Lamp shall stand
> In the great history of the land,
>   A noble type of good,
>   Heroic womanhood.

"Daybreak," a short poem in rhyming couplets, shows the poet's delicate fancy: the wind from the sea touches enough aspects of life in rapid succession to suggest the full pageantry of human life on earth. "The Children's Hour," written in 1819, only two years before his wife's death, is a delightful picture of his three daughters and of the playful but understanding relationship between the poet-father and the little girls.

As Longfellow grew older, and particularly after he gave up his Harvard duties, he tended to devote himself more to long poems and less to short lyrics. However, he continued to turn occasionally to the shorter forms, and never lost his ability to write them. In 1864, with the Civil War nearing its end but with heavy fighting still going on, he wrote the much beloved "Christmas Bells," with its effective use of the refrain "Of peace on earth, good-will to men!" In 1866, the war over, he wrote his best war poem, "Killed at the Ford," a lyric similar in content to Whitman's well-known "Come up from the Fields Father." This poem compares not too badly with Whitman's, though Longfellow could not match Whitman's simple and sincere pathos.

In 1873, Longfellow published *Aftermath,* a volume containing the last part of *Tales of a Wayside Inn* and miscellaneous poems. He wrote a short title poem for it which is one of his finest lyrics; it deserves quotation in its entirety:

> When the summer fields are mown,
> When the birds are fledged and flown,
>   And the dry leaves strew the path;
> With the falling of the snow,
> With the cawing of the crow,
> Once again the fields we mow
>   And gather in the aftermath.

> Not the sweet, new grass with flowers
> Is this harvesting of ours;
>   Not the upland clover bloom;
> But the rowen mixed with weeds,
> Tangled tufts from marsh and meads,
> Where the poppy drops its seeds
>   In the silence and the gloom.

The "rowen," like the "aftermath," is an after-mowing, an end-of-season crop. In this poem, Longfellow was wise enough to let the simple lyric expression stand without didactic interpretation.

In 1879, when he was seventy-two and only three years from death, he wrote the lovely "The Tide Rises, The Tide Falls," a poem reminiscent of "My Lost Youth." He returns again to his boyhood in Portland, where he had loved to listen to the sough of the waves and to the gentle rush of the tide coming in. As he visualized in old age the phenomena of water behavior, it became symbolic of life. Once again, as in the early "Psalm of Life," he uses the figure, "footprints in the sands." By now he seems not very certain that he has made lasting footprints in the sands of life, but the tone implies that it does not greatly matter. This lyric too invites full quotation:

> The tide rises, the tide falls,
> The twilight darkens, the curlew calls;
> Along the sea-sands damp and brown
> The traveller hastens toward the town,
>   And the tide rises, the tide falls.
>
> Darkness settles on roofs and walls,
> But the sea, the sea in the darkness calls;
> The little waves, with their soft, white hands,
> Efface the footprints in the sands,
>   And the tide rises, the tide falls.
>
> The morning breaks; the steeds in their stalls
> Stamp and neigh, as the hostler calls;
> The day returns, but nevermore
> Returns the traveller to the shore,
>   And the tide rises, the tide falls.

It is interesting to compare this poem with Robert Frost's "Stopping by Woods on a Snowy Evening." There is a difference of only one line in the length; both feature a traveler proceeding through life. Longfellow uses sea imagery; Frost, woods and snow. Frost's lyric is the better, but Longfellow's came first and is good.

Only two weeks before his death, Longfellow wrote his last poem, "The Bells of San Blas." It is one of his finest lyrics; he had kept his poetic vision to the end. This poem can be compared with

Arnold's "Dover Beach" and with other late nineteenth-century lyrics lamenting the passing of an age of religious faith. Longfellow, like Arnold, joins the lament; but unlike Arnold he accepts change with an unshaken and confident personal faith:

> O Bells of San Blas, in vain
> Ye call back the Past again!
> The Past is deaf to your prayer;
> Out of the shadows of night
> The world rolls into light;
> It is daybreak everywhere.

Although the short lyrics are only a small part of his total poetic production, if Longfellow had written only these, he would still have been a notable nineteenth-century American poet.

III Ballads

Longfellow early became interested in ballads and balladry. He read the old English ballads, and in *Hyperion* he includes ballads among the forms of German poetry studied by Paul Flemming. Later in this story, Flemming courts Mary Ashburton partly by reading Uhland's ballads to her. On January 2, 1840, the year after he published *Hyperion* and *Voices of the Night*, Longfellow wrote to his friend Greene: "I have broken ground in a new field; namely, ballads; beginning with the 'Wreck of the Schooner Hesperus,' on the reef of Norman's Woe, in the great storm of a fortnight ago. I shall send it to some newspaper. I think I shall write more. The *national ballad* is a virgin soil here in New England, and there are great materials. Besides, I have a great notion of working upon the *people's* feelings ... I desire a new sensation and a new set of critics" (*Life*, I, 342-43).

Longfellow was here, as frequently, sizing up a situation shrewdly, and he seemed to have a natural talent for ballad writing. It is somewhat surprising, then, that he won no great distinction in this field, much less, in fact, than his contemporary, Whittier. The explanation, however, is simple: he proved to have less interest in the ballad than his first enthusiasm suggested; moreover, he tended to write too diffusely in this traditionally compressed form. However, he did write several ballads deserving mention.

"The Wreck of the Hesperus," which he wrote and published with such satisfaction, is probably the best known, but it made little positive contribution to Longfellow's reputation. It is prolix, sentimental, unconvincing. It has been among the most parodied of all Longfellow's poems, one of the parodies reputedly being Holmes's amusing "Ballad of the Oysterman." Longfellow's poem, recounting the death in a storm of a bold sea captain and his young daughter, is one of the few which he elected to write in conventional ballad meter. He managed the form readily enough, and this ballad has other traditional ballad characteristics, such as use of superstition and of dialogue; but Longfellow's ballad is twice the length of "Sir Patrick Spence," on which it was apparently modeled, and it has far less impact. Perhaps he realized shortly that he had not done as well as he had first thought.

Another early ballad, however, is much better. "The Skeleton in Armor," which, like the "Hesperus," was based on local materials, may still be read with enjoyment and the sense of possibility if not full plausibility. It took its origin from Longfellow's ruminations on an old Round Tower at Newport, reportedly built by the Norsemen centuries earlier, and from the then recent discovery of the "Fall River Skeleton," which wore a breastplate of brass and was possibly a Norseman. On the basis of these materials, Longfellow constructed a thrilling narrative of a Viking abduction and pursuit, the later death of the maiden, and the suicide of her lover in the strange new land to which they had fled from her father's wrath. It is not didactic as is the "Hesperus," and, although not written in strict ballad meter, it is far more successful as a ballad.

Shortly after composing "The Wreck of the Hesperus," Longfellow wrote a poem which he first called "a new Psalm of Life" and then "a kind of ballad." This is the famous "The Village Blacksmith." It probably should be included with his ballads, though it lacks the traditional superstition and dialogue and is not written in strict ballad meter. Its six-line stanza, however, is only a variant on the ballad quatrain, and the poem has the swing and movement of a ballad. This sympathetic portrait of the humble but virtuous, bereft workman has had wide appeal, stimulated somewhat perhaps by the fact that Longfellow had a blacksmith ancestor, and certainly later by the presentation to him by Cambridge school-children of the famous armchair made from the wood of the "spreading chestnut-tree." In this poem, Longfellow shows his technical dexterity by using as an opening line in one stanza "Toiling,—rejoicing,—sorrowing," a radical departure from the iambic tetrameter ordinarily found, but still satisfactory to a reader's ear.

Three of the seven "Poems on Slavery" are written in what would be regular ballad meter except that Longfellow rhymes the first and third lines as well as the second and fourth. These poems are "To William E. Channing," "The Good Part," and "The Quadroon Girl." None is strictly a ballad; "The Quadroon Girl," which tells a story of a planter's selling his own quadroon daughter, comes closest. It was probably the most effective of his little group of anti-slavery poems.

Another poem, a very famous one, loosely classifiable as a ballad, is "Paul Revere's Ride," the first "tale" in *Tales of a Wayside Inn*. It is not written in ballad meter and does not use superstition or dialogue, but it does tell a swiftly moving story very successfully. It will be discussed with the other "tales" in the next chapter.

Longfellow's balladry is worth mentioning, but perhaps as much for the small extent of it as for actual accomplishment in a field where he meant to do much more.

IV Odes

In a century given to the writing of odes and elegies, Longfellow was not especially devoted to these types. Yet a search through his poems shows that he was by no means unaware of these, the most ambitious and elaborate of lyric forms.

His first serious attempt at an ode seems to have been "To a Child," on which he was working in late 1845, at about the time of the birth of his own second child. For more than a month he tried to shape the poem, which had the working title of "Ode to a Child," but he found the material refractory. He completed the poem, however, and was pleased that it was one of the best-received poems in the volume in which it was published. In length and subject matter, it suggests comparison with Wordsworth's famous "Ode on Intimations of Immortality," published some forty years earlier. Both poems use childhood as a starting point in order to make philosophical observations on life. Longfellow's poem has much the same tone as Wordsworth's, but not the imaginative lift and unity of thought. Even so, it has good phrases: "O new-born denizen / Of life's great city!"; "The wisdom early to discern / True beauty in utility."

One of Longfellow's best odes, and by far the best-known one, is "The Building of the Ship." Although narrative in form, this medium-length poem has many of the characteristics of classic English odes. As with many of the most famous odes, its title does not immediately suggest its theme. Keats's "Ode on a Grecian Urn" is actually about the imperishability of beauty; Shelley's "Ode to the West Wind" is about the spirit of human liberty. "The Building of the Ship" is an ode to political union and patriotism, with particular reference to the United States of America, the ship symbolizing the nation. Structurally, the poem has the variety of stanzas we expect in an ode. How much of its popularity was due to the incorporation of a romantic love story is conjectural, but certainly most of its solid fame rests on the imaginative way in which Longfellow managed to present a lofty concept of nationalism.

Longfellow's most remunerative poem, "The Hanging of the Crane," is really an ode to family life—the pageantry of establishing a home and of bringing up children. He is said to have received his inspiration for the poem while visiting in 1867 in the home of the newly wed Thomas B. Aldrich, who was destined to become one of the famous *Atlantic Monthly* editors.[6] Apparently Longfellow's poem was not written until shortly before its first publication in the New York *Ledger* in 1874. In it Longfellow uses the hanging of the crane in the fireplace to symbolize the establishment of the home, the progressive enlargement of the family dining table to symbolize the family's growth, and the shrinking of the table later to represent the scattering of the family to repeat the process in a new generation. Smoothly wrought, the poem presents a pleasing exposition of its simple theme; but it does not quite reach the imaginative heights we expect in an ode.

A much better effort is "Morituri Salutamus," which he wrote about the same time. This poem, written for his fiftieth college class reunion at Bowdoin and read by him on the occasion, was one of his few occasional poems and is deservedly the most famous one. It is an ode to old age and to the spirit of acceptance and resolution which should accompany it. It is somewhat reminiscent of Tennyson's "Ulysses," written a generation earlier; but it is not an imitation. Longfellow praises the beauty and aspiration of youth, but he points out that old age also has its merits:

> Ah, nothing is too late
> Till the tired heart shall cease to palpitate.
>
> . . . .
>
> Chaucer, at Woodstock with the nightingales,
> At sixty wrote the Canterbury Tales;
> Goethe at Weimar, toiling to the last,
> Completed Faust when eighty years were past.
>
> . . . .
>
> The night hath not yet come; we are not quite
> Cut off from labor by the failing light;
> Something remains for us to do or dare;
>
> . . . .
>
> For age is opportunity no less
> Than youth itself, though in another dress,
> And as the evening twilight fades away
> The sky is filled with stars, invisible by day.

Three years later, in 1877, when he was seventy years old, Longfellow wrote another of his finest odes, "Kéramos," an ode to art.

In it he harked back once more to his early recollections of Portland, this time to his boyish observation and admiration of an old potter who kept a shop there. As he progresses through his poem, Longfellow surveys the parts of the world where notable pottery has been produced, all the way from Delft, Holland, to Japan. From his survey the didactic Longfellow concludes:

> All that inhabit this great earth,
> Whatever their rank or worth,
> Are kindred and allied by birth,
> And made of the same clay.

Of more literary interest are his observations that

> Art is the child of Nature . . .
> in whom we trace
> The features of the mother's face.
> .   .   .   .
> He is the greatest artist, then,
> Whether of pencil or of pen,
> Who follows Nature.

The well-maintained smoothness of the verse, the considerable imaginative lift, the use of a refrain of musical stanzas, and the skillful embodiment of the theme of the ode all combine to make this one of the most successful of Longfellow's middle-length poems.

V Elegies

With his early interest in Thomas Gray and his lifelong concern with death, it might be expected that Longfellow would have written outstanding elegiac verse. Actually, he never completed a full elegy, but he did write a number of death pieces, some of which have an elegiac quality.

One of Longfellow's earliest elegiac poems was "Tegnér's Drapa," the death-song he wrote for Esaias Tegnér, the Swedish poet whom he had greatly admired and translated. This dirge is devoted largely to a comparative description of the old warlike mythology of the Scandinavians and of the newer poetry of human love and brotherhood; Balder symbolizes the earlier; Tegnér, the later: "The law of force is dead! / The law of love prevails." It is a good example of Longfellow's interest in Scandinavian materials, but it is not a great poem and is more of a funeral piece than an elegy.

More of a true elegy is "Resignation," written a year later in 1848, after the death of his first daughter, Fanny. Longfellow did not write easily of his personal losses, and he and his wife both felt the death of this namesake child very keenly. However, the poet's meditation ultimately took elegiac form. Recovering from the deep grief of his loss, he arrived at a reconciliation with the larger plan: "oftentimes celestial benedictions / Assume this dark disguise," and

> There is no Death! What seems so is transition;
>   This life of mortal breath
> Is but a suburb of the life elysian,
>   Whose portal we call Death.

The poem is prolix and does not compare favorably with Emerson's similarly inspired "Threnody," but it has some merit.

Another notable funeral piece is "The Warden of the Cinque Ports," the memorial for the Duke of Wellington that Longfellow wrote in October, 1852, a month after the famous Duke's death. It contains some of Longfellow's finest imaginative responses to his material. With none of his too-frequent didacticism, he invokes the highlights of Wellington's career and suggests the importance of his exploits to England. The quiet ending of the poem is especially artistic:

> Meanwhile, without, the surly cannon waited,
>   The sun rose bright o'erhead;
> Nothing in Nature's aspect intimated
>   That a great man was dead.

The best of his several funeral pieces is undoubtedly the tribute to Hawthorne which he wrote only a month after Hawthorne's death. It has a fine restraint and shows a just estimate of the novelist's genius. The poem is too long to quote entirely; here are choice stanzas:

> How beautiful it was, that one bright day
>   In the long week of rain!
> Though all its splendor could not chase away
>   The omnipresent pain.
>
> For the one face I looked for was not there,
>   The one low voice was mute;
> Only an unseen presence filled the air,
>   And baffled my pursuit.
>
> There in seclusion and remote from men
>   The wizard hand lies cold
> Which at its topmost speed let fall the pen,
>   And left the tale half told.
>
> Ah! who shall lift that wand of magic power,
>   And the lost clew regain?
> The unfinished window in Aladdin's tower
>   Unfinished must remain!

One other funeral piece may be mentioned: "Charles Sumner," his tribute to his long-time friend, the well-known Massachusetts senator. Although brief, this is almost an elegy in structure. It begins with the funeral tribute, moves to contemplation of the relation between life and death, and concludes with an attempt to reconcile the present loss with the larger plan:

> Alike are life and death,
> When life in death survives,
> And the uninterrupted breath
> Inspires a thousand lives.
>
> . . . .
>
> So when a great man dies,
> For years beyond our ken,
> The light he leaves behind him lies
> Upon the paths of men.

Longfellow was by no means a great elegist, but he wrote enough elegiac verse to deserve recognition in this field. The truth seems to be that he was not enough of a philosopher to compose an elegy of the first rank.

VI Sonnets

However much critics of Longfellow may disparage particular poems or his total achievement as a poet, none denies him considerable ability as a sonnet writer. In fact, he is universally admitted to be the finest sonneteer in America prior to the twentieth century. His high rank is the more remarkable because he wrote no sonnet cycle, no conventional nature or love sonnets, and no sonnets in other than the Petrarchan form. Even his total output of about eighty sonnets is considerably below the three hundred of Wordsworth and the totals of a good many other poets. He did, however, have a great deal of interest in the form, and wrote sonnets from about his thirty-fifth year until the end of his career.

His first important sonnet seems to have been "Mezzo Cammin," discussed and quoted in Chapter 4. This poem had been partly inspired by Dante; hence it is not surprising that one of his next sonnets, three years later, was addressed to Dante. It is a worthy tribute to the great Italian poet:

> Tuscan, that wanderest through the realms of gloom,
> With thoughtful pace, and sad, majestic eyes,
> Stern thoughts and awful from thy soul arise,
> Like Farinata from his fiery tomb.
> Thy sacred song is like the trump of doom;
> Yet in thy heart what human sympathies,
> What soft compassion glows, as in the skies
> The tender stars their clouded lamps relume!
> Methinks I see thee stand with pallid cheeks

> By Fra Hilario in his diocese,
> As up the convent-walls, in golden streaks,
> The ascending sunbeams mark the day's decrease;
> And, as he asks what there the stranger seeks,
> Thy voice along the cloister whispers "Peace!"

It is interesting that Longfellow would note in Dante the combination of stern thoughts with soft compassion.

In his Petrarchan sonnets, Longfellow showed a natural preference for Italian topics. In 1849, however, he wrote a notable sonnet which did not touch Italy except in the use of the form of the sonnet: his fine tribute to Fanny Kemble and her readings from Shakespeare. Longfellow and the famous actress had become very good friends. He particularly appreciated her highly effective public reading of his "The Building of the Ship." He seems to have missed no opportunity to hear her series of Shakespearean readings in Cambridge. After one of these the Longfellows entertained her with a supper, and the poet read his newly written sonnet tribute to her afterward (*Poems*, 112). It is a good sonnet, and she must have been pleased. It begins "O precious evenings! all too swiftly sped!" and ends

> O happy Poet! by no critic vext!
> How must thy listening spirit now rejoice
> To be interpreted by such a voice!

The next notable sonnets returned to the Italian locale with "Giotto's Tower" and the six sonnets (two for each of the three parts) he wrote to preface his translation of the *Divine Comedy*. The *Comedy* sonnets are often considered the finest poetry Longfellow wrote, and with reason. The first is perhaps the best. It takes on added value to the reader who recognizes that it not only commemorates the intensive labor that Longfellow had been engaged in for years in translating a favorite poet whom he greatly admired, but also reflects the comfort he derived from that labor during a period of personal grief. It must be quoted in its entirety:

> Oft have I seen at some cathedral door
> A laborer, pausing in the dust and heat,
> Lay down his burden, and with reverent feet
> Enter, and cross himself, and on the floor
> Kneel to repeat his paternoster o'er;
> Far off the noises of the world retreat;
> The loud vociferations of the street
> Become an indistinguishable roar.
> So, as I enter here from day to day,
> And leave my burden at this minster gate,
> Kneeling in prayer, and not ashamed to pray,

The tumult of the time disconsolate
To inarticulate murmurs dies away,
While the eternal ages watch and wait.

The final sonnet is also very fine, especially in its opening quatrain:

O star of morning and of liberty!
O bringer of the light, whose splendor shines
Above the darkness of the Apennines,
Forerunner of the day that is to be!

Two other sonnets on Italian subjects may be mentioned. In 1874 he wrote in English about the Old Bridge at Florence; but then, to show that he had not lost his mastery of Italian, he wrote the sonnet again in Italian, with the title, "Il Ponte Vecchio Di Firenze." Two years later he wrote a sonnet in tribute to Venice, always a wonder city to him. It begins "White swan of cities, slumbering in thy nest / So wonderfully built among the reeds."

Longfellow turned more toward English subjects in the frequent sonnet writing of his last years. The final part of his *The Masque of Pandora, and Other Poems,* published in 1875, was a "Book of Sonnets," consisting of a group of fourteen, four of them tributes to English authors. His selections are interesting: Chaucer, Shakespeare, Milton, and Keats. These are clearly poets with whom he felt a kinship of spirit. All are discerning tributes, but the one on Keats—because of its epitomizing of the brilliant and tragic career of the young poet in rich imagery incorporating allusions to his life and writings—seems most deserving of quotation.

The young Endymion sleeps Endymion's sleep;
The shepherd-boy whose tale was left half told!
The solemn grove uplifts its shield of gold
To the red rising moon, and loud and deep
The nightingale is singing from the steep;
It is midsummer, but the air is cold;
Can it be death? Alas, beside the fold
A shepherd's pipe lies shattered near his sheep.
Lo! in the moonlight gleams a marble white,
On which I read: "Here lieth one whose name
Was writ in water." And was this the meed
Of his sweet singing? Rather let me write:
"The smoking flax before it burst to flame
Was quenched by death, and broken the bruised reed."

When Longfellow was seventy, he wrote "The Three Silences of Molinos," a sonnet tribute to Whittier to be read at the now famous Whittier birthday dinner. The same year, 1877, he wrote "Wapentake," a sonnet tribute to his kindred spirit, Lord Tennyson. Other notable sonnets of his later life—besides "The Cross of Snow" quoted in Chapter 5—include "The Broken Oar" and "My Books." In "The Broken Oar" he returns to his Scandinavian studies to illustrate his feeling of happy weariness in his protracted toil on Dante, referring to a beach traveler's finding a broken oar with the inscription: "Oft was I weary, when I toiled at thee." In "My Books" he takes a pensive farewell of the volumes which have meant so much in his life of scholar and poet. The poem begins, "Sadly as some old mediaeval knight / Gazed at the arms he could no longer wield," and it ends:

> So I behold these books upon their shelf,
> My ornaments and arms of other days;
> Not wholly useless, though no longer used,
> For they remind me of my other self,
> Younger and stronger, and the pleasant ways
> In which I walked, now clouded and confused.

Longfellow wrote "My Books" in 1881, within a year of his death. He must have known then that his association with these beloved companions was nearly finished. Some five years earlier, however, he had written "Nature," the sonnet which is in tone the nearest to a farewell poem. It stands comparison with such famous poetic farewells as Emerson's "Terminus," Whitman's "Good-bye, My Fancy!" and Tennyson's "Crossing the Bar." It is one of Longfellow's finest poems in its simple but sustained imagery and obviously sincere feeling:

> As a fond mother, when the day is o'er,
> Leads by the hand her little child to bed,
> Half willing, half reluctant to be led,
> And leave his broken playthings on the floor,
> Still gazing at them through the open door,
> Not wholly reassured and comforted
> By promises of others in their stead,
> Which, though more splendid, may not please him more;
> So Nature deals with us, and takes away
> Our playthings one by one, and by the hand
> Leads us to rest so gently, that we go
> Scarce knowing if we wish to go or stay,
> Being too full of sleep to understand
> How far the unknown transcends the what we know.

This sampling from Longfellow's shorter, chiefly lyric poems indicates a remarkable versatility and a considerable accomplishment. Poems of these types alone, however, would not have sufficed to make him the poet most widely read in America and to place him among the top in world readership of all the poets of his age. Some of the long narrative poems were even more popular, whether or not they represent a greater poetic achievement.

CHAPTER 8

Verse Narrative, Indian Saga, Idyl, Framework Tales, Drama, Translations

> Come, read to me some poem
> Some simple and heartfelt lay
> That shall soothe this restless feeling,
> And banish the thoughts of day.
>
> . . . .
>
> And the night shall be filled with music,
> And the cares, that infest the day,
> Shall fold their tents, like the Arabs,
> And as silently steal away.
> —"The Day Is Done"

I *Longfellow and the Major Types of Poetry*

LONGFELLOW, by the mid-1840's, had published several volumes of prose and verse. Among these were *Hyperion*, the prose romance loosely classifiable as a novel, and *The Spanish Student*, a verse drama which he had some hope might prove suitable for stage production. Both had considerable success, but the greater part of his fame up to this point had come from his short poems. Although by now less obsessed than he had been in his college days by the burning urge to become eminent, Longfellow was still the shrewd economist. Comfortably settled with his wife and children in Craigie House, he seems to have surveyed the situation and decided that it was time for him to undertake a poem of major scope. He cannot have failed to observe that his great masters, Dante and Goethe, had written epic and drama, as had the truly great English poets, including Shakespeare and Milton. Longfellow would need a larger canvas to paint upon. Fortune was with him; it was not long until the first of several appealing subjects for major poems was suggested to him.

II *A Sentimental Journey:* Evangeline

His friendship with Hawthorne provided Longfellow with the idea for his world-famous verse narrative of the Acadian maiden Evangeline. Hawthorne's *American Notebooks* and Samuel Longfellow's *Life* agree on how the central part of the plot of his narrative was laid ready to his hand. Here is Samuel Longfellow's version:

> Mr. Hawthorne came one day to dine at Craigie House, bringing with him his friend Mr. H. L. Conolly, who had been the rector of a church in South Boston. At dinner Conolly said that he had been trying in vain to interest Hawthorne to write a story upon an incident which had been related to him by a parishioner of his, Mrs. Haliburton. It was the story of a young Acadian maiden, who at the dispersion of her people by the English troops had been separated from her betrothed lover; they sought each other for years in their exile; and at last they met in a hospital where the lover lay dying. Mr. Longfellow was touched by the story, especially by the constancy of its heroine, and said to his friend, "If you really do not want this incident for a tale, let me have it for a poem;" and Hawthorne consented. Out of this grew Evangeline, —whose heroine was at first called Gabrielle (*Life*, II, 70-71).

There has been conjecture, some of it playful, as to why Hawthorne or Whittier, who also knew of the Acadian material, did not elect to use the Evangeline story. Whittier implied in his review of Longfellow's poem that his indignant sympathy with the persecuted Acadians would have prevented him from writing as Longfellow did. Hawthorne, it has been remarked, could not use the story because it did not have enough gloom or sin in it. A paradox has also been observed in the fact that the most Victorian poet of the nineteenth century had the maiden doing the pursuing.

The historical background of *Evangeline* involved the series of French and Indian wars with the English for possession of northern and mid-America. The peninsula of Acadia (Nova Scotia, as the English called it), with its situation between New England and the mouth of the St. Lawrence River, was strategic. The English had won political possession before the final French-English war broke out in 1755, but the loyalty of the Acadians to the English naturally continued to be suspect. As a military measure, then, the wisdom and justice of which were to become and continue to be controversial, the English in 1755, early in the war, dispersed the Acadian settlers. They were scattered all along the Atlantic Coast and the Gulf of New Mexico as far as southern Louisiana, where the only group to preserve its identity found new homes.

Longfellow's journals show that Conolly and Hawthorne paid their visit to him on October 27, 1846, and that he had begun work on *Evangeline* before November 12, kept himself at the poem in spite of distracting college duties in the ensuing weeks, and finished it on his birthday, February 27, 1847. He also recorded that it was published October 30, 1847, and that by January 10, 1848, it was in its sixth edition. On July 2, 1847, while he was reading the proofs, Fanny wrote to a friend: "I suppose I can now tell you that he is correcting the proofs of a long poem called *Evangeline,* written in hexameters, describing the fortunes and misfortunes of an Acadian damsel driven to this country from Canada by the British in the olden time. It is a very beautiful, touching poem *I* think and the measure gains upon the ear wonderfully. It enables greater richness of expression than any other, and is sonorous like the sea which is ever sounding in Evangeline's ears."[1]

True to his usual custom, Longfellow made no attempt to do on-the-scene research for *Evangeline;* instead he read the best printed sources he could find. According to his own statement, he drew heavily upon Thomas C. Haliburton's *An Historical and Statistical Account of Nova Scotia,* with its quotations from the Abbé Raynal, for descriptions of Acadia (*Poems,* 70). Apparently the three books which helped him most for the second part of the poem were John Fremont's *Expedition to the Rocky Mountains,* Charles Sealsfield's *Life in the New World,* and W. I. Kip's *Early Jesuit Missions in North America.*[2] By an almost incredibly lucky stroke of fortune, John Banvard's diorama of the Mississippi arrived in Boston soon after Longfellow had begun work on the poem. On December 17, he wrote in his journal: "I see a panorama of the Mississippi advertised. This comes very *à propos.* The river comes to me instead of my going to the river: and as it is to flow through the pages of the poem, I look upon this as a special benediction" (*Life,* II, 67-68). On December 19, he wrote, "Went to see Banvard's moving diorama of the Mississippi. One seems to be sailing down the great stream, and sees the boats and the sandbanks crested with cottonwood, and the bayous by moonlight. Three miles of canvas, and a great deal of merit."

The impressions he gained from this evening's viewing of Banvard's series of painted scenes obviously stood him in good stead when he came to write his own descriptions; but it should be noted also that, as a boyhood resident of Maine, he was familiar with an area not very distant and not too different from Nova Scotia. Moreover, his visit to Sweden had familiarized him with another similar country. Indeed Andrew Hilen believes his descriptions of Acadia are based largely on his observations in Sweden: "the pine forests and rocky fields of the Swedish countryside were not inconsistent with his idea of Acadia and he had already idealized the Swedish peasantry in the same way that he wished to idealize the equally 'lumpish' Acadians."[3] It is interesting to find Longfellow providing scenery in the manner of today's movie industry, which sometimes

films scenes thousands of miles away from the places ostensibly
pictured.

One of the most controversial aspects of *Evangeline* proved to be
the dactyllic hexameter in which it was written. Some of Longfellow's friends, including the historian J. L. Motley, thought he had
made a mistake; and even Whittier said it would have been at least
as effective in "the poetic prose of the author's *Hyperion*."[4] Longfellow seems never to have had serious doubts that he had chosen
rightly, though to reassure himself he once paraphrased a passage
in blank verse, with a clearly inferior result (*Poems*, 71). He had
long admired the meter of *Evangeline* in Greek and Latin classics;
it is noteworthy that he was rereading Homer while working on
the poem. More modern influences on his choice were doubtless his
familiarity with Tegnér's *The Children of the Lord's Supper*, which
was written in this meter and translated by Longfellow in the same
meter in 1841, and with Goethe's *Hermann und Dorothea*, which
was not only written in hexameters, but provided a significant
parallel for his plot since it centered on the expulsion of the Pro-
testants from Salzburg following a decree by the archbishop.

For his plot, Longfellow did little more than expand Conolly's
anecdote, but he expanded it at great length. First comes a brief
invocation to affection and hope and "the beauty and strength of
woman's devotion," beginning with the famous lines:

> This is the forest primeval. The murmuring pines and the hemlocks,
> Bearded with moss, and in garments green, indistinct in the
> twilight,
> Stand like Druids of eld, with voices sad and prophetic,
> Stand like harpers hoar, with beards that rest on their bosoms.
> Loud from its rocky caverns, the deep-voiced neighboring ocean
> Speaks, and in accents disconsolate answers the wail of the forest.
>
> (71)

These opening lines are followed by a detailed description of the
French settlement on "the shores of the Basin of Minas" where the
peasants live in bucolic happiness. The harvest has been gathered
in, and the settlers are looking forward to a winter even colder than
ordinary, for the Indian hunters have noticed that "thick was the
fur of the foxes."

Presently the principal characters are introduced: "the gentle
Evangeline," running the household of "the farmer of Grand-Pré,"
who "lived on his sunny farm"; and Gabriel Lajeunesse, "the son of
Basil the Blacksmith, / Who was a mighty man in the village, and
honored of all men." Longfellow took the name of his hero directly
from Fremont's *Expedition*, where the original was a French

voyageur;[5] but the origin of the heroine's name is less certain. Tradition has it that the inspiration for Evangeline Bellefontaine was Emmeline Labiche, whose adventures largely paralleled those of her fictional counterpart.[6] According to his brother, Longfellow first called his heroine Gabrielle, but all his journal entries call the story *Evangeline*.

The story itself begins with Longfellow's description of the gathering in the Bellefontaine home for the signing of the marriage contract, which was customarily done, apparently, the night before the actual marriage took place. The aged notary, "Father of twenty children was he, and more than a hundred / Children's children rode on his knee," arrives to lend the proper legal sanction. While he is there, he reports gossip that the ships in the harbor are there with "evil intention," but he expresses his own confidence that the peace will continue. After the notary has drawn up his papers and been paid thrice the customary fee, he rises and blesses the prospective bride and bridegroom, lifts a tankard of ale and drinks to their health, and solemnly takes his leave. The fathers play draughts while the lovers whisper apart. Then Gabriel and his father leave, and the lovers expect to meet on the morrow at the church for the priest's blessing.

The sun rises pleasantly the next day, but not to grace the wedding. Instead, a drumbeat summons all the men to the church to hear a message from his Majesty, the King of England. The message proves to be no less than an order for the confiscation of all property and the dispersal of the Acadians. Longfellow describes the result of this pronouncement in one of his few Homeric similes:

As, when the air is serene in sultry solstice of summer,
Suddenly gathers a storm, and the deadly sling of the hailstones
Beats down the farmer's corn in the field and shatters his windows,
Hiding the sun, and strewing the ground with thatch from the
    house-roofs,
Bellowing fly the herds, and seek to break their enclosures;
So on the hearts of the people descended the words of the
    speaker. (80)

But there is no recourse. The removal takes place so rapidly and cruelly that husbands are separated from wives and children from parents; Basil La Jeunesse is thrust on one ship; Gabriel, on another. Evangeline and her father are not put on the first ships. While they wait, they witness the burning of their village, a catastrophe which Evangeline's father does not survive. With lover gone and father dead, Evangeline is left to face an anxious, uncertain future.

At the opening of Part II, "Many a weary year had passed since the burning of Grand-Pre," but still the exiles are seeking to restore broken family ties: "Long among them was seen a maiden who waited and wandered, / Lowly and meek in spirit, and patiently suffering all things." She has sought her lost Gabriel "From the bleak shores of the sea to the land where the Father of Waters / Seizes the hills in his hands, and drags them down to the ocean" (84), but with only tantalizing results. Many times she arrives where Basil has been not long before—on the prairies with the Coureurs de Bois or "a Voyageur in the lowlands of Louisiana." Friends counsel her to forget Gabriel and to marry another fair youth, but her love is constant. In the month of May she courses down "the Beautiful River, / Past the Ohio shore and past the mouth of the Wabash," and on "Into the golden stream of the broad and swift Mississippi" to the Louisiana "Acadian coast, and the prairies of fair Opelousas" (85-86).

It is in the Acadian settlement in Louisiana that Longfellow gives his rapt readers their greatest thrill, first the expectancy of love's fulfillment and then the chill of disappointment. Evangeline's party arrives at a village and finds Gabriel's father Basil, who tells Evangeline that Gabriel had left only the day before with a party going to the Ozark Mountains to trade for mules with the Spaniards. Their boats must have passed each other on the bayou. Evangeline had indeed sensed Gabriel's nearness on the previous day and so informed Father Felician, but destiny was not with them. However, Basil assures Evangeline that, if she will follow immediately, her party can surely overtake Gabriel's in a matter of days; so she sets out again. The return voyage up the river is beautiful, but they are following a will-o'-the-wisp.

> Meanwhile, apart, at the head of the hall, the priest and the herdsman
> Sat, conversing together of past and present and future;
> While Evangeline stood like one entranced, for within her
> Olden memories rose, and loud in the midst of the music
> Heard the sound of the sea, and an irrepressible sadness
> Came o'er her heart, and unseen she stole forth into the garden.
> Beautiful was the night. . . .
> "Patience!" whispered the oaks from the oracular caverns of darkness:
> And, from the moonlit meadow, a sigh responded, "To-morrow!"
> (91)

But they do not find him the next day, or the next, or the next. They reach the Ozark Mountains, where Longfellow's secondhand knowledge of geography becomes very hazy; he apparently visualized the Oregon (Columbia) River as rising in the Ozarks. As they get farther and farther from Louisiana, Evangeline has mounting misgivings:

> Filled with the thoughts of love was Evangeline's heart, but a secret,
> Subtile sense crept in of pain and indefinite terror,
> As the cold, poisonous snake creeps into the nest of the swallow.
>
> (93)

Their Shawnee Indian guide conducts them to a mission on the western slope of the mountains. Here the black-robed Jesuits also have tantalizing news:

> "Not six suns have risen and set since Gabriel, seated
> On this mat by my side, where now the maiden reposes,
> Told me this same sad tale; then arose and continued his journey!"
> Soft was the voice of the priest, and he spake with an accent of kindness;
> But on Evangeline's heart fell his words as in winter the snowflakes
> Fall into some lone nest from which the birds have departed. (94)

The priest assures her, however, that the party will return to the mission in autumn when the hunting season is over. The weary Evangeline decides to accept the priest's advice to await her lover at the mission. But the autumn comes and passes, with no Gabriel; so she again resumes her pursuit:

> Thus did the long sad years glide on, and in seasons and places
> Divers and distant far was seen the wandering maiden;—
> .   .   .   .
> Fair was she and young, when in hope began the long journey;
> Faded was she and old, when in disappointment it ended. (95)

Evangeline is nothing if not persistent. It apparently never occurred to the Victorian Longfellow that anyone would question the virtue of a maiden who would voyage for years unchaperoned with the rough men of the frontier and even spend a summer and autumn as the only woman in a mission full of men. He may have been entirely right, for there appears to be no evidence that any contemporary reviewer did question it. Longfellow and his readers apparently shared Milton's concept of the unassailable defense of the chaste heart.

Finally, even Evangeline tires of pursuing the elusive Gabriel and decides to spend her remaining years as a Sister of Mercy, nursing in hospitals. In this role, she finally meets Gabriel when he is on his deathbed and unable even to whisper her name; but he does recognize her.

> Sweet was the light of his eyes; but it suddenly sank into darkness,
> As when a lamp is blown out by a gust of wind at a casement.
> All was ended now, the hope, and the fear, and the sorrow,
> All the aching of heart, the restless, unsatisfied longing,
> All the dull, deep pain, and constant anguish of patience!
> And, as she pressed once more the lifeless head to her bosom,
> Meekly she bowed her own, and murmured, "Father, I thank thee!" (97)

It is impossible in this unsentimental age to imagine or understand the reception given to Longfellow's poem, though even the cynical modern reader is likely to find an indefinable charm in it. Longfellow was of course elated with its success, but he had his explanation: "I had the fever a long time burning in my own brain before I let my hero take it. 'Evangeline' is so easy for you to read, because it was so hard for me to write."[7]

The contemporary reception was remarkable. The British *Fraser's Magazine* commented: "This is an American poem; and we hail its appearance with the greater satisfaction, inasmuch as it is the first genuine Castalian fount which has burst from the soil of America." The *Metropolitan* had this verdict: "No one with any pretensions to poetic feeling can read its delicious portraiture of rustic scenery, and of a mode of life long since defunct, without the most intense delight." His esteemed literary contemporaries Hawthorne, Whittier, and Holmes were unstinting in their praise. In an article in the *Literary World*, F. Blake Crofton wrote: "Evangeline has proved, in fact, one of the decisive poems of the world." In 1865 it was translated into French alexandrines by a Canadian, M. Le May.[8]

The poem continued to win adherents long after it was published. By 1857, sales had mounted to nearly 36,000 copies (*Life*, II, 295). The same year the poet's friend Sumner wrote him from Scotland after a visit with the Duke and Duchess of Sutherland: "Driving with the Duchess . . . I read at her request several of your poems and parts of 'Evangeline,' all of which she admired and enjoyed almost to tears" (*Life*, III, 52). Further on in the same letter he mentions meeting at the country seat of Sir William Stirling Maxwell a beautiful lady who "has read 'Evangeline' some twenty times, and thinks it the most perfect poem in the language."

Even though the poem is not itself so much read—or wept over—today as it used to be, it has been assimilated into the American tradition in a variety of ways. The first state park to be established in Louisiana was the Longfellow-Evangeline State Park (1934). Driving through the area some years ago, I was momentarily startled when I overtook a huge transport truck emblazoned with the unpoetic sign, "Evangeline Canned Okra." Even without such memorials, *Evangeline* would continue to live, most of all for the sympathetically conceived and delicately portrayed central character and her embodiment of steadfast human love, but also for making possible vicarious travel through picturesque scenery and for the sheer musical charm with which Longfellow managed to imbue his refractory hexameters.

III   *Quasi-Epic:* Hiawatha

Eight busy years intervened between the publication of *Evangeline* (1847) and *Hiawatha* (1855). During this time Longfellow published his final attempt at a novel, *Kavanagh* (1849); a volume of short poems (1850); and *The Golden Legend,* the middle part (written first) of his religious epic (1851). He was full of other projects, but his heavy duties at Harvard, together with various distractions, made it extremely hard for him to proceed with major writings. Free at last from his Harvard obligations, he pushed forward his work on *Hiawatha* with dispatch and enthusiasm. Apparently he had been brooding over the poem for years. His interest in the Indians in college-student days has been mentioned. Also, he had been much impressed by a visit in Boston in 1837 of the famous Black Hawk and other Indians.[9] According to Edward Everett Hale, this interest was actively revived during his early Harvard years: "It is said that one of Mr. Longfellow's Harvard pupils, of one of those early classes which were favored with much of his personal care, returned to Cambridge a few years after graduating, fresh from a summer on the plains among the Indians. Meeting Professor Longfellow at dinner one day, he eagerly told his kind friend some of the legends of lodge and camp-fire, and begged him to rescue them from the extinction which seemed almost certain, by making them the subject of a poem."[10] In his journal for February 26, 1849, Longfellow recorded that "an Ojibway preacher and poet came to see us. The Indian is a good-looking young man. He left me a book of his, an autobiography" (*Life*, II, 135).

It was Longfellow's way to brood over a poetic idea for a long time, until he could hit upon the right metrical form for it and find the opportunity to let his creative imagination give it shape and substance. On June 5, 1854, he recorded in his journal: "I am reading with great delight the Finnish Epic Kalevala. It is charming" (*Life,* II, 247). By June 25, he could record his beginning on "Manabozho," his first title for the poem. The next day he spent reading "Schoolcraft's great book on the Indians; three huge quartos, ill-digested, and without any index." By July 31, he was calling the poem *Hiawatha,* and he recorded working on it, along with reading "to the boys the Indian Story of the Red Swan." On September 19 he wrote, "Working away with Tanner, Heckewelder, and sundry books about the Indians." By November 13, he was trying out some pages of *Hiawatha* on an unnamed correspondent: "He fears the poem will want human interest. So does F. So does the author. I must put a live beating heart into it" (*Life,* II, 251).

He was not able to do this at once, apparently, for he broke off work on it for two months. But by January he was writing again, and by March 21 he could notify Fields that he would bring in an engraving of his portrait "and also the 'Song of Hiawatha,' which I finished to-day at noon. Of course the bells rang!" (*Life,* III, 44). By mid-April he was "Busy copying and rewriting Hiawatha for the press" (*Life,* II, 256). June 4 he was reading proof-sheets, with this result: "I am growing idiotic about this song, and no longer know whether it is good or bad." By October it was in press, and it was published on November 10, 1855, by Ticknor and Fields. Five days later, he could record "Hiawatha makes some sensation" and by November 18, "Some of the newspapers are fierce and furious about Hiawatha, which reminds me of the days when Hyperion first appeared."

Shortly afterward, Hawthorne wrote him that he was reading it "with great delight." About the same time, the Quaker poet Bayard Taylor wrote him at length, mostly in praise, but he also observed shrewdly: "It will be parodied, perhaps ridiculed in many quarters, but it will live after the Indian race has vanished from our Continent" (*Life,* II, 264-65). Fanny Longfellow, a remarkably acute judge of her husband's writings, made a similar observation: "It is very fresh and fragrant of the woods and genuine Indian life, but its rhymeless rhythm will puzzle the critics, and I suppose it will be abundantly abused."[11]

But Longfellow may have found the most exciting commentary in sales figures. The poem sold 10,000 copies the first four weeks and 30,000 in six months. Kennedy says: "Perhaps no poem in the English language was ever so immediately popular. It furnished topics to the sculptor, the *litterateur,* the ethnologist, and the philologist."[12] The poet must have been especially gratified at receiving a highly complimentary letter from H. R. Schoolcraft, to whom he had sent a copy. The man who had lived with the Indians and whose books had been Longfellow's principal source praised the fidelity to the Indian, "a warrior in war, a savage in revenge, a stoic in endurance, a wolverine in suppleness and cunning. But he is also a father at the head of his lodge, a patriot in the love of his country.... There has been no attempt, my dear sir, before 'Hiawatha' to show this" (*Life*, III, 45).

Longfellow planned and wrote *Hiawatha* basically in much the same way he had composed *Evangeline*. However, his instinct told him that, for primitive folk materials, he would need a meter very different from the classic hexameter. Here his interest in Scandinavian culture stood him in good stead. The short, unrhymed, musical lines of the Finnish epic *Kalevala* ("Land of Heroes") were most promising. Soon he had decided on this form, probably with no expectation that the choice would result in criticism and even charges of plagiarism. It was nevertheless a fortunate choice, as the great success of the poem attests.

The setting of *Hiawatha*, principally the environs of Lake Superior, was even less accessible to Longfellow than the setting of *Evangeline*, which he had not visited. There is no indication that he considered journeying to the land of the Ojibway Indians. But again, fortunately for him, good printed sources were available. He had known John Heckewelder's books on Indians from college days. Since then more pertinent sources had appeared. He specifically mentioned Tanner and Schoolcraft in his journal. The Tanner book was *A Narrative of the Captivity and Adventures of John Tanner*, published in 1830. John Tanner had been United States interpreter to the Indians at Sault Sainte Marie, which was Ojibway country. Schoolcraft's work was even more relevant and useful. Henry Rowe Schoolcraft became Indian agent to the Ojibway Indians in 1822 and was later Superintendent of Indian Affairs. He lived with the Indians, married an Ojibway halfbreed woman, and became well acquainted with Indian history and traditions. Longfellow must have realized that he himself knew next to nothing about Indians, but he made sure that he had a highly qualified expert to lean on. Schoolcraft wrote about Indians throughout his life, but the books which Longfellow used most were his *Algic Researches*, (1839); *Oneóta, or Characteristics of the Red Race of America*, (1844-45); and probably the first four volumes of his *Historical and Statistical Information ... of the Indian Tribes* (1851-54).[13]

No Banvard's Diorama of the Lake Superior country came to Boston while Longfellow was working on *Hiawatha*, but he probably found a partial equivalent in the works of the famous artist on Indian life, George Catlin, three hundred of whose engravings were published in two volumes in 1841 as *Manners and Customs of the North American Indians.*

Hiawatha has epic qualities, but can hardly be classifed as an epic. The Indians it portrays are not a great people harking back to primitive origins but a group on the point of losing its identity. Moreover, although it presents their folk materials authentically, it is not written in their own language. Longfellow, to be sure, knew he was not writing an epic of the Indians, but rather a collection of mythological materials exhibiting a primitive people giving way to a not necessarily nobler but more accomplished people destined to succeed them as occupants and rulers of their lands. Like Cooper, Longfellow wanted to preserve a noble concept of the red man for the white man who would follow him and tend to forget him.

Although *Hiawatha* has proved highly quotable in fragments, it is of course best understood when considered carefully as a whole. Often the "Introduction" is omitted, but in it Longfellow explains his purpose. He is writing a commemorative poem for those

> who love a nation's legends,
> Love the ballads of a people,
> That like voices from afar off
> Call to us to pause and listen.

And for those

> Who have faith in God and Nature,
> Who believe that in all ages
> Every human heart is human,
> That in even savage bosoms
> There are longings, yearnings, strivings
> For the good they comprehend not,
> That the feeble hands and helpless,
> Groping blindly in the darkness,
> Touch God's right hand in that darkness. (114)

The poem is too long and has too many episodes for full summarization, but an attempt will be made to convey some of its flavor. The first scene shows a great congregation "On the Mountains of the Prairie," presumably in the Pictured Rocks area on the shore of Lake Superior. Here have come tribes whose homes range all the way from the New York-Pennsylvania area to the Rocky Mountains of the West. They have been summoned by "Gitche Manito, the mighty," who enjoins them to lay aside their destructive quarrels and to unite in peace under a Prophet, a Deliverer, whom he will send them. The red stone of the region is formed into Peace-Pipes, and the smoke curls upward in good omen.

The Prophet does not come immediately or in a simple manner. After the great peace council, the scene shifts to an epic battle between Mudjekeewis, who comes from the regions of the North-Wind, and the Great Bear of the mountains. Mudjekeewis is victorious, and for his victory he is to be henceforth the West-Wind, with dominion "Over all the winds of heaven."

Hiawatha is not born by immaculate conception nor does he spring full grown from the brow of a god, but he does have a supernatural origin. The "beautiful Nokomis," who is "a wife, but not a mother," through the act of a jealous rival falls from the moon to a beautiful meadow on earth, where she gives birth to a winsome daughter, Wenonah. Nokomis warns Wenonah against the West-Wind, but vainly; so she "Bore a son of love and sorrow. / Thus was born my Hiawatha." His mother dies deserted by the faithless West-Wind, and the "child of wonder" is reared by his grandmother Nokomis and educated by his animal neighbors:

> Then the little Hiawatha
> Learned of every bird its language,
> Learned their names and all their secrets,
> How they built their nests in Summer
> Where they hid themselves in Winter,
> Talked with them whene'er he met them,
> Called them "Hiawatha's Chickens."
> Of all the beasts he learned the language,
> Learned their names and all their secrets,
> How the beavers built their lodges,
> Where the squirrels hid their acorns,
> How the reindeer ran so swiftly,
> Why the rabbit was so timid,
> Talked with them whene'er he met them,
> Called them "Hiawatha's Brothers." (120)

Quickly the wonder boy grew into an equally wondrous young man:

> Swift of foot was Hiawatha;
> He could shoot an arrow from him,
> And run forward with such fleetness,
> That the arrow fell behind him! (121)

Grown into manhood, Hiawatha questions old Nokomis until he finds out about his mother and his fickle father. Despite Nokomis' attempts to dissuade him, he sets out to find his father, and he does. Mudjekeewis welcomes him because he brings back memories of "the beautiful Wenonah." After they have talked for days, Hiawatha remembers his quarrel with his father, and they have a prodigious battle, resulting in a draw, since neither can be killed. Hiawatha then returns to his people with his father's injunction:

> Go back to your home and people,
> Live among them, toil among them,
> Cleanse the earth from all that harms it
> Clear the fishing-grounds and rivers,
> Slay all monsters and magicians. (123)

He pauses only once on the way home, to purchase arrows from the ancient arrow maker at the Falls of Minnehaha in the land of the Dacotahs. Here he becomes enamored of the arrow maker's dark-eyed daughter, for whom the falls are named. He proceeds without her, but

> Who shall say what thoughts and visions
> Fill the fiery brains of young men?
> Who shall say what dreams of beauty
> Filled the heart of Hiawatha? (124)

One of the most pleasing and memorable episodes of the book is Hiawatha's fasting, which ends in the gift of the Indian corn to his people. Hiawatha fasted not for "renown among the warriors, / But for profit of the people, / For advantage of the nations" (124). What they seem to need most is more variety of food; wild fruits and game are not enough. So as he lies exhausted in his wigwam on the fourth day of his fast, he has a revelation:

> And he saw a youth approaching,
> Dressed in garments green and yellow,
> Coming through the purple twilight,
> Through the splendor of the sunset;
> Plumes of green bent o'er his forehead,
> And his hair was soft and golden. (124)

The youth asks Hiawatha to wrestle with him. They wrestle three times "In the glory of the sunset, / Till the darkness fell around them," until Hiawatha conquers; and the youth asks the victor to bury him "Where the rain may fall upon me, / Where the sun may come and warm me" (125). By the end of summer, from this extraordinary planting "Stood the maize in all its beauty," and the Indians gathered the ripened ears in autumn. As Longfellow tells the story of the origin of the corn, which had become central in the Indian economy, it is a beautiful myth.

Famous passages in the poem include the description of Hiawatha's making of his canoe:

> Give me of your bark, O Birch-tree!
> Of your yellow bark, O Birch-tree!
> Growing by the rushing river,
> Tall and stately in the valley!" (128)

All the trees essential to the making of a good canoe willingly yield tribute, and the hedgehog gives his quills for decorations.

Like Beowulf, Hiawatha must perform an underwater exploit. His is killing the Sturgeon, King of Fishes, which he manages successfully with the help of a friendly squirrel. A still more involved exploit is killing Pearl-Feather, the wicked magician who sends the fiery fever. This he does in

> the greatest battle
> That the sun had ever looked on,
> That the war-birds ever witnessed.
> All a Summer's day it lasted,
> From the sunrise to the sunset. (133)

Hiawatha's wooing of Minnehaha is delayed until almost the middle of the poem, but it is described delightfully, beginning with the famous passage:

> "As unto the bow the cord is,
> So unto the man is woman;
> Though she bends him, she obeys him,
> Though she draws him, yet she follows;
> Useless each without the other!" (135)

Minnehaha is a charming heroine, and is very willing to be carried off by her strong lover:

> Over wide and rushing rivers
> In his arms he bore the maiden.
>
> .   .   .   .
>
> From the sky the moon looked at them,
> Filled the lodge with mystic splendors,
> Whispered to them, "O my children,
> Day is restless, night is quiet,
> Man imperious, woman feeble;
> Half is mine, although I follow;
> Rule by patience, Laughing Water!" (137)

At the wedding feast, they have varied entertainment provided by the merry mischief maker Pau-Puk-Keewis and the singer Chibiabos.

Another pleasing section is the "Blessing of the Cornfields." Longfellow followed Schoolcraft in having the Indians plant the corn and then work a charm on it by selecting one of the women (in the poem, it is Minnehaha, at Hiawatha's bidding) to walk naked around it in the darkness of night, " 'Covered by your tresses only, / Robed with darkness as a garment' " (143).

Tragic losses come to Hiawatha. First he loses his good friend, the sweet-singing Chibiabos, who follows the deer onto the ice of the Big-Sea-Water, which breaks beneath him, enabling the Evil Spirits to drag him down. So Hiawatha "In his wigwam sat lamenting, / Seven long weeks he sat lamenting" (147). Then the cunning "Little People," who are the only ones who know how the strong man Kwasind is vulnerable, manage to kill him. We are not told how long Hiawatha weeps for Kwasind. The greatest blow of all is the death of Minnehaha, who dies during a great famine. For her Hiawatha weeps "Seven long days and nights." Probably Longfellow and most readers did not notice that Hiawatha wept seven times as long for Chibiabos as for Minnehaha.

It is not long after the loss of Minnehaha, and with her the joyful mood of the poem, that the white men come to the Indian land in their "great canoe." Hiawatha is perceptive enough to realize that he has not been able to make his people sufficiently strong to withstand this invasion. In fact, he sees the hand of destiny in the coming of the whites, and he enjoins his own people to

> "Listen to their words of wisdom,
> Listen to the truth they tell you,
> For the Master of Life has sent them
> From the land of light and morning!" (164)

With this injunction, Hiawatha launches his birch canoe westward and takes his leave:

> Thus departed Hiawatha,
> Hiawatha the Beloved,
> In the glory of the sunset,
> In the purple mists of evening,
> To the regions of the home-wind,
> Of the Northwest-Wind, Keewaydin,
> To the Islands of the Blessed,
> To the Kingdom of Ponemah,
> To the Land of the Hereafter! (164)

Thus the leader of his people, having served them capably, takes his leave—just as King Arthur in Tennyson's "Morte d'Arthur" (1842) departs for Avalon to be healed of his grievous wound. Arthur is expected to return, and Longfellow's source intimates that Manabozho will come again; but there is no clear intimation of this in the poem. It is interesting that Longfellow, who admired Tennyson and who displayed much interest in Old and Middle English writings, never chose to use the Arthurian materials, unless in this remotely allusive way.

Hiawatha was, as has been noted, enormously popular. Dr. Holmes gave a technical explanation of part of its appeal: "The eight-syllable trochaic verse of Hiawatha, like the eight-syllable iambic verse of the Lady of the Lake and others of Scott's poems, has a fatal facility.... The recital of each line uses up the air of one natural expiration, so that we read, as we naturally do, eighteen or twenty lines in a minute without disturbing the normal rhythm of breathing."[14] But there were other reasons for its appeal including interest in an exotic land still little known to most readers and in the culture of an apparently vanishing race. Besides this, the story presents a very sympathetic cast of characters, especially the winsome heroine and the noble hero.

The furore over the poem is possibly best compared to that over the Ossianic poems in England a century earlier. Later ages seem to derive a peculiar kind of pleased excitement from discoveries that point to the existence of rather charming and accomplished personages in a much earlier time. And an element of quaintness always enhances the appeal. Too, perhaps mid-century America was ripe for a new wave of romanticization of the Indian, after the decline of the initial one centering on Cooper's Leather-Stocking Tales.

Like *Evangeline, Hiawatha* has its memorials. Children and schools were named Hiawatha; Hiawatha Avenue is a thoroughfare in Minneapolis, where the lovely Minnehaha Falls are situated. According to Higginson, "The best tribute ever paid to it ... was the actual representation of it as a drama by the Ojibway Indians on an island in Lake Huron, in August, 1901, in honor of a visit to the tribe by some of the children and grandchildren of the poet."[15] One of the most amusing testimonials to the poem's popularity was provided Longfellow by his friend Sumner, who wrote from Scotland, October 22, 1857, reporting a visit to Sir William Stirling Maxwell, famous for his fine cattle: "His cattle take the great premiums. Among them is a famous bull named Hiawatha, and a cow named Minnehaha" (*Life,* III, 55). Whether the appeal is serious or comic, *Hiawatha* promises to live as long as Arthurian romance or any other cherished body of myth and legend.

IV *New England Idyl:* The Courtship of Miles Standish

In a sense, Longfellow's *The Courtship of Miles Standish* was an extra and unexpected dividend from his investment in studies of early New England history and literature. His journal entries show that his main poetic ambition in the two years following *Hiawatha* was verse drama based on the early colonial conflicts between the Quakers and the Puritans, material which he hoped to fit into his scheme for the religious epic of which he had already written part in *The Divine Tragedy*. Eventually his *New England Tragedies* grew from this ambition, but at this time the poet found it very hard to work on them. More to his taste was the idyllic material he used in his Puritan love story of his own remote ancestors, John Alden and Priscilla Mullins.

On December 2, 1857, he wrote in his journal: "Soft as spring. I begin a new poem, 'Priscilla'; to be a kind of Puritan pastoral; the subject, the courtship of Miles Standish" (*Life*, II, 310). The next day he wrote: "My poem is in hexameters, an idyl of the Old Colony times. What it will turn out I do not know; but it gives me pleasure to write it; and that I count for something." Apparently he did not progress very rapidly at first, but by March 1 he could report: "Keep in-doors, and work on 'Priscilla,' which I think I shall call 'The Courtship of Miles Standish.'" On March 22, he recorded finishing the poem, which needs revision, "But in the main I have it as I want it." On April 23, he could record that "Miles Standish" was being printed, with its defects staring at him from the type: "It is always disagreeable when the glow of composition is over to criticise what one has been in love with. We think it is Rachel, but wake to find it Leah." By June 3, he could write to Sumner, "I have just finished a poem of some length—an idyl of the Old Colony times; a bunch of Mayflowers from the Plymouth woods." On July 10, he wrote Sumner saying the poem was "founded on the well known adventure of my maternal ancestor, John Alden," and mentioning the "well known anecdote" of Priscilla's interruption of Alden's recital of Standish's virtues. On October 16 it was published, with the original print order of ten thousand doubled and a sale of five thousand copies in Boston alone on the first day. It brought the author new compliments, but apparently the satisfaction it gave Longfellow's public was reflected more in sales than in testimonials, which had been so abundant when *Evangeline* and *Hiawatha* appeared. In any case, he was painting this time on a much smaller canvas.

Longfellow's resolution of a triangular romantic situation in the early days of the little Pilgrim Colony of Plymouth is one of his most perfectly realized poems. He found his return to the dactyllic hexameter very satisfactory for giving the mood of this early time; and the plot, apparently ready to his hand in popular tradition, gave him little difficulty. His extensive readings in colonial writings and history had provided him with the necessary saturation in the material.

The opening of the poem transports the reader immediately to the setting, and involves him in the central situation:

In the Old Colony days, in Plymouth the land of the Pilgrims,
To and fro in a room of his simple and primitive dwelling,
Clad in doublet and hose, and boots of Cordovan leather,
Strode, with a martial air, Miles Standish the Puritan Captain.
Buried in thought he seemed. . . .
Near him was seated John Alden, his friend and household
    companion,
Writing with diligent speed at a table of pine by the window;
Fair-haired, azure-eyed, with delicate Saxon complexion. (165)

The talkative Captain Standish presently brings us up to date on
his military exploits and his arrangements for keeping the Indians in
subjection, quoting a proverb or a bit of Scripture from time to time.
It soon becomes apparent, however, that he is not interrupting
"the hurrying pen of the stripling" just to make idle conversation;
he has a weighty matter on his mind, no less than a request that
the young fellow shall carry a proposal of marriage from him to the
maiden Priscilla Mullins—the very same person that Alden had just
been hymning in his letters, which were "Full of the name and the
fame of the Puritan maiden Priscilla!"

Alden naturally tries to refuse the commission, quoting back to
the Captain his adage, " 'If you would have it well done,—I am only
repeating your maxim,— / You must do it yourself, you must not
leave it to others!' " (168). But the Captain is obdurate; so Alden
proceeds with heavy heart on "The Lover's Errand." As he sets off
through the woods, he tries, Puritan-like, to find a reason why his
cherished dreams should have recoiled in this bitter manner. He
attempts to convince himself that it is because his heart is deceitful
and he cherishes "the misty phantoms of passion," so that now,

"This is the hand of the Lord; it is laid upon me in anger,
For I have followed too much the heart's desires and devices,
Worshipping Astaroth blindly, and impious idols of Baal.
This is the cross I must bear; the sin and the swift retribution."
                                                    (168-69)

Though bitter, he is not oblivious to the beauty of the New England spring. The May flowers he encounters in the woods move
him to soliloquy: " 'Puritan Flowers,' he said, 'and the type of
Puritan maidens, / Modest and simple and sweet, the very type of
Priscilla!' " (169). Wistfully he plucks some to take to her as a
parting gift.

Priscilla welcomes her visitor, and receives his flowers while he
stands speechless: "Then they sat down and talked of the birds and
the beautiful Springtime, / Talked of their friends at home, and the
Mayflower that sailed on the morrow" (170). As she describes the

beauty of Old England at this time of year and wishes herself back there, Alden sees an opening and blurts out his message:

> "Stouter hearts than a woman's have quailed in this terrible winter.
> Yours is tender and trusting, and needs a stronger to lean on;
> So I have come to you now, with an offer and proffer of marriage
> Made by a good man and true, Miles Standish the Captain of
>   Plymouth!" (170)

Priscilla may be homesick, but she is still spirited enough to resent the roundabout manner of the proposal—from the wrong man. If the Captain wants her for his wife, let him take the time and trouble to come to her and say so. When Alden tries to make out a case for the busy and doughty Captain, he is stopped in an apparently unexpected way:

> But as he warmed and glowed, in his simple and eloquent language,
> Quite forgetful of self, and full of the praise of his rival,
> Archly the maiden smiled and, with eyes overrunning with laughter,
> Said, in a tremulous voice, "Why don't you speak for yourself,
>   John?" (171)

Priscilla's natural, if perhaps coquettish, question has of course long been part of the popular parlance of America; perhaps no literary bit has been quoted more, mainly in situations quite different from the original one. Alden is too upset to answer. Instead, he rushes into the open air like a man insane. He tries, Puritan fashion, to find the hand of the Lord in the outcome of his mission; and he decides, tentatively, that it is a way of showing him that he ought to leave temptation and return to England. When he reports to the Captain, Standish is, not too surprisingly, beside himself with rage, and he calls Alden the Brutus to his Caesar. A chance circumstance helps resolve the situation. A message from hostile Indians threatens an attack, and the disciplined soldier Miles Standish immediately begins to make plans to break up the Indian expedition before it forms.

The next day Standish and his army of eight men and a friendly Indian guide march northward "to quell the sudden revolt of the savage." Meanwhile, Alden goes forward with his plans to sail on the Mayflower. After a sleepless night, he hurries to the seaside "eager to go, and thus put an end to his anguish." But when he sees Priscilla in the crowd, with a look which seems to implore him not to leave her, he wavers and presently decides to stay, for, " 'There is no land so sacred, no air so pure and so wholesome / As is the air she breathes, and the soil that is pressed by her footsteps' "

(176). So he will remain and protect her. He continues to look at the *Mayflower* until its sail vanishes. When he turns to follow the others, he finds that "Priscilla was standing beside him." After delicate word fencing, they manage a reconciliation.

The idyl continues, with Standish and his men still away and with John and Priscilla enjoying their "friendship":

> Oft when his labor was finished, with eager feet would the dreamer
> Follow the pathway that ran through the woods to the house of Priscilla
> Led by illusions romantic and subtle deceptions of fancy,
> Pleasure disguised as duty, and love in the semblance of friendship.
>
> (181)

As she plies her spinning wheel, he is reminded of the virtuous woman described in the Proverbs and also of "beautiful Bertha, the spinner, the queen of Helvetia." In the midst of this happy scene, with John holding the skein of yarn while Priscilla winds it for knitting, a messenger enters to announce the death of Miles Standish in Indian warfare.

With this obstruction to love's fulfillment removed, John and Priscilla make plans to be married. On their wedding day, an un-invited guest appears—Standish, of course, who has not been killed after all—but he proves not unwelcome; for he promptly gives them his blessing, reciting another adage in explanation: "No man can gather cherries in Kent at the season of Christmas." So they are married, and Alden proudly transports his bride to her new home on his snow-white bull, Raghorn, his proudest possession:

> Gayly, with joyous laugh, Priscilla mounted her palfrey. . . .
> Like a picture it seemed of the primitive, pastoral ages,
> Fresh with the youth of the world, and recalling Rebecca and Isaac,
> Old and yet ever new, and simple and beautiful always,
> Love immortal and young in the endless succession of lovers.
> So through the Plymouth woods passed onward the bridal procession.
>
> (184)

On November 3, 1858, two weeks after the poem was published, Longfellow noted: "I give a dinner to Ticknor and Fields, the publishers, in honor of the success of Miles Standish" (*Life*, II, 327). But no other entries on it follow, at least in the *Life*. Though pleasantly excited about its success, Longfellow apparently considered it something of a *jeu d'esprit,* and was soon busy on other projects for which he had greater ambitions. But the idyl has passed into the cultural heritage of America.

V *Framework Narrative:* Tales of a Wayside Inn

After the brilliant popular successes of *Hiawatha* and *The Courtship of Miles Standish* in his first three years of full-time writing, Longfellow must have been a little disappointed in his production during the three years before the loss of his wife interrupted his writing. Probably the gathering of the Civil War clouds worried him more than is generally recognized. There are numerous references to the events of these politically troubled year; however, his writing did not wholly stop.

The next major project, *Tales of a Wayside Inn*, was to prove another popular one. Obviously indebted to Chaucer's *Canterbury Tales*, it originated in much the same way. That is, Longfellow wrote a number of the poems separately and apparently with no thought of assembling them into a collection. Also, his "The Saga of King Olaf," like Chaucer's "The Knight's Tale," is so long that it unbalances the collection. Many of the poems were published in magazines before they were collected for a volume.[16]

Apparently he worked first on "The Saga of King Olaf." His birthdays seem to have been especially good occasions for producing ideas for literary works. On his fifty-second (February 25, 1859), he noted in his journal: "The thought struck me this morning, that a very good poem might be written on the Saga of King Olaf, who converted the North to Christianity" (*Life*, II, 332). On November 30 he noted that he had completed " 'The Saga of King Olaf,' in a series of lyrics." "Paul Revere's Ride," the opening story of the published *Tales*, was written in 1860. The work was far enough along before Mrs. Longfellow's death in mid-1861 to permit the first part, despite this interruption, to be published in late 1863. The other two parts followed in 1872 and 1873 as portions of volumes of new poems.

Contrary to his usual practice of relying solely on written sources and his imagination, he drove on October 31, 1862, with Fields to the old Red Horse Tavern in Sudbury, about twenty miles from Cambridge, for local color. They found "A rambling, tumble-down old building, two hundred years old; and till now in the family of the Howes, who have kept an inn for one hundred and seventy-five years. In the old time, it was a house of call for all travellers from Boston westward" (*Life*, II, 388). By November 11, he could report to Fields that "The Sudbury Tales go on famously." On August 25, 1863, he wrote Fields that it had been a mistake to change the title and asked to revert to "The Wayside Inn."

Although there is evidence that Longfellow had Chaucer's *Canterbury Tales* in mind, his scheme is closer to Boccaccio's in the *Decameron* than to Chaucer's. Longfellow has assembled in an inn a small but varied group of characters who tell stories for their mutual amusement. Longfellow was well acquainted with Sudbury, and several of the originals of his characters spent their summers at the Red Horse Inn (*Poems*, 204; Higginson, 215). Longfellow himself identified the originals of two of his characters, and the others have also been identified: "The poet is T. W. Parsons, the translator of Dante; the Sicilian, Luigi Monti, whose name occurs often in Mr. Longfellow's *Life* as a familiar friend; the theologian, Professor Daniel Treadwell, a physicist of genius who had also a turn for theology; the student, Henry Ware Wales, a scholar of promise" (*Poems*, 204). Those identified by Longfellow are Ole Bull, the famous Norwegian violinist who became the poet's good friend; and the Spanish Jew, Israel Edrehi, whom Longfellow also knew personally (204). The Landlord was Longfellow's own creation, but he is in the tradition of the Howe family which operated the Inn.

Like Chaucer, Longfellow wrote a prologue (which he calls "Prelude") to introduce the characters. It is not in pentameter couplets, however, but in the faster-moving iambic tetrameter. Longfellow's descriptions are good, if not as memorable as Chaucer's. After this introduction, the Landlord's tale of "Paul Revere's Ride" gets the fireside entertainment off to a promising start. Longfellow's narrative has been shown to be historically inaccurate, but his lively ballad has proved, despite criticisms of it, to have a lasting appeal to American patriotism: "through the gloom and the light, / The fate of a nation was riding that night."

After an interlude in which Longfellow's sense of humor flashes in his comment on the Landlord's view of history—"those who had been longest dead / Were always greatest in his eyes"—the Student retells a tale from Boccaccio as "The Falcon of Ser Federigo." Monna Giovanna, an attractive young widow, has a son who admires Ser Federigo's falcon. When the boy falls ill, the lady goes to Ser Federigo to ask for the falcon. Before she reveals her mission, Federigo, wanting to show hospitality and having no other way, has the falcon cooked for the meat dish of a feast—the sort of story twist later to be made famous by O. Henry. But not all is lost in Love's sacrifice. The child dies, but after a period of grief Monna Giovanna becomes the beautiful bride of Ser Federigo.

The Sicilian's tale of "King Robert of Sicily," retold by Longfellow from the medieval *Gesta Romanorum*, was destined to become a great favorite. It is a verse sermon on the text: "Pride goeth before destruction and an haughty spirit before a fall." The arrogant King Robert falls asleep in a cathedral. He is found there in the night by a sexton who disbelieves his identity, and he is unable to win back his kingship until thoroughly humbled. The poem contains the famous line, adapted from St. Paul's Espistle to the Hebrews, "He entertained the Angel unawares," and its story is told with a simple charm which is quite effective.

Longfellow has the Musician relate "The Saga of King Olaf," a poem in twenty-two parts. The poet had been intrigued by Scandinavian culture ever since his visit to Sweden and Denmark in 1831, and the story of King Olaf, the eleventh-century Norwegian king who according to tradition converted the Northland to Christianity by force, especially appealed to him. The poem opens with the war god Thor proclaiming, "Force rules the world still," and challenging the Galilean. After the introduction of much Norse mythology and scenes of more violence than Longfellow ordinarily portrayed, it ends with Olaf dead and the voice of Saint John:

> Stronger than steel
> Is the sword of the Spirit;
> Swifter than arrows
> The light of the truth is,
> Greater than anger
> Is love, and subdueth![17] (235)

In the "Interlude" the Theologian thanks God that, "The reign of violence is dead / Or dying surely from the world." It is ironic that Longfellow wrote this line on the very eve of the Civil War.

The Theologian then proceeds to tell the grim story of Torquemada and the Spanish Inquisition as a further illustration of the perversions to which the spread of Christianity has been subject. This is followed by the Poet's delightful tale of "The Birds of Killingworth," based on a legend of the old English town of Kenilworth. The citizens decide to destroy the birds of the town as useless nuisances, but they miss their songs and are overrun by insects. This lighter tale, offsetting the grim ones of the misdeeds of Christianity, brings the first day's tale telling to a close. The guests retire, and the Landlord rakes the embers of the fire as "Far off the village clock struck one."

After a second Prelude, the Sicilian resumes the tale telling with "The Bell of Atri"—the bell representing the claim of every creature, beast as well as man, to justice. The second day's narratives are less remarkable than the first's, but they include the Poet's tale of "Lady Wentworth," in which humble Martha Hilton, twenty years old, weds the governor of the province on his sixtieth birthday—in defiance of Chaucer and others who have thought little of December-May marriages. Another, the Theologian's tale of "The Legend Beautiful," shows Longfellow's continuing interest in Catholic religious practices. Still another, the Student's tale of "The Baron of St. Castine," is a characteristic Longfellowian minor idyl, containing such lines as "For man is fire and woman is tow, / And the Somebody comes and begins to blow," and "No day is so long / But it comes at last to vesper-song."

Part Three also has its Prelude, interesting partly for the phrase E. A. Robinson used for an early volume of poems—"Children of the Night." Remarkable in this final part is the Student's tale of "Emma and Eginhard." Longfellow goes back to the age of Charlemagne when Eginhard, "a youth of Frankish race, / Whose face was bright with flashes that forerun / The splendors of a yet unrisen sun," studied the Trivium, with other promising young men, as higher education. But Eginhard takes time from studying to win the heart of the Princess Emma and often visits her in her tower at night. They are happy and undetected until a snowy night when Eginhard's returning footprints would be incriminating. But Emma, no slender maiden apparently, is equal to that! She carries her lover homeward through the snow and retraces her footsteps. The emperor has been a witness, however, and recognizes his daughter. But he is sympathetic with the young lovers, and the poem ends pleasantly with a description of what must have been one of the happiest of shotgun weddings. The emperor places his daughter's white hand in Eginhard's and says,

> "My son,
> This is the gift thy constant zeal has won;
> Thus I repay the royal debt I owe,
> And cover up the footprints in the snow."

It is significant that Longfellow made no attempt to emasculate this robust legendary story.

The Sicilian's tale of "The Monk of Casal-Maggiore" is another instance of Longfellow's delight in retelling medieval legends—and in modern versions worthy of the old. This one is based on "the deadly sin of gluttony." A gluttonous Brother Timothy seeks to hide his vice by claiming to have been turned from a donkey into a man. The new identification gets established so well that when a real donkey dies, he is lamented as Brother Timothy, relapsed into his old vice. As Longfellow tells it, the tale is amusing.

There are several additional tales, but none that seem to invite comment. With the third day's story telling concluded, Longfellow supplies a short Finale, in which the portly Landlord bids his parting guests "Farewell!" and the poet, apparently writing considerably later, calls the roll of the guests, of whom "Two are beyond the salt sea waves, / And three already in their graves." But perhaps those still living, and presumably many other readers, will want to look

> Into the pages of this book
> And see the days of long ago
> Floating and fleeting to and fro.

Although Longfellow's framework for *Tales of a Wayside Inn* was not to prove especially convincing, it did help unify a large body of very diverse material. This fact, combined with competent versification in a variety of meters and a generally pleasing tone, serves to explain, at least in part, why this collection of verse tales was destined to become one of Longfellow's most popular works.

VI *Verse Drama*

Apparently Longfellow made little effort to write prose drama, but he was more seriously interested in verse drama than has generally been recognized. While still at Bowdoin, he considered writing a drama on the Haitian hero Toussaint l'Ouverture "that thus I may do something in my humble way for the great cause of Negro emancipation" (*Life*, I, 424). Nothing came of this, but it was not long before he was entertaining other ideas for dramatic treatment. Longfellow had a wide-ranging interest in all the literary forms; hence his interest in the drama is not particularly surprising, especially since much of the foreign-language literature he studied was in this form. In time he had to recognize that, like Tennyson, whom he so much resembled, he did not have much dramatic ability. Also, he was writing in an unproductive period of the American drama. The chief stage fare in the mid-1800's was the melodramas played by Edwin Forrest and others, and little solid achievement was made until after Longfellow's death. Whether Longfellow could have done better in an age more conducive to playwriting is conjectural, but none of his attempts show a strong flair for the stage.

The earliest of his plays to be completed was *The Spanish Student*, a drama deriving in part from Cervantes' *La Titanilla* and Thomas Middleton's *The Spanish Gypsy* (*Poems*, 23). He seems to have begun work on this about the time *Hyperion* and *Voices of the Night* were published. On December 20, 1840, in a letter to his grandfather, after mentioning "The Wreck of the Hesperus," he wrote: "I have also written a much longer and more difficult poem, called 'The Spanish Student,'—a drama in five acts; on the success of which I rely with some self-complacency. But this is a great secret, and must not go beyond the immediate family circle; as I do not intend to publish it until the glow of composition has passed away, and I can look upon it coolly and critically. I will tell you more of this by and by" (*Life*, I, 367).

Longfellow was probably inspired to write the play, whose heroine is a Spanish gypsy dancing girl, by his interest in Fanny Ellsler, the famous dancer whose performances in Boston had greatly impressed him (Thompson, 317ff.). He thought her artistic, but the Yankee in him was also impressed by her monetary success. He wrote to his father on October 4, 1840: "We have nothing new here, save Fanny Ellsler the dancing girl, who is a beauty, and an admirable dancer. She has excited great enthusiasm among the Bostonians. Her Spanish dances are exquisite; and remind me strongly of days gone by. She has five hundred dollars a night; consequently makes with her heels in one week just what I made with my head in one year" (319). The success of his fellow native of Portland, N. P. Willis, with plays could have been an added inducement; while he was working on his play, Longfellow wrote to Greene: "Nat Willis . . . says he has made ten thousand dollars the last year by his writings. I wish I had made ten hundred" (323). But the mixed feelings about the play which he had expressed in the letter to his father continued; and, when he left for Europe in 1842, it still had not been published. While he was abroad, it appeared serially in *Graham's Magazine* and in 1843 as a book. It was considered mildly scandalous, but it had only a moderate success.

It is not hard to see why. Longfellow managed his blank verse smoothly, as always, and the central character—the student Victorian and the dancer Preciosa—have some vitality. But the Count of Lara is a stock roué, and Preciosa's supposed gypsy father and her gypsy lover, rival of Victorian, are also stock characters. Very much in love, Victorian and Preciosa meet nightly, but chastely, in her Juliet bower. Don Carlos and the Count debate the dancer's chastity. Some lines from their debate are interesting for what they reveal of the lonely author-widower's thoughts:

Count Lara: would you persuade me
    That a mere dancing-girl, who shows herself
    Nightly, half naked, on the stage, for money,
    And with voluptuous motions fires the blood
    Of inconsiderate youth, is to be held
    A model for her virtue? (24)

Don Carlos: I believe
   That woman, in her deepest degradation,
   Holds something sacred, something undefiled,
   Some pledge and keepsake of her higher nature,
   And, like the diamond in the dark, retains
   Some quenchless gleam of the celestial light. (25)

Count Lara sets about to prove by seducing her that his low opinion of Preciosa is justified. He is not successful, but he does manage to taint her good name and to make Victorian so suspicious that he abandons her. There is a measure of suspense when her supposed gypsy father tries at this juncture to force her to accept her returned gypsy lover. But she continues loyal to Victorian, and finding that he has been tricked into suspecting her, he returns to her. To make everything perfect, Longfellow has Preciosa discover that her actual father is a wealthy nobleman who is seeking her and is about to be reunited with her. She had been stolen away by gypsies; so she is not a gypsy at all. Also, her unwanted gypsy suitor is killed in a mêlée at the end, so the Spanish student and his dancing bride are bound to live happily ever after.

Longfellow creates some excitement, and there is interest in the trial of the gypsy and her dance, by a cardinal and an archbishop of the church (who applaud the dance as not vice but art). But, on the whole, the play is much too facile and saccharine for modern taste and was apparently somewhat so even for Longfellow's time. He had hopes of its being staged, and it was performed in German at a theater in Dessau in 1855 (*Poems*, 23), but no American producer was ever interested. Despite its lack of stage success, however, Longfellow must have derived some satisfaction from the continuing demand for it as a poem. By 1857 it had sold over 38,000 copies, which left it still leading the somewhat more recent but more famous *Evangeline* (*Life*, II, 295).

In 1841, Longfellow made only a single entry in his journal, but, as his brother says, it was a highly significant one. On November 8 he wrote: "This evening it has come into my mind to undertake a long and elaborate poem by the holy name of CHRIST; the theme of which would be the various aspects of Christendom in the Apostolic, Middle, and Modern Ages" (*Life*, I, 388-89). Whether or not he had a drama in mind at this time is not certain. An examination of the pattern of his life and writing at this period makes it seem logical that he would turn to a major poetic work of a religious nature; since he was fresh from attempting drama in *The Spanish Student*, a play or series of plays would be natural.

The years 1839-43 were the most crucial of Longfellow's entire life. At the beginning of this period, it seemed very doubtful that he would have a substantial literary career at all, despite his early aspirations; by the time of his second marriage in 1843, it was certain that he *would* have a literary career, but its nature was still not clear. He wrote little in 1840 except *The Spanish Student*. The next year, still fighting depression because of his personal life, he was much preoccupied with somber and religious subjects: "The Rainy Day," "God's Acre," "Blind Bartimeus" (Blind Bartimeus has a section in *The Divine Tragedy*), and his translation of Tegnér's *The Children of the Lord's Supper*. His near breakdown in health and his final European residence followed the next year. While at Marienburg, he wrote little, but that he was still thinking of his long poem is shown by an entry in his notebook:

> CHRISTUS, a dramatic poem, in three parts:
> Part First. The Times of Christ. (Hope.)
> Part Second. The Middle Ages. (Faith.)
> Part Third. The Present. (Charity.) (*Life,* I, 403)

The only poem he completed while at Marienburg seems to have been the sonnet "Mezzo Cammin," with its reference to the "tower of song with lofty parapet" which he had wanted to build but had not achieved by middle life. The quoted entries from the 1841 journal and the Marienburg notebook comprise the first reasonably clear picture he had of the tower he wanted to build. Nearly all the rest of his life he kept returning to this "lofty" project; he wrote a great deal of verse for it, but never really succeeded in building a tower that satisfied either himself or his readers. This was the great failure in his otherwise largely successful life.

In 1843 he began his translation of Dante's *Divine Comedy*, possibly in part to ready himself for writing his own religious epic. He worked assiduously on this project for a time, but presently put it aside, apparently to get time and energy for new writing. On February 2, 1846, he recorded that "F[anny] read to me Browning's Blot on the 'Scutcheon; a play of great power and beauty.... He is an extraordinary genius, Browning, with dramatic power of the first order" (*Life,* II, 65). Longfellow must have been thinking still of his own dramatic project, but soon he was working instead on *Evangeline*. By March 16, 1848, however, he was contemplating drama again—not, however, religious drama but a "dramatic romance" on the age of Louis XIV, but "F evidently does not think very well of the plan" (110). Because of her lack of enthusiasm, or for other reasons, he did not complete this then or ever. His next major project was the novel *Kavanagh*. With it published, he confided to his journal on November 19, 1849. "And now I long to try a loftier strain, the sublimer Song whose broken melodies have for so many years breathed through my soul in the better hours of life, and which I trust and believe will ere long unite themselves into a symphony not all unworthy the sublime theme, but furnishing 'some equivalent expression for the trouble and wrath of life, for its sorrow and its mystery'" (*Life*, II, 151-52).

Finally, he managed to settle down on the middle part of the project, which he completed and published in 1851 as *The Golden Legend*. This section won considerable praise and popularity, but he could not go on, although he tried. First he was distracted by his Harvard resignation and then by the writing and publication of *Hiawatha*. When he tried to return to it, he got as far as a rough draft of *Wenlock Christison*, his original title for the first of *The New England Tragedies*. This time he was interrupted by writing *The Courtship of Miles Standish*, which he drafted first as a drama, then by work on *Tales of a Wayside Inn*, the death of his wife, and the translation of Dante. So it was not until 1868 that *The New England Tragedies*, which were intended to serve as the final part of the epic, were published.

With this part completed, he was able to tackle the first. Early in 1871 he wrote: "The subject of The Divine Tragedy has taken entire possession of me, so that I can think of nothing else" (*Life*, II, 456-57). He completed it in a few weeks, but when it went to press he began to have misgivings: "I never had so many doubts and hesitations about any book as about this." It was published in December, 1871, and the three parts together appeared as *Christus: A Mystery* in 1872. Shortly after *The Divine Tragedy* was published, he wrote to Greene: "The Divine Tragedy is very successful, from the bookseller's point of view. . . . That is very pleasant, but that is not the main thing. The only question about a book ought to be whether it is successful in itself" (*Life*, III, 176-77). Obviously he had his misgivings. He had contemplated at one time writing still another drama, on the Moravians, "to harmonize the discord of the New England Tragedies, and thus give a not unfitting close to the work" (*Life*, II, 458). He never did this, realizing perhaps that it was beyond his power to achieve the integration in this work that Dante and Milton had wrought in theirs. Certainly, although it was logical to end his drama in modern times and in America, his *New England Tragedies* do not serve to bring the work to a climactic conclusion.

More because it occupied so central a place in Longfellow's poetic intentions than because it had intrinsic merit, the *Christus* calls for a somewhat detailed analysis. The three parts will be considered in the order of subject matter rather than of composition.

An "Introitus" presents an angel bearing the Prophet Habakkuk through the air, for his charity to the needy and his battle for truth make him a fitting person to witness "The coming of its Redeemer" to a bewildered world. Part I, *The Divine Tragedy*, meant to symbolize Hope, is essentially the coming of the Messiah, largely drawn from the Four Gospels and written in verse of irregular length. Lucifer is also introduced, but he is a pale character beside Milton's Satan; there are also one Manahem, an Essenian; and Helen of Tyre, consort of Simon the Magician. Christus himself plays much the same role as Jesus of Nazareth in the Gospels. A section is devoted to Mary Magdalene and another to Simon the Pharisee. The ending of the tragedy closely follows the Bible. After The Resurrection, Longfellow uses the Apostles' Creed as epilogue. The play reads easily, and Longfellow displays considerable imagination in working with the scriptural materials; but he does not manage to produce either dramatic intensity or highly imaginative poetry.

An "Interlude" shows the Abbot Joachim in his convent reflecting that strength lies in faith, hope, and charity; that Hate is death; and that Love is life. Part II, *The Golden Legend*, symbolizing Faith, has greater novelty, introducing as it does subject matter from the thirteenth century, with a German and Italian setting. As early as 1839, Longfellow had been intrigued by the story of *Der Armer Heinrich* (Poor Henry), written by a twelfth-century German minnesinger, Hartmann von der Aue (*Poems*, 361). He used for the nucleus of his plot the saving of the life of the leprosy-stricken Henry by faith expressed in the voluntary blood sacrifice of a pure maiden. He changed the leprosy to a mysterious illness without a name and the heroine from eight years old to a more romantic fifteen. Also, he added Lucifer, probably borrowed from Goethe's *Faust*, though he has little in common with Mephistopheles. Henry tells Lucifer that he cannot be cured because the only possible remedy is unavailable, and he has Lucifer read from the mystic scroll containing the prescription:

> "The only remedy that remains
> Is the blood that flows from a maiden's veins,
> Who of her own free will shall die,
> And give her life as the price of yours!" (411)

Lucifer agrees with Henry that such a cure is not likely to be available; he offers instead his own nostrum, which Henry refuses.

Presently the peasant girl Elsie finds Henry reading in the fields and offers flowers to him, lamenting that they will fade. He replies gallantly:

> Themselves will fade,
> But not their memory,
> And memory has the power
> To re-create them from the dust. (417)

Learning from her parents of Henry's plight, Elsie volunteers her life to save his. They set out from the region of the Castle of Vautsburg on the Rhine for Salerno, where the healing is to take place. The situation gives Longfellow the opportunity to present another sentimental journey, very different from that in *Evangeline;* for here his man and maiden are together, he guiding her on the physical journey, she as the stronger character eventually showing him the spiritual light. There is much material about medieval church practices, good and bad, but they finally arrive in Salerno, where Henry is saved, not by Elsie's blood, though she still offers it, but by her faith and the touch of St. Matthew's sacred bones. The play combines the exotic flavor of life in the Middle Ages with religious interest skillfully enough to account for much of the appeal the poem had for nineteenth-century readers, but no one has ever maintained that Longfellow succeeded in making his material highly dramatic.

A second "Interlude" centers in Martin Luther, appropriately enough since the Quakers and the New England Puritans, central in the final part of the *Christus,* were children of the Protestant Reformation. Erasmus and Melanchthon are introduced too but, oddly, not John Calvin.

The first of the two *New England Tragedies* has its own name of *John Endicott.* Longfellow had first called it *Wenlock Christison,* after a Quaker character in it, but he probably thought the historical name would have more appeal. The play focuses on the early New England Quaker persecutions. Longfellow seeks to add interest by inventing a love affair between Governor Endicott's son and Edith, daughter of Wenlock Christison. Young John Endicott speaks sententiously but pertinently of the spirit of persecution in New England:

> A word that has been said may be unsaid;
> It is but air. But when a deed is done
> It cannot be undone, nor can our thoughts
> Reach out to all the mischiefs that may follow. (471)

In its context such a speech is moderately effective, but somehow the blank verse in which Longfellow wrote this tragedy is disappointing. It is pleasingly rhythmical, but usually the content is too obvious; it never fully achieves the tension needed for strong dramatic effect. Although Longfellow called this piece a tragedy, the appropriateness of the classification is doubtful. Young John Endicott and Edith Christison are both still alive at the end, and there is no remaining obstacle to their love. Governor Endicott is dead, and Lieutenant Governor Bellingham says, "Only the acrid spirit of the times / Corroded this true steel" (495). The plain truth seems to be that Longfellow was too religious at heart and too sympathetic with all his characters to be able to write convincing tragedy.

Giles Corey of the Salem Farms, the second of the *New England Tragedies,* is, logically enough, a dramatization of the Salem witchcraft hysteria. Most of the characters are historical: the accused Giles Corey, Judge John Hathorne, and Cotton Mather. Longfellow had been familiar from early life with some of Cotton Mather's works, including the famous *Magnalia.* On November 27, 1839, he speculated in his journal about his next literary work: "Shall it be two volumes more of Hyperion? or a drama on Cotton Mather? . . . or a drama on the old poetic legend of *Der Armer Heinrich?*" (*Life,* I, 334). He was never able to write a drama around Mather, but he did make use of his colonial studies in the two plays on the Quakers and on witchcraft. Longfellow makes Mather more central in his witchcraft play than history warrants; he has the famous colonial minister say:

> I am persuaded there are few affairs
> In which the Devil doth not interfere.
> We cannot undertake a journey even,
> But Satan will be there to meddle with it
> By hindering or by furthering. (496)

>   The spiritual world
> Lies all about us, and its avenues
> Are open to the unseen feet of phantoms
> That come and go, and we perceive them not. (498)

Both Mather and Hathorne are stern logicians. Hathorne says:

> 'T is not the part of wisdom to delay
> In things where not to do is still to do
> A deed more fatal than the deed we shrink from. (499)

A clock strikes, and Mather says:

> I never hear the striking of a clock
> Without a warning and an admonition
> That time is on the wing, and we must quicken
> Our tardy pace in journeying Heaven-ward,
> As Israel did in journeying Canaan-ward! (499)

Giles Corey, who here, as historically, is tortured to death, is also presented as superstitious. He is happy in his harvest, but still dreads Satan's menace:

> But Satan still goes up and down the earth;
> And to protect this house from his assaults,
> And keep the powers of darkness from my door,
> This horseshoe will I nail upon the threshold. (501)

His wife Martha tries to talk him out of his belief in witchcraft, but she is unsuccessful and in time is herself accused. Longfellow was compelled by his sources to have this play end tragically in the deaths of Giles and Martha Corey, but even here he does not achieve the tension of great tragedy. The modern playwright Arthur Miller has done better with the same materials in *The Crucible*. Mather is given the closing speech of the play, a recantation not fully warranted by historical accounts of his role:

> Those who lie buried in the Potter's Field
> Will rise again, as surely as ourselves
> That sleep in honored graves with epitaphs;
> And this poor man, whom we have made a victim,
> Hereafter will be counted as a martyr! (522)

A "Finale" finds Saint John wandering over the face of the earth, reflecting on the fate of mankind:

> Lo, here! lo, there, the Church!
> Poor, sad Humanity
> Through all the dust and heat
> Turns back with bleeding feet,
> By the weary road it came,
> Unto the simple thought
> By the great Master taught,
> And that remaineth still:
> Not he that repeateth the name,
> But he that doeth the will! (522)

Longfellow knew that he had been at best only partly successful in writing a religious epic—his "tower of song with lofty parapet." He had testified to his own faith in the Christian religion, despite its failures and defeats, but he had pointed no clear road toward making it more effective. His *Christus* seems rather thin and disorganized in comparison with the epic works of Dante, Milton, and Goethe, perhaps because he could not really imagine the power of evil in human living; the result is that his testimonials to goodness are lacking in strong contrast, hence unconvincing. He seems never to have been quite convinced that Satan came to America with the colonists, though he examined considerable evidence that Satan did. Religious epic material has always seemed especially difficult for American poets, from Timothy Dwight through Longfellow and William Vaughn Moody to Robert Frost and Archibald MacLeish.

In 1872, the year the *Christus* appeared, Longfellow published as part of *Three Books of Song* a short play in five acts, *Judas Maccabaeus*. He notes in his journal that he had thought about this subject as early as 1850, but he apparently did not settle down to work on it until he had finished the *Christus*. Dealing as it does with a time shortly before the coming of Christ, it is related to *The Divine Tragedy*. Longfellow evidently intended it as a treatment of Hebraism and Hellenism, but he says little about the work in journal or letters and must have known that it was not a successful undertaking.

A more important dramatic work was *Michael Angelo: A Fragment;* found in his desk after his death, it was published in 1883. Of this poem, one of his longest although called a fragment, Scudder says: "Longfellow, in building this poem and reflecting upon its theme during the last ten years of his life, was more distinctly declaring his artistic creed than in any other of his works" (*Poems*, xx). It has a tone of somber serenity, contains some of his wisest observations on art and life, and much of it is written in his best blank verse. Although the great artist Michael Angelo is the central character, Longfellow places him in a full company, including his friend the woman poet Vittoria Colonno, the young and brillant sculptor Benvenuto Cellini, the beauty Julia Gonzaga, and various representatives of the church. Michael Angelo is portrayed as a talented and devoted artist who must work in his own way, whether or not he and others are satisfied. The poem is one of Longfellow's most quotable.

> Art is the gift of God, and must be used
> Unto His glory. That in art is highest
> Which aims at this. (543)

> We ourselves,
> When we commit a sin, lose Paradise,
> As much as he did. (549)

> The men that women marry
> And why they marry them, will always be
> A marvel and a mystery to the world. (554)

> The fever to accomplish some great work
> That will not let us sleep. I must go on
> Until I die. (557)

> Alas! how little
> Of all I dreamed of has my hand achieved! (558)

> Death is the chillness that precedes the dawn;
> We shudder for a moment, then awake
> In the broad sunshine of the other life. (568)

> All great achievements are the natural fruits
> Of a great character. (574)

> When anything is done
> People see not the patient doing of it,
> Nor think how great would be the loss to man
> If it had not been done. (578)

> Sometimes I think
> The happiness of man lies in pursuing,
> Not in possessing. (584)

It could be interesting to compare some of Longfellow's thoughts and phrasings with those of Browning, who was also drawing from the well of Renaissance art for inspiration at about the same time.

VII *Translations*

The translation of foreign literature, especially poetry, was very important to Longfellow, and through his own translations he made a considerable contribution to cultural interchange. The quality of his translations has been less controversial than that of his original writings. In his own time, they were highly regarded by such American authorities as C. E. Norton of Harvard and by such critics as the German poet-scholar Freiligrath. Nearly a century after its completion, his translation of Dante remains one of the standard versions.

A noticeably large part of Longfellow's writing consisted of translations. He began extensive translating to provide materials for his college students at a time when few translations from modern foreign languages were available. He soon developed a deep interest in this activity, and over the course of his life probably had two main reasons for devoting so much time to it: (1) to bring to the attention of his fellow Americans something of the culture of their various ancestor nations; (2) to seek inspiration and models for his own literary compositions. H. E. Scudder's statement is significant: "translating played an important part in the development of Mr. Longfellow's powers. Before he had begun to write those poems which at once attested his poetic calling, and while he was busying himself with study and prose expression, he was finding an outlet for his metrical thoughts and emotion in the translation of lyrics and pastoral verse, and occasionally of epic and dramatic fragments" (*Poems,* 586).

He formed and stated his theory of translation very early in the Preface to his translation of *The Coplas de Don Jorge Manrique,* published in 1833 while he was at Bowdoin (*Works,* II, 406-7). Here he says that "The great art of translating well lies in the power of rendering literally the works of a foreign author, while at the same time we preserve the spirit of the original," and he tries to explain how the two requirements can be met simultaneously. He recognizes that it may be necessary to depart somewhat from the literal rendition of words and phrases to do justice to the foreign author's intent, just as the sculptor departs from life to present a true picture of it. It is apparent that Longfellow, even at this early stage in his career as a distinguished translator, had given considerable thought to the rationale of translation. When he was teaching Dante at Harvard and had begun to think of translating, he wrote a lengthy essay on Dante, which included the statement: "We are to consider the Divine Poem as the mirror of the age in which its author lived; or, rather, perhaps, as a mirror of Italy in that age" (*Works,* X, 58). He was always anxious to transmit the national culture, as well as the sense, of a foreign literary work.

At the same time, he recognized the limitations of translation; it could give a reader part, but not all, of the quality of the original. The most desirable result was to encourage him to learn to read the original. This is indicated in the ending of one of Longfellow's later poems, printed by Scudder as the Prelude to his translations:

> I have but marked the place,
> But half the secret told,
> That, following this slight trace,
> Others may find the gold. (*Poems,* 587)

The scope of his translations is indeed impressive: "The list includes thirty-five versions of whole books or detached poems in German, twelve in Italian, nine each in French and Dutch, seven in Swedish, six in Danish, five in Polish, three in Portuguese, two each in Spanish, Russian, Hungarian, and Bohemian, with single translations in Latin, Hebrew, Chinese, Sanskrit, Marath, and Judea-German—yielding one hundred versions altogether, extending into eighteen languages, apart from the original English."[18]

Examination of Scudder's chronological listing of the dates of compositions of his poems shows that for many years Longfellow's translations outranked in number and bulk his original poems, and that during his years at Bowdoin and his first years at Harvard he translated very extensively into verse while writing almost nothing original. The proportion of translation to original work decreased later, but it continued large. Translated poems figure importantly in *Outre-Mer* and in *Hyperion,* and he did extensive translating for his anthology *The Poets and Poetry of Europe.* After the death of his second wife, translation again became his central preoccupation for several years—with the famous blank-verse rendition of Dante's *Divine Comedy.* Even in the year of his death he was still translating; the list of writings for 1882 includes four translations. He liked to translate, and his translations were important both in themselves and for their influence on his original poetry.

VIII *Fragments and Gestures*

Longfellow's early desire to become "eminent in literature," combined with his later opportunities as multilingual college professor and translator, made him not only a versatile published author but also a writer extraordinarily fecund in projects begun and broken off or merely contemplated. Had he managed to complete his unwritten works, he might have become even more famous for them than for those he actually published. An attempt will be made here to give some idea of what he jotted down in his "Book of Suggestions."[19]

Apparently Longfellow completed most of his short poems, but much smaller portions of the drama, both prose and poetry, and the prose narratives. Thus the image we have of him as a literary figure is, in relation to his ambitions and intentions, skewed toward lyric poetry. In 1838, he and Hawthorne were planning to collaborate on a volume of fairy tales, *The Boy's Wonder Horn.* The next year he was contemplating a farce on the then new railroad, to be entitled, *Jabez Doolittle, or the First Locomotive.* We know that two years later he actually wrote and published a drama, *The Spanish Student.* For some time after this, many of his ideas were dramatic: plays featuring La Rochefoucauld, Alfieri, Sebastian Bach, Machiavelli, Louis XIV, Mazarin, and Swift's Stella and Vanessa. American materials included *The Mormon Elder,* a tragedy; and *Eliza Wharton, A Tragedy in Prose,* on the story previously novelized by Hannah Webster Foster. He also considered dramatizing Hawthorne's "The Birthmark" and other Hawthorne short stories. His most ambitious idea, however, was an elaborate drama on Fairyland, with parts on The Elixir of Life, Witchcraft and The Slave.

Unfinished prose projects included a romance about Tycho Brahe, a supplement on Fouqué's *Undine,* and some stories for children. Also, late in life, had his health permitted, he would have written his friend Sumner's biography. There were also unwritten poetic tales, most notably a series conceived by 1846, long before *Tales of a Wayside Inn.* This was to be "Poetic Tales, Told by Emigrants Crossing the Rocky Mountains. A kind of American Canterbury Tales." Tales originally listed included "The Indian's Tale," "The Trapper's Tale," "The Voyager's Tale," and "The Bois Boulé's Tale." He later added "The Starved Camp," doubtless after reading about the fate of the Donner Party in the same year. He was also an editor of some consequence, especially of *Poets and Poetry of Europe* in two editions and of the thirty-one-volume *Poems of Places.* Additional editorial projects included an anthology of lyrics of the sea, on which he was anticipated by someone else, and a collection of ghost stories.

It is apparent that Longfellow regarded literature as a house with many windows. It was not altogether his own choice that he looked most successfully through the windows of poetry, especially lyric, and that the world has tended to suppose that he was interested in no others. A versatile writer in accomplishment, he was far more versatile in interest and intention. Even so, he must have been more contented in late life with the "tower of song" he had built than he had been in mid-life with such foundations as he had managed to construct up to that time.

CHAPTER 9

Longfellow in Literary History
and in Literature

I *Longfellow's America and Ours*

IT HAS NOW BEEN more than a century and a half since Longfellow was born and over eighty years since his death. Although a modern writer if we consider the total history of literature, he lived in an age so different from ours and wrote for an audience so unlike present-day readers that it is impossible in the 1960's to imagine his situation clearly. And to understand an author, we need to understand his background and his audience. Shakespeare may have written not for an age but for all time, but for an appreciation of even Shakespeare an informed knowledge of the Elizabethan period is very helpful. A new evaluation of Longfellow, then, can hardly end without referring to the changed and changing spirit of America.

Constitutional government in the United States was only eighteen years old when Longfellow was born and less than a century old when he died. He lived in a young America, conscious of its youth and still uncertain whether to feel inferior to its parents, the older nations of Europe, or superior to them because of its free institutions in a land of vast untapped natural resources. The inevitable result, of course, was a wavering between the two attitudes. This ambivalence was reflected in the nation as a whole and in individuals who were, as Longfellow was, self-consciously representative.

Longfellow did not live in our age of instantaneous communication and rapid transportation, of houses incomplete without a built-in garage and a television room. He spent most of his youth in a territorial, outpost city. He received his higher education in a little college not yet a generation old. His first three voyages to Europe were made in sailing ships. He was within a year of beginning his Bowdoin professorship when the first railroad was built, and the first transcontinental line was not completed until he was past sixty. He was middle-aged when the telegraph began to come into use;

the telephone was still experimental when he died. When he lived in Cambridge, he either walked to Boston or went by horsecar; when he visited Portland, he went by boat or stagecoach. He did all of his writing with quill pens.

All of this seems remote to us now, and yet Longfellow grew up in a society of considerable sophistication. He thought himself exceptionally fortunate to live in the only nation he ever wanted to make his permanent home, and in a well-situated city. He could criticize the lack of literary patronage, especially in his early years; but in time he achieved a happy working relationship with a conveniently located and extraordinarily enterprising publisher, the Boston firm of Ticknor and Fields, which in his time patronized contemporary writers more successfully than any other American firm has ever managed to do. He valued the accessibility of the Harvard Library, which he continued to use after he severed his official connection with Harvard. He enjoyed and profited from his associations in the Saturday Club and the Atlantic Club of Boston, and he felt honored to be invited to the Goethe Club in New York City. There was the excitement of cultural discovery in the air which he could not have failed to feel.

Longfellow was also singularly fortunate, or extraordinarily canny —or both—in his personal friendships. Early in life he formed associations with the historian George Greene and the politician Charles Sumner, both literary men and extremely helpful as sources of or sounding boards for his ideas through the years. He doubtless enjoyed these friendships, and they were useful too. Other noteworthy friendships were his Harvard ones with C. C. Felton, Professor of Greek; and with C. E. Norton, like himself a translator of Dante.

His associations with his fellow authors must have proved marvelously satisfactory and stimulating. He and his former classmate Hawthorne became very friendly, in their mutually reserved way. There are numerous entries in his journals about going to hear Emerson lecture, and less frequent ones refer to visits with him. At the Saturday Club and elsewhere, he saw a great deal of Whittier, Holmes, and Lowell, to name only the most famous. Other friends included his brother-in-law, the cosmopolitan traveler and wit Tom Appleton, and the financier Sam Ward, who at times served informally as Longfellow's financial counselor and literary agent, being associated with him somewhat as H. H. Rogers would be later with Mark Twain.

Longfellow had casual friendships also with notable English and European writers of his time. Although he met and visited with Carlyle, Tennyson, the Brownings, and other contemporary English literary personalities, Dickens seems to have been the only English author with whom he developed a close friendship, one resulting in extensive visiting at Craigie House and at Gadshill. On the Continent, his closest of several literary friends was Ferdinand Freiligrath, a major German poet, critic, and translator. Life at Craigie House must have been frequently brightened by the appearance of illustrious visitors from abroad who were touring America in their professional capacities. Some of the best known of these were women, including the actress Fanny Kemble and the singer Jenny Lind, both of whom he greatly admired.

It is a common mistake to suppose that Longfellow lived and thought exclusively in the world of literature and art. It is true that he preferred discussion of literature to politics and science. Once he even complained in his journal that a Saturday Club meeting had been mostly on politics and did not get around for hours to anything really interesting (*Life*, II, 276). But he was not uninterested in politics. His friend Sumner, a United States Senator, would have reminded him of politics if that were necessary, but this seems not to have been the case. His journals show that he voted conscientiously, even going through the rain to do so; and there are many references to political affairs. As for science, one of his best friends was the famous Harvard Professor of Natural History, Louis Agassiz, and Longfellow's literary interests included Paracelsus. In no sense did he live in an ivory tower of art.

He did, however, live in an age of decorum and restraint. Even so, he seems to have been no more than mildly shocked at the frankness of Chaucer's language or by the French fabliaux, though he did deplore the latter as a literary waste since readers could spend their time more profitably. There are occasional, but not a great many, references in journals, in letters, and in *Outre-Mer* to coarseness and licentiousness in Spain and Italy. As has been mentioned above, in *Tales from a Wayside Inn* he could even bring himself to tell with apparent enjoyment a comic tale of gluttony and a frank (and charming) story of nightly assignations. Longfellow was not unaware of all the aspects of human living, but he simply thought it bad taste to discuss some of them, as Howells did a little later. In this, of course, he was Victorian; he lived in an age when restrained language and behavior were the fashion, and he thought the fashion a good one.

Conversely, although there were Victorian restrictions on vocabulary and subject matter, it was an age that believed in simplicity. It did not believe in metaphysical complexities of thought or in involved language that would puzzle the reader. Today's readers, accustomed to narrative filtered through the minds of retarded men or nymphomaniac women and to poetry depending for its appreciation on knowledge of obscure myths or ability to interpret abstruse symbols, find Longfellow disturbingly simple and forthright. He wrote in an age that believed in poetry for enjoyment and for instruction. He took this as his assignment, and did his homework well. Probably few poets have provided more sheer enjoyment, in musical line and in clear observations on life. Even today, readers can derive much pleasure from both his lyrics and his narratives; and many may welcome the absence of the profanity and obscenity which some modern writers and readers quaintly believe indicate robustness and sophistication.

Closely related to Longfellow's sense of decorum is his Puritanism, which has been mentioned from time to time throughout this book. It is important to recognize, first, that his Puritan background is significant; second, that the fortunes of his literary reputation have been inseparably tied in with the changing attitudes toward Puritanism in America. His was an age when the descendants of the colonial Puritans were still proud of their ancestry. Some of them—such as Richard Hildreth of Harvard and Boston—were writing its history from what another more remote descendant, Charles Francis Adams, would later call the filio-pietistic point of view. But it was also an era when most of the bigotry and authoritarianism in colonial and early national Puritanism had given way to the liberalism of Channing and Emerson—a much happier time when God had come to seem more benevolent than terrible, when free men in a land of opportunity found it easy to forget the Fall of Man and the loss of Eden.

However, Longfellow's Puritan background more than any other one factor accounted for his steady industry, which resulted in substantial attainments as educator and author, and for his conviction that literature at its best should serve the cause of morality—a conviction that sometimes, though not always, resulted in a didacticism which detracted from the effectiveness of his writings. Mainly, however, Longfellow wrote in the *Zeitgeist;* America was still more Puritan than not. To be sure, even before his death the moral earnestness had shown signs of changing into a desire for wealth and power; but the drive engendered by Puritanism was still there.

This drive is not extinct yet, of course, and probably never will be. It is not reasonable to suppose that a force once so important in America will ever totally disappear. But a pronounced wave against Puritanism, led especially by H. L. Mencken and his school, accompanied the great decline in Longfellow's reputation in the 1920's and 1930's, and contributed to it. Mencken's vogue passed quickly, long before his death; but the revolt against Puritanism which hurt Longfellow is still with us, though it is subsiding. As twentieth-century writers like Arthur Miller and William Faulkner portray anew various aspects of Puritanism in America, Hawthorne and Longfellow begin to show up better again; Longfellow does not now seem as out of date as he did a generation ago. Longfellow, then, lived in a world very different from ours, but one so responsible for ours that we cannot reasonably consider him obsolete.

II *Literary Virtuoso*

Besides his role as the leading spokesman of an age which still has a good deal to say to ours, there is the matter of Longfellow's natural abilities and acquired skills as a poet. In this respect, he has been much misunderstood and undervalued, partly because of the tendency of readers to be arbitrary or whimsical in what they choose to read from a given author's works. No writer can coerce the generations of readers who come after him to accept him at his own valuation or even to read the works by which he would prefer to be known. Poe has been identified overmuch as the melancholy jingle man of "The Raven" and "Annabel Lee," to the neglect of such pure lyrics as "To Helen" or the musical "Ulalume." Whitman was long represented in anthologies only by his untypical rhymed and metrical "O Captain! My Captain!" instead of by such more artistic free-verse poems as "Out of the Cradle Endlessly Rocking" and "When Lilacs Last in the Dooryard Bloom'd." Carl Sandburg has lamented that the little cat feet of his "Fog" have been remembered at the expense of his more fully developed poems. Similarly, Longfellow would likely have wished the twentieth century to remember him less for "A Psalm of Life," "The Midnight Ride of Paul Revere," and *Hiawatha,* and more for "My Lost Youth," "Kéramos," "Morituri Salutamus," and *Christus.*

To be well informed on Longfellow as a poet, a student must read widely in his works, for he was a poet of extraordinary natural talent and accomplishment. He had an excellent ear for meter and rhyme. He could handle dexterously all the verse forms he attempted. He was by no means limited to the iambic foot which prevails in English poetry, but he handled trochees, anapests, and dactyls frequently and with great skill. His lines range in length from trimeter to octameter; his range of stanzaic patterns includes couplets, triplets, simple quatrains and ballad meter, the varied patterns of the ode and the elegy, sonnets, and blank verse. Apparently he was not interested in the Chaucerian or Spenserian stanzas or in the English sonnet forms; if so, he would have written them too.

Not only could he handle a wide range of verse forms successfully; he was also able to impress his own style on each of them so well that a Longfellow poem is readily identifiable. He achieved his characteristic artistry partly because his wide and careful reading gave him such a large vocabulary that diction was never a problem. Much of his appeal must have been due also to his prevalent and felicitous imagery. He is hardly one of the most figurative of poets, and yet his similes, metaphors, personifications, and symbolism are abundant enough to lend an extraordinary imaginative quality to many of his poems. He was always a competent artisan: a reader who examines his metrical forms closely will find almost no inversions or other evidence of amateurishness. Directness, gently imaginative quality, and a quiet charm—these are the hallmarks of Longfellow's poetry.

He had considerable talent for writing poetry to begin with. He fostered it through his steadfast love for poetry, his interest in achieving a variety of effects through the choice of suitable forms, and his study of the techniques which had been developed not only in English but also in the other leading languages of Europe. The importance of this third point is emphasized in a quotation from C. E. Norton: "And the charm which his verse exercises over its readers, especially over its American readers, continued to be enhanced by the variety and abundance of its sources. From Sicily to Norway, from the castles of Spain to the vineyards of France, from the strongholds of the Rhine to the convents of Italy, the poet was everywhere at home, not as a passing guest, but as an intimate familiar with the landscape, the life, and the legends of the land."[1] Longfellow wrote poetry not as a neophyte or provincial, but as an accomplished virtuoso and citizen of the world of Western culture.

III *Transmitter of Old World Culture*

Longfellow's permanent place in American literary history will, of course, have to be determined most of all by his own writings—his original contribution to American and thereby to world literature. However, he made a more important secondary contribution as a transmitter of Old World culture than is true of any of our other writers, with the possible exception of Emerson. His services as a pioneer in pointing out the importance of comparative literary study and in furthering it through his work as teacher and as translator were very great.

It is probably not possible to account fully for the breadth of Longfellow's cultural outlook, but some relevant points may be mentioned. He was—and this is important—that eager type of child who finds any reading exciting, whatever it may be. Fortunately, part of Longfellow's early reading was in the classics; consequently, he began to acquire an extraordinary breadth of outlook from childhood. We do not have full information on how he developed his interest in the modern languages or what evidence, other than his proficiency in Latin and some study in French, the Bowdoin trustees had for believing him to be interested in them. We do know that he intended to study French and Italian during his contemplated year of postgraduate study at Harvard.

In any event, he arrived in Europe at the age of nineteen so ópen-eyed and eager to study several languages that he had difficulty deciding which one to study first. In turn he was to find French, Spanish, and Italian exciting; but he was not immediately so enthusiastic about German, which, as events proved, was ultimately to occupy and influence him most of all.

When he returned to assume his professorship, he was aglow not only with his new knowledge of the languages and the people but also with a zest for communicating what he had learned. His enthusiasm was infectious; he was able to enlist the interest of his students. He prepared his own texts not only because existing text material was scarce or unsuitable, but also because presentation in an attractive form had become vital to him. His efforts were directed toward bringing his students to an appreciation of the total cultural outlook of the people whose language and literature they were studying. Thus it is apparent that he was extremely modern in outlook. Had his attitude spread promptly through the American educational system, it seems unlikely that there would have been so much basis for "ugly American" books later. As it was, he has earned a high place, with Thomas Jefferson and George Ticknor, in pioneering modern language study in America; and his total contribution is probably the greatest of the three. His work and that of other pioneers in the study of European languages and cultures must also have helped somewhat to prepare America for the great flood of European immigrants who were coming to America before he died.

Longfellow's interest in the languages and peoples of Europe was not whimsy for the exotic or dilettantism. His journals and letters are replete with evidence that he early recognized the heterogeneous origin of American culture and thereby the necessity for ascending the various tributaries of the cultural stream to find the nature of their origin and growth. Longfellow had a genuine interest in both the people and the art of a nation. He has been criticized for his lack of affiliation with foreign universities and for his failure to avail himself of tutors when he was on his first, and longest, stay abroad. But he was following an intuition which proved to be right. He associated with all levels of society, from peasants and inn-keepers to the writers and socially prominent persons to whom he had borne letters of introduction; listening perhaps more than he spoke, he studied the oral language along with the written. Thus he came to know the people who used the languages quite as well as the languages themselves. And, since he made friends in every country he visited, he must have convinced the people of his friendly interest. Often considered an aristocratic snob, Longfellow was certainly a democrat when he lived abroad.

Though it is true that European influences are strong in his work, accusations that, as a writer, he lived in a house with only Eastern windows are certainly not supported by evidence in his letters and journals or by the subjects he chose for his literary works. He did, to be sure, write a great deal based on his European travels. His first two books of prose stem mainly from his European residence, but the first is influenced more in form by the American Irving than by European writers. Many of his poems draw from the European literary treasury, which is not surprising if we consider that Long-fellow was consciously trying to bring to Americans the culture of their parent nations. Even so, it is remarkable how much of his writing is American in subject matter: one of two novels, all of the three most successful long narrative poems, most of the ballads, and a fair share of the long and short lyrics, including the sonnets. In his own writings, then, as well as in his capacities as teacher and translator, Longfellow served importantly as transmitter of Old World Culture to the New and as ambassador of a burgeoning New World Culture to the Old. This role we cannot rightly overlook when we discuss his place in literary history.

IV *Absorption in American Culture*

It is a well-known phenomenon of cultural history that the con-tributions to a given culture may become lost or distorted primarily because they have been so assimilated that people no longer know where they came from. It is equally well known that readers believe what they want to believe. And so a generation living in the United States between 1915 and 1945—an age of rebellion from a variety of forms of restraint, including decorum—developed a pronounced dis-like for the ideals and idols of earlier times. Longfellow was identi-fied with an authoritarian and moralistic Puritanism which had become anathema in an age of iconoclasm and candor. Disillusioned thinkers reasoned that the proper course of action would be first to ridicule the ideals and idols of the past and then, presumably, to forget them. Thus the same generation which scoffed at American Puritanism also tended to pity and ridicule Longfellow as an archaic remnant of a fumbling infant culture.

The colonial American Puritans and their vision of a new Canaan in America are being looked at more judiciously today. The Puritans still appear to have been often bigoted, frequently hypocritical, and sometimes cruel. But such modern writers as Henry Nash Smith,[2] R. H. B. Lewis,[3] and Frederic I. Carpenter[4] have effectively pointed out that the best of America in the twentieth century rests upon the substructure of the three preceding centuries. In all of these centuries Puritanism and its natural progeny such as Unitarianism, Transcendentalism, and pragmatic idealism have been of fundamental importance. Without the moral seriousness which produced Longfellow and his enthusiastic and devoted readers, America would not have had the dream of the American Garden of Eden, which in its original form and in the misgivings it induced—with a stubborn persistence in the face of them—became a dominant force in the colonies and in the nation.

Longfellow has been assimilated into American culture almost as completely as Puritanism has been into our general pattern of living. There is little awareness today of how his ideas and even his phrases have worked themselves into our lives. Probably no day goes by without his being cited or even quoted by dozens of Americans; it is doubtful if even Shakespeare is quoted more often. Following are only a few of the lines and phrases from his poetry which have become household sayings: "And the night shall be filled with music"; "Lives of great men all remind us"; "Under a spreading chestnut-tree"; "This is the forest primeval"; "Sail on, O Union, strong and great!"; "There is no Death! What seems so is transition"; "As unto the bow the cord is, / So unto the man is woman"; "Why don't you speak for yourself, John?"; "A boy's will is the wind's will"; "sweetness as of home-made bread"; "I heard the bells on Christmas Day / Their old, familiar carols play"; "While the eternal ages watch and wait"; "And as the evening twilight fades away / The Sky is filled with stars, invisible by day"; "But in ourselves, are triumph and defeat"; "Art is the child of Nature"; "The tide rises, the tide falls"; "Out of the shadows of night / The world rolls into light." There are many more. A few, to be sure, are themselves derivative; but for most if not all of them, Longfellow's wording is the one we know.

As the quotations suggest, Longfellow developed an extraordinary faculty for phrasing neatly what his contemporaries already believed. Believing it, even if only nebulously, they could easily memorize his smooth phrasing. Hence he came to be quoted until some quotations became household phrases with their sources forgotten. However, he deserves to be remembered not merely as a source of quotations, some of which have become trite. He did not write to be quoted—although he was pleased that people would want to quote him—but to have his works read and enjoyed in their entirety. Much of him can be read today with that same sense of quiet enjoyment which his contemporaries cherished. His importance, then, is now twofold: (1) historical, for what has been assimilated; (2) esthetic, for what can still be enjoyed.

V A Clean, Well-Lighted Place

This book has made no attempt to establish Longfellow as a major poet, nor will it dismiss him as a minor or second-rate poet. He was what he was, and he is what we can make of him. He was a good man and a talented poet. He loved his country and his fellow men. As a young man, he started out with a burning desire to become eminent, preferably in literature, but at any rate in something. By middle life he had concluded that it was not so important to become eminent as to be devoted to one's work, one's friends, one's country, one's fellow men. But he always loved art and sought its meaning. His late-life poem "Kéramos" and the fragment *Michael Angelo* are proof enough of that.

A patriot, he wanted his country to recognize literature and to encourage it, but he did not believe that literary art is primarily national. Rather, it is universal, and each nation can contribute most by understanding first the general nature of humankind and then its own special nature.

He was a greatly beloved and almost universally respected man. Probably few other authors have had such affection and loyalty from family and friends. Longfellow's friends were of both sexes and of many nations. There is no record that he was ever ungenerous or disloyal. Without apparent effort, he seems to have been the center of any group he was in, even though others were more loquacious and more eloquent. The discerning W. D. Howells, who became acquainted with him as a young invited guest at the meetings of the celebrated Dante Club, has perhaps, as nearly as anyone, revealed the secret of the esteem in which he was held: "He did not talk much himself, and I recall nothing that he said. But he always spoke both wisely and simply, without the least touch of pose, and with no intention of effect, but with something I must call quality for want of a better word; so that at a table where Holmes sparkled, and Lowell glowed, and Agassiz beamed, he cast the light of a gentle gayety, which seemed to dim all those vivider luminaries."[5]

At Longfellow's funeral, the aged Emerson, then within a month of his own death, called his deceased friend "a sweet and beautiful soul." The Concord sage's mind had grown too dim for him to recall the name of his friend, but he had not lost his wizardry with words. In an age when it was still honorable to do so, Longfellow sweetly and beautifully lived the life of a Christian gentleman; and he devoted his considerable talent to contributing memorable writings to a country and a human race he loved. The size of the niche he ought to occupy in the mansion of national and world literature may remain uncertain for some time, but one thing is already certain: whatever its size, it will always be a clean, well-lighted place.

Notes and References

Notes and References

Abbreviations: Following is a list of works cited parenthetically in the text, with the short form used:

The Works of Henry Wadsworth Longfellow. New York: The Davos Press, 1909. 10 vols. Cited as *Works*.

The Complete Poetical Works of Longfellow. Boston: Houghton Mifflin Company, 1893. Cited as *Poems*.

Longfellow, Samuel. *Life of Henry Wadsworth Longfellow*. Boston: Ticknor and Company, 1886, 2 vols. Cited as *Life*, I or II.

Longfellow, Samuel. *Final Memorials of Henry Wadsworth Longfellow*. Boston: Ticknor and Company, 1887. Cited as *Life*, III.

Thompson, Lawrance. *Young Longfellow (1807-1843)*. New York: Macmillan Company, 1938. Cited as Thompson.

Chapter One

1. V. L. Parrington, *The Colonial Mind* (New York, 1927), p. 98.

2. Newton Arvin, *Longfellow: His Life and Work* (Boston, 1962), p. 325.

3. From the Prelude to "Among the Hills," *The Complete Poetical Works of Whittier* (Boston, 1892), p. 85.

4. Ernest Wadsworth Longfellow, *Random Memories* (Boston, 1922), p. 13.

5. William Dean Howells, *Literary Friends and Acquaintance* (New York, 1911), p. 208.

6. Edward Wagenknecht, *Longfellow: A Full-Length Portrait* (New York, 1935), p. 7.

7. Charles E. Norton, *Henry Wadsworth Longfellow* (Boston, 1907), p. 27.

8. Thomas Wentworth Higginson, *Henry Wadsworth Longfellow* (Boston, 1902), p. 287.

9. Helen A. Clarke, *Longfellow's Country* (New York, 1909), p. 14.

10. William Sloane Kennedy, *Henry W. Longfellow* (Cambridge, Mass., 1882), p. 308.

11. H. S. Gorman, *Longfellow: A Victorian American* (New York, 1926), pp. 313-14.

12. John Greenleaf Whittier, *The Poetical Works* (Boston, 1892), p. 216.

13. Kennedy, *Henry W. Longfellow*, p. 326.

14. *Ibid.*, p. 331.

15. *Ibid.*, pp. 307-34. There were doubtless many which Kennedy did not include.

16. Harold Blodgett, "Heard from the New World," *Literary History of the United States* (New York, 1948), I, 628-29. For an account of the remarkable circulation of his works in Great Britain, see Clarence Gohdes, "Longfellow and His Authorized British Publishers," *PMLA*, LV (December, 1940), 1165-79.

17. Higginson, *Henry Wadsworth Longfellow*, p. 7.

18. Ludwig Lewisohn, *Expression in America* (New York, 1952), p. 65.

19. Howard Mumford Jones, "Longfellow," *American Writers on American Literature* (New York, 1934), p. 111.

20. Odell Shepard, Introduction, *Henry Wadsworth Longfellow: Representative Selections* (New York, 1934), p. liv.

21. Albert Mordell, *Quaker Militant: John Greenleaf Whittier* (Boston, 1933).

Chapter Two

1. Kennedy, *Henry W. Longfellow*, pp. 12-14. See also the genealogical chart in Samuel Longfellow, *Life*, III, 419.

2. Kennedy, *Henry W. Longfellow*, p. 18.

3. *Ibid.*, pp. 19-23.

4. Higginson, *Henry Wadsworth Longfellow*, p. 14.

5. Wagenknecht, *Longfellow*, p. 27.

6. *Life*, I, 23. See also Thompson, pp. 18-19. Thompson thinks the poem was essentially a refutation of another poem on the same subject by Thomas Cogswell Upham, a young Dartmouth graduate. Upham had implied that the heroes of the battle had been forgotten; Longfellow maintained that they would never be. Thompson prints Upham's poem, with Longfellow's, in his Notes, pp. 346-47.

7. Higginson, *Henry Wadsworth Longfellow*, p. 15.

8. *Ibid.*, p. 17.

9. Andrew R. Hilen, *Longfellow and Scandinavia* (New Haven, 1947), p. 137.

10. Higginson, *Henry Wadsworth Longfellow*, p. 19.

11. *Ibid.*, pp. 30-36.

Chapter Three

1. See, however, Thompson's view: "during this first European visit, Longfellow was not primarily interested in study and scholarship." *Young Longfellow*, p. 366.

2. James T. Hatfield, *New Light on Longfellow* (Boston, 1933), pp. 20-22.

3. *Ibid.*, p. 23.

4. Wagenknecht, *Longfellow*, p. 217.

5. Andrew R. Hilen, ed. *The Diary of Clara Crowninshield* (Seattle, 1956), p. xxiii. Other entries, however, show that Clara and Mary were companionable.

6. Wagenknecht, *Longfellow*, p. 217.

7. Hilen, *The Diary of Clara Crowninshield*, pp. 182-85.

8. Carl L. Johnson, *Professor Longfellow of Harvard* (Eugene, Ore., 1944), p. 4. Lawrance Thompson in *Young Longfellow, Chapters* XVI-XVII, treats in full detail Longfellow's efforts to leave Bowdoin.

9. Johnson, *Professor Longfellow of Harvard*, pp. 4-5.

10. *Ibid.*, pp. 7-8.

11. *Ibid.*, pp. 13-14.

Chapter Four

1. Hilen, *Longfellow and Scandinavia*, p. 28.

2. Hilen, *The Diary of Clara Crowninshield*, p. xxii.

3. Hilen, *Longfellow and Scandinavia*, p. 8.

4. *Ibid.*, p. 19.

5. Hilen, *The Diary of Clara Crowninshield*, p. 198.

6. *Ibid.*, pp. 198-99.

7. *Ibid.*, p. 264.

8. *Ibid.*, p. 238.

9. Johnson, *Professor Longfellow of Harvard*, p. 14.

10. *Ibid.*, p. 23.

11. See *ibid.*, 19-20, for Ticknor's letter commending the method, and p. 23 for Longfellow's success with it. See also Esther Cloudman Dunn, "Longfellow the Teacher," *North American Review*, CCXI (February, 1920), 259-65.

12. Hatfield, *New Light on Longfellow*, p. 53.

13. Kennedy, *Henry W. Longfellow*, p. 43.

14. William Winter, *Old Friends* (New York, 1909), p. 48.

15. Johnson, *Professor Longfellow of Harvard*, pp. 50-51.

16. *Ibid.*, p. 53.

17. *Ibid.*, pp. 43-44.

18. Edward Wagenknecht, ed., *Mrs. Longfellow: Selected Letters and Journals of Fanny Appleton Longfellow (1817-1861)* (New York, 1956).

19. *Ibid.*, p. 32.

20. *Ibid.*, p. 36.

21. See Thompson, *Young Longfellow*, pp. 255, 402. Papers which might clarify this point have not yet been released for publication.

22. Hatfield, *New Light on Longfellow*, p. 70.

23. Wagenknecht, *Mrs. Longfellow*, p. 58.

24. *Ibid.*, p. 64.

25. Hatfield, *New Light on Longfellow*, pp. 90-109, gives the best account of Longfellow's third European visit.

26. Wagenknecht, *Mrs. Longfellow*, p. 83.

27. Wagenknecht, *Longfellow*, p. 236.

28. *Ibid.*, p. 257.

29. Wagenknecht, *Mrs. Longfellow*, p. 106.

30. Wagenknecht, *Longfellow*, p. 50.

31. Johnson, *Professor Longfellow of Harvard*, p. 29.

32. *Ibid.*, p. 40.

33. Wagenknecht, *Mrs. Longfellow*, p. 199.

34. Johnson, *Professor Longfellow of Harvard*, p. 82.

35. *Ibid.*, p. 90.

Chapter Five

1. Their birth dates: Charles, June 9, 1844; Ernest, November 23, 1845; Fanny, April 7, 1847 (died September 11, 1848); Alice Mary, September 22, 1850; Edith, October 22, 1853; Annie Allegra, November 8, 1855.

2. Edward Waldo Emerson, *The Early Years of the Saturday Club, 1855-1870* (Boston, 1918), p. 19.

3. Wagenknecht, *Longfellow*, p. 322. Professor John Webster of the Harvard Medical School, on November 23, 1849, killed George Parkman, uncle of Francis Parkman, the historian. It was the scandal of the age for the Boston area and a great shock to Longfellow and his wife, along with the rest of the community, but Longfellow's brother elected to omit letters referring to it from his biography.

4. *Ibid.*, p. 253.

5. Howells, *Literary Friends and Acquaintance*, p. 195.

6. E. W. Longfellow, *Random Memories*, p. 69.

7. Wagenknecht, *Longfellow*, pp. 257-58.

8. Higginson, *Henry Wadsworth Longfellow*, p. 225.

9. While still in his early years at Bowdoin, Longfellow had published a translation of Jorge Manrique's *Coplas de Manrique*; and, as has been noted, he had by 1845 accumulated enough translations to provide a large part of the translated material in his compendious *Poets and Poetry of Europe*. Higginson says (p. 269): "As a translator, he was generally admitted to have no superior in the English tongue."

10. Kennedy, *Henry W. Longfellow*, p. 102.

11. Wagenknecht, *Longfellow,* p. 307.

12. *Ibid.,* p. 309.

13. Kennedy, *Henry W. Longfellow,* p. 113.

14. E. W. Longfellow, *Random Memories,* p. 68.

15. Wagenknecht, *Longfellow,* pp. 275-76. The estate continued to grow after he died; Alice's share was worth $1,500,000 in 1928.

16. Longfellow was an excellent reader of poetry. See *Life,* II, 464. He tested the poems for *Poems and Places* upon listeners, one of whom observed: "He was a fine reader, the melody of his voice giving a sweetness to his expression that was charming, and his eyes glowing with the rapture of the thought. He would sometimes . . . read with all the impression [sic] of the professional actor." Kennedy, *Henry W. Longfellow,* p. 116.

17. Wagenknecht, *Longfellow,* pp. 324-27.

18. *Ibid.,* p. 312.

19. Kennedy, *Henry W. Longfellow,* pp. 276-77.

Chapter Six

1. All are printed in the Davos edition of Longfellows *Works,* II, 351-88.

2. Although Longfellow and Tegnér did not meet in Sweden, they were to carry on an extensive correspondence. Each had a high regard for the work of the other, and Tegnér was obviously disappointed that Longfellow, who had rendered parts of his "Saga" so well, did not translate all of it into English. Higginson (p. 135) says that "Frithiof's Saga" is thought by some critics to contain Longfellow's finest descriptive prose. A shorter piece which Longfellow wrote to introduce his translation of *The Children of the Lord's Supper* was later incorporated into his "Frithiof's Saga."

3. All quotations from *Outre-Mer* are from the Davos edition of Longfellow's *Works,* I, 25-349. Page references are supplied in parentheses.

4. Higginson, *Henry Wadsworth Longfellow,* p. 124.

5. Quotations from *Hyperion* are from the Davos edition of the *Works,* II, 5-345.

6. Hilen, *The Diary of Clara Crowninshield,* pp. 227ff.

7. Higginson, *Henry Wadsworth Longfellow,* pp. 124-25.

8. Editorial note, Davos edition of *Works,* III, 7. Quotations from *Kavanagh* are from the Davos edition of the *Works,* III, 7-169.

9. Higginson, *Henry Wadsworth Longfellow,* p. 199.

10. *Ibid.,* p. 200.

11. Wagenknecht, *Mrs. Longfellow,* p. 146.

Chapter Seven

1. The standard treatment of Longfellow's prosody is G. W. Allen, *American Prosody* (New York, 1935), Chapter VI. For other elements of poetic structure, the discussion in George Arms, *The Fields Were Green* (Stanford, 1953) is provocative and useful. All quotations of poetry are from *The Complete Poetical Works of Longfellow*, ed. H. E. Scudder (Boston, 1893). Cited elsewhere as *Poems*.

2. Allen, *American Prosody*, p. 157.

3. Dorothea Brande, *Becoming a Writer* (New York, 1934), p. 20.

4. To make this point, Allen quotes from "Tegnér's Drapa": "They laid him in his ship,/With horse and harness,/As on a funeral pyre./Odin placed/A ring upon his finger,/And whispered in his ear." *American Prosody*, p. 173.

5. Allen, *American Prosody*, pp. 191-92.

6. Kennedy, *Henry W. Longfellow*, p. 106.

Chapter Eight

1. Wagenknecht, *Mrs. Longfellow*, p. 132.

2. M. G. Hill, "Some of Longfellow's Sources for the Second Part of *Evangeline*," *PMLA*, XXI (June, 1916), 170.

3. Hilen, *Longfellow and Scandinavia*, p. 36.

4. In Whittier's review, *Works* (Boston, 1892), VII, 366.

5. Newton Arvin, *Longfellow: His Life and Work* (Boston, 1962), p. 107n.

6. Carolyn Ramsey, *Cajuns on the Bayous* (New York, 1957), p. 5.

7. Kennedy, *Henry W. Longfellow*, p. 230.

8. *Ibid.*, pp. 75-79.

9. Higginson, *Henry Wadsworth Longfellow*, pp. 129-30.

10. Kennedy, *Henry W. Longfellow*, p. 85.

11. Wagenknecht, *Mrs. Longfellow*, p. 201.

12. Kennedy, *Henry W. Longfellow*, p. 85.

13. The most detailed study of Longfellow's use of Schoolcraft is Chase S. Osborn and Stellanova Osborn, *Schoolcraft-Longfellow-Hiawatha* (Lancaster, Pa., 1942). Chase Osborn, a former governor of Michigan, is more an advocate of the Michigan area and Longfellow defender than a scholar; but reprints from newspapers and, especially, excerpts from Schoolcraft in juxtaposition with relevant passages from the poem are useful. The work also includes a biography of Schoolcraft. The most essential parts of the bulky work were reprinted in 1944 as *"Hiawatha" with Its Original Indian Legends*.

14. Kennedy, *Henry W. Longfellow*, pp. 89-90.

15. Higginson, *Henry Wadsworth Longfellow*, p. 209.

16. Kennedy, *Henry W. Longfellow*, p. 90.

17. For a full account of "The Saga of King Olaf" and its background, see Hilen, *Longfellow and Scandinavia*, pp. 94-103.

18. Higginson, *Henry Wadsworth Longfellow*, p. 5.

19. Wagenknecht, *Longfellow*, Appendix A, pp. 315-20, gives fuller information.

Chapter Nine

1. C. E. Norton, *Henry Wadsworth Longfellow*, p. 33.

2. Henry Nash Smith, *Virgin Land* (Cambridge, Mass., 1950).

3. R. H. B. Lewis, *The American Adam* (Chicago, 1955).

4. Frederic I. Carpenter, *American Literature and the Dream* (New York, 1955).

5. Howells, *Literary Friends and Acquaintance*, p. 184.

Selected Bibliography

Selected Bibliography

PRIMARY SOURCES

Complete Works. Standard Library Edition. Boston: Houghton Mifflin Company, 1891. 14 vols. The first definitive edition and still standard. Based on the Riverside Edition of 1866 in 11 vols., but adds illustrations and the 3-volume *Life* by Samuel Longfellow.

The Works of Henry Wadsworth Longfellow. New York: The Davos Press, 1909. 10 vols. A limited edition, nearly complete except for the Samuel Longfellow *Life. Contains* some rare prose material. References in the present study of prose works are to this edition.

The Complete Poetical Works of Longfellow. Boston: Houghton Mifflin Company, 1893. Based on the Riverside Edition of 1886, this is the standard edition of Longfellow's poems.

The Poetical Works of Henry Wadsworth Longfellow. Boston: Houghton, Osgood and Company, 1879-80. 2 vols. An elaborate edition, testifying to Longfellow's fame in his last years. Hundreds of illustrations by Darley and others.

Representative Selections. Introduction, Bibliography, and Notes by Odell Shepard. American Writers Series. New York: American Book Company, 1934. Has an incisive 45-page introduction, concluding with a stout defense.

Longfellow. Ed Howard Nemerov. Laurel Poetry Series. New York: Dell Publishing Company, 1959. A judicious selection of poems by a modern American poet; also a good twenty-page introduction.

The Continental Tales of Longfellow. Selected by J. I. Rodale. New York: A. S. Barnes and Company, 1960. A misleading publication, for the tales are not newly discovered, as implied. Two were published as short stories in his *Works;* the others are taken from *Outre-Mer* and *Hyperion.*

SECONDARY SOURCES

ALLEN, G. W. *American Prosody.* New York: American Book Company, 1935. The standard work on this subject. Chapter VI is devoted to Longfellow.

ARMS, GEORGE. *The Fields Were Green.* Stanford: University Press, 1953. One of the most penetrating analyses of Longfellow as poet.

ARVIN, NEWTON. *Longfellow: His Life and Work.* Boston: Little, Brown and Company, 1962. The most recent general study. Presents Longfellow as a humane, talented person; ranks him as only a minor poet.

BLODGETT, HAROLD. "Heard from the New World." Chapter 37, Vol. I, of *Literary History of the United States.* New York: Macmillan

Company, 1948. Especially useful for its vivid picture of Longfellow's contemporary fame.

CLARKE, HELEN A. *Longfellow's Country*. New York: Baker and Taylor Company, 1909. A handsome illustrated volume dedicated to Alice Longfellow. Has some helpful treatments of poems and their sources.

DUNN, ESTHER CLOUDMAN. "Longfellow the Teacher." *North American Review*, CCXI (February, 1920), 259-65.

EMERSON, EDWARD WALDO. *The Early Years of the Saturday Club, 1855-1870*. Boston: Houghton Mifflin Company, 1918. The son of the author Emerson presents Longfellow favorably in his own milieu.

FIELDS, ANNIE. *Authors and Friends*. Boston: Houghton Mifflin Company, 1893. The wife of Longfellow's chief publisher devotes sixty pages of anecdotes and reminiscences to him as a gentleman of wit and charm.

GOHDES, CLARENCE. "Longfellow and His Authorized British Publishers." *PMLA*, LV (December, 1940), 1165-79. A thorough study of the very great popularity Longfellow's poetry had in great Britain. Includes his business dealings with British publishers.

GORMAN, H. S. *Longfellow: A Victorian American*. New York: George H. Doran Company, 1926. An impressionistic life of Longfellow. Makes much of his Puritan background and Victorian outlook.

HAMMER, CARL, JR. *Longfellow's "Golden Legend" and Goethe's "Faust."* Baton Rouge: Louisiana State University Press, 1952. An informative brochure.

HATFIELD, JAMES TAFT. *New Light on Longfellow: With Special Reference to His Relations to Germany*. Boston: Houghton Mifflin Company, 1933. A detailed study of Longfellow up to the time he relinquished his Harvard professorship. Two appendices give much information on German friends and studies.

HIGGINSON, THOMAS WENTWORTH. *Henry Wadsworth Longfellow*. Boston: Houghton Mifflin Company, 1902. Based on the *Life* by Samuel Longfellow, but includes additions and new interpretations.

HILEN, ANDREW R. *Longfellow and Scandinavia*. New Haven: Yale University Press, 1947. Presents Longfellow more as a figure in literary history than as an important poet. Says he went to Scandinavia as a philologist rather than as a poet, but derived inspiration and material for later poems, especially *Evangeline* and *Hiawatha*.

————, ed. *The Diary of Clara Crowninshield: A European Tour with Longfellow, 1835-1836*. Seattle: University of Washington Press, 1956. This full account kept by one of the members of Longfellow's party on his second trip to Europe throws new light on his studies and way of life abroad.

HOWELLS, WILLIAM DEAN. "The White Mr. Longfellow." Chapter VI of *Literary Friends and Acquaintance*. New York: Harper &

Brothers, 1911. This intimate, admiring sketch did much to create the image of a poet who was venerable and kindly rather than great.

JAPP, A. H. "The Puritan Element in Longfellow." *Living Age*, CLV (November 4, 1882), 306-15. Has helpful comments on a number of poems, including *The New England Tragedies*.

JOHNSON, CARL L. *Professor Longfellow of Harvard*. Eugene, Ore.: University of Oregon Press, 1944. Johnson sees Longfellow as a conscientious, very successful teacher of languages who never found the academic road easy.

JONES, HOWARD MUMFORD. "Longfellow." Chapter IX of *American Writers on American Literature*. New York: Tudor Publishing Company, 1934. One of the earliest and also one of the best modern attempts to apply a measuring stick of common sense to Longfellow.

KENNEDY, WILLIAM SLOANE. *Henry W. Longfellow: Biography, Anecdote, Letters, Criticism*. Cambridge: Moses King, Publisher, 1882. An informative biography, especially valuable for materials published in connection with Longfellow's death.

LONG, ORIE C. *American Literary Pioneers: Early American Explorers of European Culture*. Cambridge: Harvard University Press, 1935. Chapter V, on Longfellow, is the best short account of his relationship to Germany and the German language.

LONGFELLOW, ERNEST WADSWORTH. *Random Memories*. Boston: Houghton Mifflin Company, 1922. An autobiographical interpretation by a son divided between admiration of and condescension toward his famous parent.

LONGFELLOW, SAMUEL. *Life of Henry Wadsworth Longfellow*. Boston: Ticknor, 1886. 2 vols. Until the complete letters and journals are published, this will be the one indispensable source for biographical studies. Longfellow's younger brother, a clergyman, made extensive use of letters and journals to establish a favorable portrait. Supplemented by *Final Memorials*, 1887.

————, ed. *Final Memorials of Henry Wadsworth Longfellow*. Boston: Ticknor and Company, 1887. Compiled because the two-volume *Life* had not covered the last fifteen years of the poet's life adequately, and there was a demand for more information. Much journal and letter material. Printed as Vol. III of the *Life* in 1891 and thereafter.

MACMECHAN, ARCHIBALD. "Evangeline and the Real Acadians." *Atlantic Monthly*, XCIX (February, 1907), 202-13.

NORTON, CHARLES E. *Henry Wadsworth Longfellow*. Boston: Houghton Mifflin Company, 1907. In a forty-page sketch, a long-time friend and fellow-translator of Dante presents a sympathetic, charming portrait of the poet, followed by autobiographical poems.

OSBORN, CHASE S., and STELLANOVA. *Schoolcraft-Longfellow-Hiawatha*. Lancaster, Pa.: Jacques Cattell Press, 1942. A formidable collection of materials, but indispensable for a thorough study of *Hiawatha*. Includes sources and a biography of H. R. Schoolcraft.

SCHRAMM, WILBUR L. "Hiawatha and Its Predecessors." *Philological Quarterly*, XI (October, 1932), 321-43. Discusses eleven poems on American Indians produced by American writers between 1790 and 1849.

SMEATON, OLIPHANT. *Longfellow & His Poetry*. London: G. Harrap & Co., 1919. A sympathetic study by a lecturer on Shakespeare in Heriot-Watt College of Edinburgh. Good interpretation, but has some factual errors.

STEDMAN, C. C. *Poets of America*. Boston: Houghton Mifflin Company, 1885. Chapter VI is on Longfellow. The most notable American critic of American poetry in the late nineteenth century treats "our poet of grace and sentiment" fully and favorably.

THOMPSON, LAWRANCE. *Young Longfellow (1807-1843)*. New York: Macmillan Company, 1938. Thompson attempts to rescue Longfellow from his flowing white beard and its connotations. Full notes testify to extensive research.

WAGENKNECHT, EDWARD. *Longfellow: A Full-Length Portrait*. New York: Longmans, Green & Co., 1955. Before Newton Arvin's *Longfellow* appeared in 1962, this was the only modern scholarly book on Longfellow. It is partly a defense of Longfellow against his modern critics.

————, ed. *Mrs. Longfellow: Selected Letters and Journals of Fanny Appleton Longfellow (1817-1861)*. New York: Longmans, Green & Co., 1956. Makes available for the first time liberal selections from the well-written, informative letters and journals of Longfellow's second wife.

Index

Index